THE POLITICS OF

FREEING MARKETS

IN LATIN AMERICA

— Judith A. Teichman —

THE POLITICS OF

CHILE

FREEING MARKETS

ARGENTINA

IN LATIN AMERICA

AND MEXICO

The University of North Carolina Press
Chapel Hill and London

Designed by Heidi Perov
Set in Bembo and Officina Sans
by Tseng Information Systems, Inc.
Manufactured in the United States of America

The paper in this book meets the guidelines for permanence
and durability of the Committee on Production Guidelines
for Book Longevity of the Council on Library Resources.

LIBRARY OF CONGRESS CATALOGING-IN-PUBLICATION DATA
Teichman, Judith A., 1947–
The politics of freeing markets in Latin America :
Chile, Argentina, and Mexico / by Judith A. Teichman.
p. cm.
Includes bibliographical references (p.) and index.
ISBN 0-8078-2629-4 (cloth : alk. paper)
ISBN 0-8078-4959-6 (pbk. : alk. paper)
1. Free trade—Political aspects—Chile.   2. Free
trade—Political aspects—Argentina.   3. Free trade—
Political aspects—Mexico.   4. Democracy—Economic
aspects—Chile.   5. Democracy—Economic aspects—
Argentina.   6. Democracy—Economic aspects—Mexico.
7. Chile—Economic policy.   8. Argentina—Economic
policy.   9. Mexico—Economic policy.   I. Title.
HF1956 .T45   2001
382′.71′098—dc21   2001023409

05   04   03   5   4   3   2

To the memory of my father,
William Charles Wells

contents

tables

Market reform in Latin America has signified a dramatic reversal in widely accepted values and practices. It usually faced stiff opposition from many quarters, not just from groups in society but also from within the state. Indeed, market reform has involved fierce political struggles with important contingents of losers and potential losers, at least in the short term. Among those losers were state bureaucrats and businessmen, as well as populist party die-hards and trade unionists. Moreover, by the early 1990s, in most cases the process was well understood to be one largely insulated from public scrutiny, not fully discernible from the print media, the public pronouncements of government leaders, or government documents. The role of multilateral lending institutions, the International Monetary Fund and the World Bank, has added another dimension to the process, one that raised the always politically sensitive issue of external involvement in domestic policy choices. Given this context, much of the research incorporated in this book was acquired through open-ended interviews with key actors. Interviews were carried out in each of the three countries: Mexico in 1991 and 1999, Argentina in 1995, and Chile in 1996. In addition, interviews of World Bank and International Monetary Fund officials involved in the policy reforms of each of the three countries were undertaken in 1997. Appendix 1 provides a descriptive breakdown of the interviews for each country and for the multilateral officials interviewed. Because of the political sensitivity of the issues being raised and my wish to encourage respondents to speak openly and frankly, interviewees were given a pledge of confidentiality. This was especially important for officials currently holding government posts and for the officials of multilaterals. Almost all of my informants appeared grateful for the promise of anonymity. Hence, citations will not identify interviewees by name but will give descriptive nonidentifying details. The term "senior official" when used in the text refers to respondents at the ministerial rank, to those at one of the two levels below this rank, or to the personal advisers of ministers. I have used this generic term to identify sources in this category when to give more detail would reveal the identity of the source.

This book would not have been possible without the generosity of those many individuals directly involved in the market reform experience — government and multilateral officials, business and labor leaders, and politicians

—who gave generously of their time to share their viewpoints and experiences with me. I also owe a debt of gratitude to the academic communities at home and in the places where I carried out field research. Gustavo Indart, of the University of Toronto's Centre for International Studies, was enormously helpful in facilitating contacts in Argentina, Chile, and Washington. I also thank Sylvia Ostry, Gerry Helleiner, Dipak Mazumdar, Edgard Rodríquez, Carol Wise, Jorge Nef, Aldolfo Canitrot, Juan Carlos Torres, Jorge Schvarzer, Ricardo Sidicaro, Oscar Ozlak, Rafael Agacino Rojas, Fernando Leiva, Orlando Caputo, Manfred Wilhelmy, Blanca Heredia, Luis Rubio, Gonzalo Hernández Licona, Jorge Buendia, Rodolfo de la Torre, Felix Veliz, Benito Nacif, and María Amparo Casar. Their advice and insights contributed in important ways to this endeavor. Special thanks are due to Getulio Steinbach who arranged office space for me at the Instituto de Desarrollo Económico y Social and offered valuable counsel as my field research in Argentina progressed and to Ricardo Israel Zipper and María Eugenia Morales for their advice and for making me feel at home at the Instituto de Ciencia Politica, Universidad de Chile.

I could not have carried out the research for this project without the invaluable work of my research assistants, Carlos Briceño Sotelo (Chile), Ana Margheritis (Argentina), and Luis Pablo Hinojosa Azaola (Mexico). Without their dogged persistence I would most certainly not have obtained the information that made this project such an exciting one. My research assistant in Canada, Michelle Bonner, carried out the tedious but essential task of checking information and finding references in the final stages of the writing. Thanks are also owed to my friend and colleague Judith Adler Hellman for helpful comments and to the two anonymous reviewers of the manuscript for their constructive advice. All errors and omissions are, of course, my own.

The Social Sciences and Humanities Research Council of Canada provided financial support that made the field research possible. A Connaught Research Fellowship afforded additional financial support and the luxury of release time to complete the writing of the manuscript. Finally, a special debt is owed my family, husband, George, and daughter, Sarah, for their support, patience, and resilience.

BHC	Mortgage Bank of Chile
CAP	Pacific Steel Company (Chile)
CCE	Business Co-ordinating Council (Mexico)
CEA	Argentine Business Council
CESEC	Center for Social and Economic Studies (Chile)
CFE	Federal Electricity Commission (Mexico)
CGE	General Economic Confederation (Argentina)
CGT	General Confederation of Labor (Argentina)
CHILECTRA	Chilean Electricity Company
CIEPLAN	Corporation for Economic Research on Latin America (Chile)
CMHN	Mexican Council of Businessmen
CNC	National Confederation of Peasants (Mexico)
CNOP	National Confederation of Popular Organizations (Mexico)
CODELCO	State Copper Company (Chile)
CORFO	Production Development Corporation (Chile)
COSENA	National Security Council (Mexico)
CPC	Confederation of Production and Commerce (Chile)
CT	Labor Congress (Mexico)
CTM	Confederation of Mexican Workers
CUT	Single Workers' Central (Chile)
DINIE	National Administration of State Industries (Argentina)
ECLA	Economic Commission for Latin America
EFF	Extended Fund Facility
ENAP	National Petroleum Company (Chile)
ENDESA	National Electricity Company (Chile)
ENTEL	National Telecommunications Company (Argentina)
FESEBES	Federation of Unions of Goods and Services Workers (Mexico)
FOBAPROA	Bank Fund for the Protection of Savings (Mexico)
FRAP	Popular Action Front (Chile)
FREPASO	Country Solidarity Front (Argentina)
FSTE	Federation of Unions of State Workers (Mexico)
IAPI	Argentine Institute for the Promotion of Trade

IDP	Interamerican Development Bank
IEERAL	Institute for Economic Studies on the Argentine and Latin American Reality (Argentina)
IMF	International Monetary Fund
IMSS	Mexican Institute of Social Security
ISSSTE	Institute of Security and Social Services for State Workers (Mexico)
ITAM	Mexican Autonomous Institute of Technology
LAC	Latin American and Caribbean Regional Division (World Bank)
LAN	National Airlines (Chile)
MAPU	Movement for United Popular Action (Chile)
MERCOSUR	Southern Common Market
MIDEPLAN	Social Planning Ministry (Chile)
MIR	Movement of the Revolutionary Left (Chile)
MYRA	Multiyear rescheduling agreements
NAFINSA	National Financiera (Mexico)
NAFTA	North American Free Trade Agreement
ODEPLAN	National Planning Office (Chile)
PAN	National Action Party (Mexico)
PDC	Christian Democratic Party (Chile)
PEMEX	Mexican Petroleum Company
PPD	Popular Party for Democracy (Chile)
PRD	Party of the Democratic Revolution (Mexico)
PRI	Institutional Revolutionary Party (Mexico)
PROGRESA	Education, Health, and Food Program (Mexico)
PRONASOL	National Solidarity Program (Mexico)
PS	Socialist Party (Chile)
SALS	Structural adjustment loans
SECALS	Sectoral adjustment loans
SECOFI	Ministry of Commerce and Industrial Development (Mexico)
SEDESOL	Ministry of Social Development (Mexico)
SEFOFA	Society to Promote Manufacturing (Chile)
SEMIP	Ministry of Energy, Mines, and Parastate Industry (Mexico)
SEPAFIN	Ministry of Natural Resources and Industrial Development (Mexico)
SICARTSA	State steel company (Mexico)

SOMISA	Mixed Argentine Steel Corporation
SOQUIMICH	Chemical and Mining Company of Chile
SPP	Ministry of Budget and Planning (Mexico)
TELMEX	Mexican Telephone Company
UP	Popular Unity (Chile)
YPF	State Petroleum Deposits Company (Argentina)

THE POLITICS OF

FREEING MARKETS

IN LATIN AMERICA

chapter one

POLITICS AND MARKET REFORM IN LATIN AMERICA

GLOBALIZATION, IDEAS, AND POLICY CHANGE

The energy crisis of 1973–74 initiated important changes in the world economic order: an increase in trade competition, the decline in U.S. economic dominance, and the struggle by multinationals to lower costs through reorganizing production. These changes, involving the elimination of economic borders and an increase in international exchange, are at the core of what has become known as globalization. The energy crisis and its attendant economic difficulties also triggered a reassessment of the role of the state in the economy. Ideas that had germinated in the academic community for years now began to reach policy makers. With the elections of Ronald Reagan in the United States and Margaret Thatcher in Great Britain policies geared to bring about a greater reliance on market forces (trade liberalization, privatization, and deregulation) gained increasing recognition worldwide. Indeed, policy prescriptions calling for a greater reliance on market forces and the withdrawal of the state came to represent a new "international policy culture" (Ikenberry 1990, 103–4; Kahler 1992, 124).

Latin America, with the notable exception of Chile, proved stubbornly resistant to this new international policy culture, however. Indeed, the opportunities for foreign borrowing made possible by the increase in price and demand for petroleum probably prolonged the resistance to change in many countries of the region. With the 1973–74 energy crisis, OPEC (Organization of Petroleum Exporting Countries) petrodollars channeled through the commercial banks aggressively sought borrowers in Latin America. Confronted with a variety of needs, both real and perceived (high oil bills, pressures for state spending, industrial needs for inputs, public demand for consumer goods), the largest Latin American states embarked on a binge of borrowing that culminated in the 1981–82 international debt crisis. That crisis forced highly indebted countries into negotiations with the International Monetary Fund (IMF) and produced agreements putting in place stabilization programs, which involved a variety of short-term austerity measures (devaluation, reduction in government spending, restriction of wage and salary increases) seen as necessary to rectify trade imbalances, reduce inflation, and initiate economic recovery to ensure the repayment of debt. When, by the mid-1980s, recovery eluded highly indebted countries, attention turned to the institution of longer-term market reform measures (structural adjustment) such as trade liberalization and privatization, while austere stabilization programs continued to be negotiated and implemented simultaneously.[1] Latin American policy reform, therefore, has been marked by the important contextual feature of economic crisis and, oftentimes, harshly austere government policies.[2]

While the multilateral lending institutions encouraged policy reform, the debt crisis also provided an opportunity for domestic critics of statism, whose voices had been subdued during the binge years of proliferative borrowing, to press for policy change. By the second half of the 1980s, the persistence of economic difficulties in the region gave growing legitimacy to the viewpoints of market reformers and propelled the new policy ideas rapidly forward among high-level state bureaucrats and politicians. At the same time, debt negotiations offered an important forum for the transfer of market reform ideas because these reforms were part of structural adjustment (market reform) packages negotiated with the International Monetary Fund and the World Bank. Country after country carried out trade liberalization, the privatization of public companies, and deregulation. By the mid- to late 1990s, countries began to undertake what has become known as "second stage reform" (Pastor and Wise 1999; Naim 1994; Torres 1997), a phase whose features, although far from uniform, include the privatization of companies remaining in state hands, regulatory reforms, changes in labor legislation, measures to combat poverty, and improvements in governance.

This book is the story of the market reform process in three Latin American countries: Chile, Argentina, and Mexico. It is a story that involves a consideration of the impact of sweeping historical forces and the acumen of individual actors; it accords an important role to both domestic and international forces. Indeed, domestic and international factors have become intertwined in new and intriguing ways in the era of globalization. By the mid-1990s, all three countries had carried out extensive market reforms under distinct regime types. Chile was the region's earliest and for many years most radical market reform case, carrying out the socially costly aspects of its reform process under highly repressive military rule (1973–89). Under the elected Concertación government (1990–present), an alliance of Christian Democrats and socialists, Chile not only maintained the reforms carried out by the military regime but moved into the privatization of sacrosanct public companies while struggling to alleviate poverty and inequality. Chile is the region's clearest case of domestically driven reform, having begun the process a decade before the full impact of the debt crisis and the new international policy environment were felt in the region. Although taking some initial steps during the 1976–82 period of military rule, Argentina implemented extensive market reform at the federal level under the elected Peronist government of Carlos Menem, in power between 1989 and 1999. Carried out in the wake of the traumatic hyperinflationary episode of the late 1980s, Argentina's reforms, which included the privatization of important public companies in such areas as petroleum and railways, were completed in a very brief time period. Post-1994 reform efforts focused on labor flexibilization[3] and privatization at the provincial level. Mexico's market reform program, led by a liberalizing authoritarian one-party-dominant regime, began slowly in 1983 and accelerated as the economic crisis renewed in 1985–86. The political fallout of the 1994–95 peso crisis, including the loss of control of Congress, stalled a number of proposed market reforms and brought increased attention to corruption and poverty issues.[4]

While it is widely recognized that the political context within which market reform has been carried out is integral to the process, the nature of the relationship between market reform and political change has been fraught with considerable controversy. The spread of market reform throughout the region demonstrates that elected regimes are capable of carrying out politically risky and socially costly reforms. But the issue of how and why they have been able to do so and what the implications are for democratic stability and practices in the longer term remains an area of ongoing research and discussion. This book aims to contribute to our understanding of the relationship between market reform and politics through examining the issue comparatively, across regime type and over time. In the following section, I sketch the major issues of the current debate and then situate this study within these broader concerns.

LATIN AMERICAN POLITICS IN THE MARKET REFORM ERA

Alongside the dramatic reversal of the statism that had come to characterize economic policy in Latin America, the decade of the 1980s also witnessed a concerted move toward political liberalization and democratization as countries shed military rule and moved to establish a variety of formal democratic practices. As we will see, this process has been examined in a variety of ways: democratization has been explored from procedural and substantive perspectives and from the point of view of responsiveness to public input. The market reform/democracy discussion has become extraordinarily intractable, involving not only differing concepts of democracy but also varying assessments of the economic and social impacts of economic reforms along with conflicting viewpoints on the possibilities opened up by such changes.

Given that Latin America's transition to democratic rule involved, in most cases, the removal from power of highly repressive military regimes, most early works focused on the acquisition of the formal attributes of liberal democracy, particularly elections (O'Donnell and Schmitter 1986; Drake and Silva 1986; Seligson 1989). Recent work agrees that impressive progress has been made in the formal procedural requisites for liberal democracy (Lowenthal and Domínguez 1996; Agüero 1998).[5] Indeed, now, more than ever before, the democratizing regimes of Latin America appear more firmly rooted and more durable, as more and more of them prove capable of surviving economic crises and transferring power through elections (Remmer 1996; Castañeda 1996, 47). The centrality of elections in much of the literature stems from their presumed role in making it possible for citizens to hold political leaders accountable through the opportunity to remove leaders from power.[6]

Early observers acknowledged that elites largely determined the conditions of transition to democracy and that they would try to determine whether liberalization would be expanded into a broader process of democratization (O'Donnell and Schmitter 1986, 7–11; Diamond and Linz 1989, 9–10). In the 1990s, as the threat of military intervention dissipated, praises for procedural advances in democracy were increasingly tempered by growing concerns about a variety of obstacles that appear to be diminishing the quality of Latin American democracy. Latin American democracies have been described as "delegative democracies" (O'Donnell 1994a), "hybrid" (Conaghan, Malloy, and Abugattas 1990, 26), and "fragile" (Hakim and Lowenthal 1993), signifying that while such regimes have electoral processes, they also have features believed to be antithetical to the spread and consolidation of democracy. Much of this literature takes a substantive rather than simply procedural definition of democracy, although there is by no means agreement on exactly what the substantive features of democracy are or should be. But clearly, for these authors, democracy involves much more than the peaceful transfer of power as a consequence of competitive elections and the protection of the basic civil liberties well known to liberal democracy. It involves such attributes as the independence of civil society and social groups from the state, free public contestation over government priorities and policies (Linz and Stepan 1996, 3–11), the operation of mechanisms that protect the weakest members of society, executive accountability to the public, the subjugation of military and police power to civilian authority, and the operation of the rule of law (Lowenthal and Domínguez 1996, 5). Others have judged democratic institutions as inadequate, pointing to corrupt and weak judiciaries and impotent legislatures.

Perhaps no issue has been more controversial than the extent to which market reform has contributed to, or detracted from, this process of democratization. On the one side, there is the by now standard argument that with the reduction of the role of the state, particularly with privatization, public policy more in tune with public interests will emerge because public bodies will now be far less permeated by corruption, rent-seeking behavior, and political manipulation (Savas 1987, 3–4; Van de Walle 1989, 606–16). In addition, there was considerable optimism that as state streamlining reduced the power of corrupt bureaucratic agencies and trade unions, the role of other, more autonomous and representative organizations would increase, allowing previously politically inactive groups a role in the political process (Williamson 1994, 13; Hausman 1994, 174). Moreover, as state intervention declines and as monopolistic state companies are eliminated, the ensuing wider array of economic actors provides a check on state power (Butler 1987). Probably the best argument on this side of the ledger is the contention that in setting the stage for future economic growth, market reforms provide the basis for democratic political stability (Remmer 1995, 115).

On the other hand, a growing number of works have argued that economic crises and market reforms are undermining the quality of democracy because both are held responsible for the increase in inequality and the rise in the numbers of people facing abject misery. Market reforms involving a dramatic cutback in state expenditures and functions—the elimination of subsidies to the poor, reduction in spending on health and education—have seriously undermined the ability of the state to protect its most vulnerable citizens. As the lives of people do not improve or, even worse, deteriorate further, there is the real danger that democracy may cease to be regarded as legitimate among those who have been economically marginalized (Borón 1998, 46). Moreover, the political instability generated by economic inequality not only threatens the continuation of democracy but also undermines business confidence and therefore economic prosperity (Vilas 1997, 21; Castañeda 1996, 55). Redistributive measures are seen as imperative and elite resistance the key obstacle (Castañeda 1996, 55). Philip Oxhorn and Graciela Ducatenzeiler believe that the inequality linked to market reforms has dangerously weakened civil society, rendering lower-class groups increasingly powerless against the middle and upper classes, a situation that militates against class compromise while encouraging elites to respond rigidly (even violently) to pressures for change (1999, 27, 35).

Inequality and the heightened vulnerability it brings are viewed as having important implications for authoritarian forms of political control: patron clientelism, "a tie between two parties of unequal wealth and influence" that "depends upon the exchange of goods and services" (Powell 1970, 412–13), and bureaucratic patrimonialism, political authority based on personalistic relationships and the distribution of material rewards, in which the property of the individual ruler and the state are indistinguishable (Lewellen 1995, 141), are likely to persist, mutate, or even strengthen under conditions of large-scale poverty and inequality (Alvarez, Dagnino, and Escobar 1998b, 22; Vilas 1997, 19; Vellinga 1998, 12). The persistence or growth of such features is regarded as an impediment to democratization because such arrangements contravene equality of access to the state and the resources it dispenses, equality of treatment by the state on the basis of rational bureaucratic criteria, and political representation based on a legal order—assumptions at the core of the democratic notion of citizenship. Moreover, clientelism is often reinforced by another hierarchical arrangement: corporatism. Like clientelism, corporatism, which provides for the incorporation of organized groups into the party or state apparatus, has operated as a mechanism of political control in Latin America, tending to contain dissent and potential dissent (Schmitter 1974, 108). Further, the mitigation of clientelism and corporatist political arrangements is important in the transition toward a more democratic ideal because both inhibit the autonomy of societal groups.[7] A concept of "civil society" involving the existence of a public life and freedom of association and political choice independent of the state exists in tension with such hierarchical principles.

Moreover, despite the expansion of democratic practices, many examining the first phase of market reform from the angle of policy formulation have emphasized the top-down, exclusionary aspects of the process, lending support to arguments emphasizing the negative implications of market reform for questions of substantive democracy, particularly public influence on policy and accountability. The ascendancy of a technocratic elite, individuals with graduate degrees in subjects such as economics, to policy predominance is widely seen as a key ingredient in the successful implementation of market reform (Williamson and Haggard 1994, 578; Haggard and Webb 1994, 13; Haggard and Kaufman 1995, 9; Pastor and Wise 1992, 91; Teichman 1997a, 37–48; Díaz 1997, 38). According to one analysis, the successful implementation of market reform requires this elite to reduce the size of its support coalition so as to exclude groups such as labor and the noncompetitive private sector that are affected negatively by the new policies and therefore can be expected to oppose them (Waterbury 1989, 40). Indeed, political difficulties can be expected at the beginning of the process because the big losers are powerful vested interests with a great deal of political clout while the beneficiaries are a diffuse, unorganized cross section of the public who lack the incentive and political resources to organize in support of market reform. The imposition of market reform through executive fiat, quickly and by surprise, often overriding democratic deliberative mechanisms, has been widely recognized as a necessary and integral part of the reform experience (Grindle 1996, 35; Morales 1996, 16; Conaghan and Malloy 1994, 145–48). According to this perspective, most Latin American governments carrying out market reform have featured formal democratic procedures alongside highly authoritarian decision-making styles in which there is neither public input nor accountability.

One key point of contention revolves around the implications of the behaviors of technocratic policy makers for the development of democracy over the longer term. On the one hand, there are those who see no necessarily negative implications springing from the concentration of political power in the hands of technocrats. Indeed, their leadership is believed to guarantee coherent, efficient, and rational economic programs laying the groundwork for economic growth, political stability, and, ultimately, democracy over the long term (Williamson 1994, 12; Galjart and Silva 1995, 273). In fact, one recent work argues that technocrats, recognizing the need to take on a political role (hence the use of the term "technopol"), have obtained public support for their economic policies and have shown a commitment to democratic values and, in some cases, social justice (Domínguez 1997, 5, 35).[8] Electoral victories won by governments that have carried out market reforms are frequently seen as evidence of the presence of a public consensual support of such programs.[9] Others, however, express growing concern for both the immediate and longer-term negative implications for democracy of economic crisis and market reform owing to the presence of a variety of features considered inimical to democratic consolidation. These features, in addition to economic inequality, include the concentration of decision-making authority in the hands of technocrats who monopolize the policy agenda combined with the increased role and policy influence of powerful economic conglomerates (Centeno and Silva 1998, 10–12; Przeworski et al. 1995, 73, 83; Haggard and Kaufman 1995, 340–41; O'Donnell 1994b, 252).

The persistence of a variety of nondemocratic features combined with a high degree of social inequality, with its attendant social problems, may threaten the state's capacity to continue carrying forward a market reform agenda in the second phase of reform. A tendency to bypass or manipulate democratic deliberative mechanisms may eventually translate into opposition that can no longer be ignored, especially if sustained economic prosperity is not in the offing. The legitimacy of market reform and of the regime that implements it becomes vulnerable especially if the public perception is that certain groups have privileged access to the policy process and have benefited inordinately from reforms in a context widely viewed as permeated by cronyism. According to Peter Evans, the state must have links of a certain type with societal groups for it to be able to transform society successfully. Evans speaks of the importance of the "embedded autonomy" of the state, involving a combination of internal coherence and external connectedness. Defined as "a concrete set of social ties which bind state to society and provides institutionalized channels for the continual negotiation and renegotiation of goals and policies" (Evans 1992, 164), embedded autonomy is generally in short supply in Latin America. Institutionalized links providing real access to the policy process exist for the private sector, but personalized inroads to the policy process are more important, and even institutionalized ones tend to be highly personalized. Such links for other groups, such as labor, rural workers, small farmers, and small business, are either weak or absent, raising the specter that policy formulation will likely ignore the interests of these groups and, in doing so, trigger political instability with its attendant negative impact on economic prosperity.

The extent to which market reform has been driven by outside pressures, thereby further removing it from contestation in the domestic political realm and democratic accountability, has not been a major concern of most work on the market reform process. Multilateral institutions such as the World Bank and the International Monetary Fund admit to extensive "policy dialogue," a purposely neutral term reflective of the extreme sensitivity of this issue and meant to signify the noncoercive nature of multilateral negotiations with indebted countries. The academic literature on the subject generally agrees that the policy pressure exerted by multilaterals has been indirect rather than direct and that direct conditionality has been largely counterproductive in forcing countries to carry through with reforms they are opposed to.[10] Nevertheless, very little has been said about the way policy discussions are conducted and the role such discussions have had in countries' market reform programs.

This book supports arguments stressing the negative implications of the market reform process for substantive democracy during the initial reform period. I argue, however, that during second-phase reform electoral democracy is making possible a wider societal input into the policy reform process—a development that has occurred largely in response to inadequacies in the outcome of market reform. Further, in both phases of reform, market reformers, including those committed to electoral democracy, tend toward authoritarian decision-making styles and attempt to isolate reform projects from outside tampering. As we will see, however, policy isolation is discriminatory and avenues to policy input are highly personalized and selective. Although the initiative for change rested with state actors, powerful private sector groups invariably acquired personal access to policy elites, and this has had an impact on the outcome of market reform. Particularly when repression was not a major feature, personalism, discretionary decision making, patron clientelism, corporatism, and patrimonialism were integral to the political management of the reform, reinforcing its exclusionary nature. Moreover, an essential part of market reform policy development involved discussions between international actors and domestic state officials, also a highly personalized process hidden from public knowledge or scrutiny and, in this sense, another aspect of the exclusionary nature of the process.

I argue that the way in which first-phase reform was carried out—in a highly discretional, personalized, and exclusionary manner—has had important consequences for the second phase, leaving a legacy of skewed policy influence by the economically powerful, monopolistic/oligopolistic ownership, and, oftentimes, corruption. In the face of these challenges, as the process of electoral democratization has taken root and opposition groups and parties become organized, the policy elite's ability to resist policy change has declined. Its priorities are being questioned and its policies revised and, at times, even blocked. Notwithstanding certain broad similarities, however, this book demonstrates that the pace, sequencing, and style of market reforms during the first phase differed in important ways among the three cases and has had implications for the opportunities and challenges of the second.

The following section looks more closely at the development of state-societal relations in Latin America. The struggle between the streams of Latin America's political history and traditions occurred between its liberal democratic institutional tradition, on the one hand, and its Iberian legacy of clientelism, corporatism, and patrimonialism, on the other. These two traditions, interacting constantly and embedded at times in each other, define the character of politics and policy making in Latin America.[11] The way in which Latin America's distinct traditions have interacted and been reformulated differs substantially from country to country. The interaction of traditions has been patterned by the structural opportunities and constraints inherent in the domestic economy and polity as well as by powerful influences exerted from beyond national borders. The market reform process in each of the three countries examined here is testimony to the resilience of both traditions and to the complex interplay between domestic development and international events and pressures. I will explore the historical evolution of the region's distinct traditions — traditions that have patterned the nature of politics and state in Latin America, setting the stage for the momentous changes of the market reform era.

STATE-SOCIETAL RELATIONS IN LATIN AMERICA

Latin America has been characterized by two constantly interacting political influences over its long and turbulent history: from the United States and non-Iberian Europe, the values and institutional features of liberal democracy, and from its Iberian heritage, an organic concept of state and society emphasizing order and hierarchy (Calvert and Calvert 1989, 100; Wiarda 1998, 40). While the former emphasizes the importance of impersonal rules and institutions, the latter conceptualizes power as embodied in the person and exercised discretionarily. Discussions of the region's Iberian heritage have invariably pointed to such persistent features as clientelism, personalism, discretionary decision making, patrimonialism, and corporatism (Wiarda 1998, 30; Vellinga 1998, 10). For some observers it is often the persistence of these features that is seen as impeding democratic progress.

The political features emanating from the Iberian strain are usually traced back to the colonial state implanted in Latin America by Spain. Described as Spanish bureaucratic patrimonialism (Sarfatti 1966), Spanish colonial rule involved an omnipotent ruler (the Spanish king), who was above the law, who exercised arbitrary and absolutist power, and who was supported by colonial officials. In return for their loyalty, these officials were allowed access to benefits and privileges. The historical roots of patron clientelism are found in the colonial state apparatus in which the exchange of loyalty for material rewards extended throughout the social order (Greenfield 1976). Corporatism, too, is said to have had its roots in Iberia and, further back, in Roman law. Under these arrangements, the rights of society's corporate units are not inherent but emanate from the king and are hierarchically arranged (Newton 1974, 41).

With the achievement of independence from Spain in the first quarter of the nineteenth century, weak states struggled against the centrifugal forces of regionalism and intraelite conflicts. "Personalism," which took the form of *caudillismo*,[12] now filled the institutional void left by the Spanish monarchy as politics fell into the hands of local strongmen, whose personal followings provided blind obedience (Lambert 1967, 152). Loyalty to the chief became the paramount value, and political victory provided personal access to state resources. Caudillismo, arbitrary authority resting on presumed personal qualities, is not guided by the rule of law and is not accountable. It became the postindependence form of patrimonialism, and its arbitrary power and dependence on the exchange of state largesse for loyalty was absolutely key in uniting territories and forcing the formation of nations (Lambert 1967, 164). Caudillismo left its legacy in a variety of ways, especially in the predisposition to give a personal character to political authority and struggles and in the persistence of exchange relations in politics. This legacy, as we will see, would become an important component of the market reform process.

By the mid-nineteenth century, liberal democratic influences were also evident. Latin American political arrangements were loosely based on the U.S. model. They were republican presidential systems with, theoretically at least, a system of checks and balances and constitutions guaranteeing basic political freedoms. In practice, the systems that evolved were far more centralized, with considerably greater power concentrated in the presidency than was the case for the model after which they were fashioned—an artifact, it has been argued, of Latin America's Iberian heritage (Véliz 1980, 151). Furthermore, Latin American presidential systems were endowed with vast emergency powers, and the ruling group's commitment to the political ideas of liberalism was imperfect at best. Into the twentieth century, property qualifications limited voting to a small segment of the population, and recourse to military intervention and brutal political repression were standard tactics to ensure that increasingly important social forces were kept out of the political game. But in most cases, elections did occur and by the early twentieth century, new groups did gain access to the political system. Political parties began to replace personal followings and politics began to take on a modern veneer. In this way distinct traditions were blended and legitimacy and authority came to rest on a combination of personal and institutional elements (Moreno 1969, 113).

The practices that came to constitute Latin America's distinct tradition were durable precisely because they proved so useful to those involved in the political game. Because personalism was an effective method of organizing political power, both for those espousing the tenets of liberal democracy and for those who did not, it persisted and strengthened. Although struggles took personalist forms, however, the interests at stake were invariably much broader: in the nineteenth century, leaders advocating economic liberalism with highly personalistic appeals and followings sought to establish the primacy of property values and to integrate their countries into the international market through the removal of trade barriers. In this endeavor, the centralist authoritarian tradition served their interests well. The state became the key instrument of economic expansion and of clientelistic political control. Under the control of liberalizing elites by 1880, the Latin American state became active in laying the basis for future economic growth based on the exportation of agricultural and mining products.[13] As states consolidated and their fiscal situations were put in order, corruption increased. Officials took kickbacks for contracts granted to the private sector or diverted funds raised by the sale of bonds for purposes other than those for which the money had been raised (Anderson 1967, 33). When elections were allowed to decide the fate of political competitions, clientelistic relations were used to ensure the election of candidates favored by landed or mining ruling elites.

The onset of the Great Depression (1929–30) triggered economic and political changes that would have far-reaching consequences. A dramatic drop in international trade occurred for the region overall, resulting in a decline in the ability of countries to import.[14] In the southern cone and in Mexico, the Great Depression initiated a form of industrialization known as import substitution, a process involving the manufacture of a variety of light consumer goods previously imported. Industrialization resulted in the emergence of new social groups whose demands for access to the political system were accommodated by multiclass political movements, commonly referred to as populist. Spanning roughly the period from 1930 to the mid-1950s, populist regimes were inclusionary in the sense that they offered the popular sectors (workers and sometimes peasants) political participation and, in most cases, some improvement in welfare.[15] But these governments were also notable for their clientelist, personalist, and often corporatist features. National leadership was often of the caudillo personalistic type.

The expansion of the state under populist regimes was a response to a variety of circumstances and pressures that played into preexisting political predilections. The multiclass nature of the populist alliance, combined with a history of foreign control of key export enclaves, gave rise to nationalist appeals that called for the takeover of foreign companies and their conversion into public enterprises.[16] The popular bases of these political movements meant inevitable pressure for the extension of social welfare services involving the establishment of government agencies to provide services for peasants and housing for workers, labor ministries involved in the setting of wages and benefits, and a plethora of boards and agencies regulating private sector behavior. The state now took on a leadership role in economic development, providing quota and tariff protection for domestic industry, loans, and infrastructural development. This direction was further bolstered by the then widely accepted developmentalist formula of the day that supported an interventionist state in economic development. In Latin America this interventionist role was conveyed to policy makers through the writing of ECLA (the Economic Commission for Latin America), which advocated industrialization stimulated by, among other things, state planning and industrial protection.

State policy responded broadly to the pressures exerted by the incorporative coalitions that constituted the basis of populist regime support— invariably some combination of factions in the private sector, the working class, the military, and, in some cases, peasants. Under these conditions, organized sectors of society became clients of the state as they permeated the state at a variety of points and received such benefits as government contracts, jobs, and urban improvements. As private interests infiltrated the public arena and captured parts of the state, internal coordination and cohesion within the state became a growing problem (Vellinga 1998, 4; Teichman 1995, 46).[17] The massive increase in the role of the state provided ample opportunity for the building of patron-client relations both within the state and between state bureaucrats and client groups in society (Véliz 1980, 189). While personalism, corporatism, and patron clientelism widened the political space for the popular classes so long excluded from the political game, these very mechanisms, usually operating in a context of electoral democracy, contained popular mobilization and ensured that radical transformation of state and society was avoided. Moreover, populist regimes were fundamentally contradictory alliances that tried to give all groups what they wanted—public sector jobs for the middle class, increased employment and wages for labor, and government contracts for business. As such, they began to falter once economies began to deteriorate and state resources declined.

For countries of the southern cone (Argentina, Chile, Brazil), the demise of populist regimes ushered in harsh periods of military rule, a new form of regime that became widely known as military bureaucratic authoritarianism. First put forward by Guillermo O'Donnell (1973) in a work dealing with the military regimes that took over in Brazil in 1964 and in Argentina in 1966, the concept linked the emergence of a new technocratic state with the requirements of continued capitalist expansion in the most developed Latin American countries. With the exhaustion of the easy import-substitution phase, an alliance of civilian, military, and public sector technocrats came to agree that painful policy choices (in particular ones involving the economic and political exclusion of the popular classes) were necessary to achieve the private investment required for the resumption of economic growth.

Bureaucratic authoritarianism was considered to be a new form of state for a variety of reasons. First, it appeared to represent an abandonment of the patronage-driven personalist populist state insofar as it claimed to favor a "technical problem-solving approach" and a preference for "rational solutions." Moreover, this new regime measured success by technocratic criteria such as growth in GDP and low levels of inflation (O'Donnell 1973, 81, 106). In place of the caudillo-like military leadership of the past, military bureaucratic authoritarianism meant that the military had taken power as an institution and that its stay in power would be long term. But even in these modernizing bureaucratic authoritarian regimes, involving highly trained technocrats, traditional political practices not only survived but were adapted to the new purposes at hand. Corporatism, particularly as a mechanism to control the working class, was a key feature of bureaucratic authoritarianism (O'Donnell 1977a; Mericle 1977). Moreover, "personalism" continued to define access to policy elites for a much narrower group of societal interests. "Bureaucratic rings," consisting of industrialists connected to small sets of individual bureaucrats, usually through some pivotal office-holder, were able to press for particularistic demands (Evans 1992, 170).[18]

By the early 1970s, it was clear that aspects of the region's Iberian political heritage had survived and had been reconstituted to carry forward new political and economic models. But, as we saw in the previous section, the 1980s would witness the initiation of a profound transformation in the role and nature of the state in combination with a process of political liberalization and invigorated electoral democracy. A cursory glance at the politics of the region during the 1980s and into the 1990s reveals the resiliency of a variety of features associated with the region's Iberian political heritage. As the cases of Carlos Menem in Argentina and Alberto Fujimori in Peru illustrate, personalism, caudillismo, and strong central political authority in the presidency have all had a part to play in the process of market reform. Such features have left their mark on the specific nature of market reform in particular countries. Below I introduce the conceptual tools that bring together the legacy of Latin America's Iberian tradition and the confluence of actors and circumstances pushing for policy change.

THE STATE AND MARKET REFORM: TRADITIONAL POLITICS, TECHNOCRATS, AND POLICY NETWORKS

Market reform involved an interplay among historical legacies, domestic economic and political realities, and international pressures. The relative importance and interaction of factors varied markedly from country to country and determined the timing, strategies, and specific nature of market reform programs. In all cases, technocrats assumed important roles in this process, dominating the domestic economic policy realm and acting as interlocutors between the state and the international financial community. But in two of the cases, technocrats were heavily dependent on caudillo-like figures who used highly personalistic mechanisms of political control. Moreover, Latin American technocrats themselves often combine specialized academic training and bureaucratic career paths and support for liberal democratic institutions, with a predilection for hierarchy, rigidity, personalism, discretionality, and, sometimes, clientelism.[19] They incline toward the building of narrow domestic personalistic support bases built on trust and personal loyalty with other technocrats of similar mind-set, and they cultivate close personal ties with powerful members of the private sector. The extent of technocrats' integration with the multilateral banking community and the nature of those ties (also highly personalistic) has made domestic technocrats important interlocutors for the transfer of external policy preferences.

The emergence of technocratic capacity and the ability to carry forward far-reaching market reforms suggest that the Latin American state has strengthened in its ability to formulate policy reform and follow through on its implementation. It is also true, however, that the Latin American state is heavily penetrated by international and domestic actors who are able to influence policy and have done so decisively in the area of market reform. While these influences have often been key in propelling reform forward, they have also determined its character and challenges. The analysis that follows conceives of the Latin American state as a state punctured by personalistic relationships with international and domestic actors, conduits of policy influence that I have termed "policy networks."

My use of the term *policy network*, a term originating in work on U.S. and British politics, differs in fundamental ways from its original usage. The term has been reformulated to "fit" the peculiarities of the Latin American context as described in the preceding section. As used in the mainstream literature, the term *policy network* assumes a pluralism of policy arenas in which a wide variety of societal groups are able, in their particular issue areas, to gain preponderant influence over policy,[20] a situation not characteristic of the Latin American policy process in general or of market reform in particular. Moreover, in its American and British usage, the term is used solely in the analysis of domestic policy formation, not contemplating the incorporation of international actors as I do in this analysis. And, in general, the concept lays emphasis on the institutional/organizational relationships between actors, particularly between organized groups and the state or particular agencies and departments of the state. The primary motivating factor in the building of such networks, and the glue that holds them together, is the recognition among participants that they share a commonality in strategic agendas (Hay 1998, 38; Peters 1998, 25). The building and establishment of personal loyalty and trust, in contrast, play virtually no role either in the construction of the policy core (the key individuals involved in policy) or in the recruitment of the wider array of network participants (Hay 1998, 45). Rather, personal relationships and loyalties are key factors in the recruitment and cohesion of policy networks in Latin America. In addition, in its standard usage, the power of policy networks emerges largely from the pooling of power resources arising from constitutionally sanctioned and institutionalized realities, with the consequence that negotiation generally occurs in a context governed by recognized rules of the game (Smith 1993, 53–64). Latin American policy networks combine institutionalized bases of power with personal power and wide discretionality. Only in the personal relationships between government officials and members of the private sector in some industrialized nations (France, Japan) do we see similarities with the Latin American case (Wilks and Wright 1987, 286).

Furthermore, in Latin America, individuals may (and often do) constitute a policy network before they obtain formal positions in the state, and networks may even survive after governmental network participants have lost their official positions. Hence the operation of these networks may not conform to the formal distribution of responsibilities in the state. Finally, the standard literature portrays policy networks, because they consist of clusters of vested interests and policy agencies, as obstacles to policy change (Rhodes and Marsh 1992, 14; Marsh and Rhodes 1992, 262). Latin American market reform policy networks, initially at least, aim to break down resistance and lead policy change. Once established, however, they are likely to become resistant to even minor alterations in direction. In short, the Latin American policy network involves individuals who either are directly involved in the formulation of market reform policy or have the opportunity to influence it in important ways. Such individuals are bound together by personal relationships, particularly trust and loyalty, and are committed to market policy reform.

While I have developed the concept of *policy network* to explain market reform, much of the work on policy formulation in Latin America has used the notion of shifting policy coalitions to explain policy change (Ames 1987, 7–8; Frieden 1991; Gibson 1997a).[21] According to this approach, shifts in policy occur in accordance with changes in the alliance of social groups backing the state. While the coalition approach can provide important insights into the market reform process, it is only a part of the story given the well-documented role of technocrats and the important place of policy ideas in these transformations (Hira 1998, 9). The era of market reform calls for a concept that incorporates both the role of policy ideas (market reform ideas), their discussion and their dissemination, *and* the policy influence of powerful societal groups. It is within policy networks that the sometimes conflicting, oftentimes coinciding, demands of market reform ideas *and* powerful vested interests interact and are translated into market reform policies.

Moreover, the policy network concept operates at a different level of analysis and is a more precise tool for explaining the development of specific policies. One of the difficulties of the coalition approach is that coalition constituencies can have qualitatively different relationships with policy makers. Some have enormously more clout than others; for example, the extent to which the electoral coalition basis of a government figures into economic policy depends heavily on the whim of the political leadership, which, in any case, can be held accountable only at election time. The military, in contrast, is cohesive, highly organized, and in a better position to veto policies it does not like even as policy networks are developing policy because the military is likely to have a direct pipeline into policy reform networks. Moreover, political calculations come into play even in military regimes when the military considers the extent of repression that may be required if a particular policy line is followed. Hence the concept of policy network goes inside the coalition, emphasizing the key actors involved, their political calculations, and their responses to powerful constituencies and to policy ideas. The policy network concept, then, can help to explain policies that do not coincide with the interests of coalition partners, and it can help us to understand why certain coalition groups appear to have triumphed over others.

In general, market reform policy networks are hierarchical, cohesive, tightly integrated, and resistant to penetration from the outside—although there are important variations in the extent and duration of these features.[22] The epicenter of domestic policy networks is the policy reform core,[23] or policy elite, a small group of anywhere from three to six officials, who especially during the first phase define the market reform agenda and is the driving force behind the policy reform. The core includes technocrats, but in two of the cases dealt with here it also involved nontechnocrats in important roles and even caudillo-like figures. From this core, policy networks radiate outward, reaching down into the state apparatus and into certain sectors of society. Networks also radiate upward into the international community, at which point they become international policy networks. During the height of the market reform process some of the most important international networks involved officials of the World Bank. While technocrats are important, often predominant actors in policy networks, the involvement of nontechnocrats (caudillo-type leaders, members of the private sector) distinguishes my use of the concept of policy network from an "epistemic community" (Haas 1990) or an "economic knowledge network" ("living social communities of like-minded professionals") (Hira 1998, 13).

Policy networks extending from the core into the state apparatus are often technocratic in nature. At the helm of a policy network is the technocratic policy clique (a tight team of three or four highly trained individuals, often economists, responsible for a policy area), backed by its loyal technocratic support base, an expanded group of trained researchers and analysts. The most important technocratic policy network is concentrated in the ministry or ministries in charge of macroeconomic policy (usually the Finance Ministry and the central bank), and during the height of the market reform process, and even thereafter, the economic policy clique and its network predominate other networks. Policy networks may not be technocratic, or may be only partially so, however, as is the case for those involving officials in ministries of labor and interior in administrations carrying out market reform. Once inside the state, market reformers, whether technocratic or not, invariably recruit people with whom they already have had long personal and professional relationships.

The increasing prevalence of graduate training in the United States in the 1960s and 1970s, particularly in disciplines such as economics, produced a generation of Latin Americans not only imbued with market reform ideas but also bound by the shared experiences and long-lasting friendships acquired during the time spent in graduate school. For these people, career advancement came to depend not just on technical competence and policy commitment but also on the maintenance of personal relationships with colleagues and with superiors. Shared values as a consequence of technocratic training and personal friendship and loyalty bind technocratic participants horizontally and vertically within policy networks.[24] Once entrenched in the state apparatus, linkages of vertical and horizontal personal ties help to ensure the coherence of policies.[25]

Members of a policy network support base may also be members of the private sector, however. Such individuals may be brought in, for example, to participate directly in the formulation of policy, through providing studies and policy recommendations (in much the way technocrats do) and through helping to formulate and write laws. There are two ways in which this participation can develop: first, core or policy clique members may involve members of the private sector informally, through chats over lunch, relationships that are by definition highly personalized, or second, the private sector may become involved through more formalized channels granted its trade association or chamber, but even these relationships tend to be highly personal interactions. Although the relationships between members of the policy elite and individuals from the private sector are personal, even developing into friendships, those relationships are certainly less hierarchical with a greater potential for conflict than is the case for the relations between the policy elite and its support base of technocrats. But as we shall see, it is precisely the combination of personal access and the potential for disagreement and conflict that gives private sector participants in policy networks their ability to influence policy.

In addition to its support base, a policy network will also have a periphery, involving groups or individuals who are consulted about policy, who are kept well informed about policy decisions, but who do not participate directly in the formulation of policy. Members of the periphery have the opportunity to influence policy in important ways. The periphery may include various ministries or agencies of the state, the private sector, certain labor leaders, party activists and loyalists, members of Congress who head up important committees, and other key political figures whom the policy elite wishes to keep on its side. The line between the support base and the periphery of a policy network may or may not be permeable. For powerful members of the private sector, the issue of permeability may vary from policy issue to policy issue, and it may vary over time. The border between support base and periphery, however, is resistant to those who wish to alter key aspects of the market reform agenda. Individuals and groups within the periphery will usually take the position that they support government policy in principle but seek some (minor) modifications.

Those outside of the periphery of policy networks have little opportunity to influence policy; if they are critical of market reform policies they are likely to be subject to various mechanisms intended to contain or thwart their objections. Indeed, the ability of the policy elite to manage opponents of market reform is usually viewed as essential to successful implementation, and the mechanisms used can be important determinants of what parts of market reform go forward and what parts remain stalled. It is usually the political (policy) network, often involving nontechnocrats, that is responsible for managing the opposition. It and the policy elite can be at the center of broad societal corporatist pact arrangements that involve the participation of officially recognized labor, business, or agricultural leaders. Where repression is not the major instrument of political control, the process may include the establishment of compensatory programs, the selective distribution of material rewards, the threat of withdrawal and the actual withdrawal of old privileges, material and political, the use of divide-and-rule tactics, and the building of personalized bases of support.

While domestic policy networks extend downward, they also reach upward, extending into multilateral lending institutions, where they take the form of "policy dialogue" over structural adjustment (market reform). Such international policy networks typically involve the most important state officials responsible for macroeconomic policy and officials in the World Bank or the International Monetary Fund. International policy networks are characterized by personal relationships of trust and often friendship, developed during years of policy dialogue. Indeed, there may also be strong ties of friendship going back to university years, which strengthen once individuals are in a position to develop policy together.[26] Members of international policy networks often share a similar educational background—usually postgraduate training in economics—and a common understanding of the causes of economic problems and of policy goals, including a belief that freeing markets will spur growth and prosperity. Strong ties of personal trust and loyalty have also developed between World Bank officials and domestic nontechnocratic officials who did not share the educational background of bank officials.

One of the most important aspects of the policy network concept is its highly personalized nature. The most important activity of policy networks is policy discussion, the purpose of which is to bring about and ensure adherence to a reform program. The dissemination of reports and studies and their discussion are integral to this process. More than anything else, face-to-face personal contact, and the consequent building of relationships of trust and even friendship, was the most important way in which market reform policy ideas and the language of market reform were transferred and strengthened and policy commitment sustained. In this way, policy ideas, when finally accepted by a key actor, could sometimes be implemented despite broader coalition resistance. At other times, technocratic reformers had to acquiesce in the stubborn resistance of a network participant—although that did not stop reformers from continuing to push their case. In the face of intense opposition pressures to abandon or modify market reform policies, the loyalty and trust that held policy networks together were key in building some certainty into what was, initially at least, a highly risky policy experiment.[27]

The concept of policy network as described in the previous paragraphs is an ideal type construction that attempts to draw out the major features of the market reform policy process. It is a concept that seeks to integrate the role of policy ideas with that of interests, and it is a concept integrally linked to key elements of Latin American political tradition—in particular, personalism, centralism, and discretionary decision making. The concept does not seek to replace the coalition approach to policy change but to provide a finer tool allowing a fuller understanding of the market reform process. Indeed, as we will see in the following chapter, the broad sweep of history and the coalition alliances to which it gave rise played a role in patterning the general timing of market reform. All three countries faced both economic and political crises by the mid-1970s. The fact that only Chile embarked on a radical reform program at this time, while such programs occurred later in the other two countries, can be understood only with reference to these historical processes. The particular way in which policy reform unfolded in each case, however, is best understood through the prism of policy networks — and these were and are embedded in each country's political culture and history.

Because the political alliances and conflicts born of history have been important in determining both the timing and the nature of reform programs, our story opens with a consideration of those historical legacies. But the international environment patterned the general direction of change, and decisions taken in multilateral institutions in opening the way for the evolution of international policy networks also played a decisive role in the way reform agendas were developed. In each of the cases examined here, the directing force for policy reform, however, was located at the pinnacle of domestic political power. Chapters 4 to 6 analyze the development of market reform by that policy elite and by the policy networks it directed, identifying the way in which policy reform responded to the interplay of ideas and interests in its ranks. These chapters also chart the policy changes that have occurred during second-stage reform as policy networks are increasingly challenged by opponents. The nature of the market reform process is also heavily influenced by the strength of its opponents and by the methods available to or chosen by the policy elite to manage that opposition. Hence Chapter 7 compares the ways in which opposition to market reform was managed and draws out the implications for the reform process and for the politics of second-stage reform. The concluding chapter will return to the broader concerns, particularly issues of democracy, raised at the beginning of this chapter.

chapter two

SETTING THE STAGE
Historical Legacies

The timing, nature, and thoroughness of market reform depend heavily on the historical development of domestic political processes. The relative political strength of societal groups, both within and outside the state, their interests, their cohesiveness, and their access to political resources not only influence the timing of reform but determine what aspects of reform go forward and what parts become stalled or remain incomplete. Political conflict and economic crisis may be managed to delay policy change, or they can be handled in such a way as to increase its likelihood. The nature of a regime, whether democratic or authoritarian, will determine what groups gain access to the policy process and through what means. All of these features influence the nature of policy networks, patterning their membership, the distribution of power within them, their openness to peripheral groups, and their handling of opposition groups. A brief journey through the political history of each of our three cases sheds considerable insight into the distinctiveness of their respective reform paths. Although their political systems and the nature of the crises they faced by the mid-1970s were markedly distinct, there remain some very broad similarities. All three were characterized by highly interventionist states involving large state enterprise sectors and heavy industrial protection. Although they all faced economic and political crises, only in the Chilean case did the bankruptcy of the old order open the way for immediate change. Reform would be initiated but stalled in Argentina until well after the return to civilian rule in 1983. And it would require repeated economic crises to drive reform forward in Mexico.

CHILE: STATE-LED INDUSTRIALIZATION AND IDEOLOGICAL POLARIZATION

For the forty years preceding the 1973 military coup, Chile was politically unique in Latin America in maintaining a competitive electoral democracy generally free of the corruption and political manipulation so characteristic of other countries of the region. Compared with Argentina, economic liberalism found scant support in state and society before 1970. And yet, in 1973, Chile took a sharp turn toward authoritarianism through the installation of a repressive military regime, and it implemented Latin America's first market reform program—a program that would ultimately alter Chilean economy, state, and society in fundamental ways. A good part of the answer as to how and why these profound changes came about so much earlier in Chile than elsewhere in the region is found in Chile's distinct economic, political, and institutional history. Until 1973, Chile had a liberal pluralist political system operating in a Latin American social and economic setting. The willingness of elites to open the political system to opposition groups through electoral politics was without doubt a key contributor to the longevity of the country's democratic political stability. But while Chile's political system gave free rein to political competition, it had neither the legitimizing societal consensus of a liberal democracy[1] nor the co-optative capabilities of Latin American clientelism and corporatism. In the absence of such integrating mechanisms, Chilean society became increasingly polarized and compartmentalized, thereby triggering the deep political and economic crises that would usher in market reform.

Like all of Latin America, Chile inherited both liberal pluralist and Iberian political strains. The country's Iberian strain appeared to fade over time, however, giving its politics a Western liberal democratic veneer characterized by parties with distinct policy positions competing for public support.[2] The electoral reforms of 1958 and 1962 were successful in reducing vote buying and fraud and in liberating the votes of rural voters from landowners' clientelist control (Angell 1988, 41). Before the 1973 coup, Carlos Ibañez (1952–58) seemed to be the last Chilean caudillo leader, a personalist/charismatic president who favored corporatism while rejecting liberal democracy and Chile's parliamentary practices as the cause of the country's decadence (Loveman 1988, 192–93, 224). By the late 1960s, Chilean politics exhibited neither the clientelist and corporatist control of the Mexican case nor the authoritarian monism of Argentina's frequent military interludes. Nor did Chilean politics display the intense personalism of Argentina's Peronist experience. And even though the state was from its inception a source of political patronage, particularly with its rapid expansion after 1939, out-and-out corruption in the form of bribery and requests for payoffs was not generally widespread (Cleaves 1974, 260).[3] The strongest residue of Chile's Iberian strain was found in its political right, in particular in the National Party (formed in 1965 with the unification of the Liberals and Conservatives) and among students and faculty at the Catholic University. The *gremialista* movement, centered at that university, sought to replace party politics with an authoritarian corporatist regime involving functional representation based on entrepreneurial and professional groups.

But if Chile was extraordinary by Latin American standards for its pluralism and in the legitimacy accorded electoral politics, the central role of the Chilean state in economic development was typical of Latin American countries at the time. The activist role of the Chilean state had its origins in the nineteenth century (Lüders 1993, 137), but the expansion of the state was particularly rapid following the Great Depression and during the government of the Popular Front in 1938. From then on, the state drove industrialization, becoming, in the words of one observer, "the main determinant of Chile's economic destiny" (Mamalakis 1976, 112). The key organization charged with leading Chile's industrial development was CORFO (Production Development Corporation), established in 1939. CORFO oversaw the development of infrastructure, provided financing to the private sector, and created enterprises in a variety of important economic sectors.[4] By 1969, the state controlled some 68 enterprises (Lüders 1993, 143) and total state expenditure exceeded 23 percent of GDP (Appendix 2, Table A.2). Under the socialist government of Popular Unity (UP) between 1970 and 1973, the state expanded to cover an even wider gamut of activities and the number of state enterprises reached 596 (Hachette and Lüders 1994, 16). CORFO acquired fourteen of the country's seventeen commercial banks, and by 1973 the government had expropriated 60 percent of the country's agricultural land (Larraín 1991, 89). By 1973, state expenditure stood at 45 percent of GDP and the public deficit at 25 percent (Appendix 2, Table A.2). The Chilean state was also highly protectionist, providing both quantitative and tariff protection for industry. By the late 1960s, average tariff protection stood at 100 percent, reaching 220 percent in some cases (Edwards 1985, 20).

Support for a highly interventionist state was widely accepted in Chilean society, including among most Chilean entrepreneurs who had grown up under the protection of the state. There had been two attempts at stabilization (1955–57 and 1958–61), and both had failed. Although most Chileans accepted the primacy of the state in economic matters, by the 1960s there was a clear lack of consensus on the issue of state protection of property rights. Economically, Chile was dominated by a powerful and highly integrated group of industrial/financial capitalists and big landowners deeply involved in the right-wing political leadership (Zeitlin and Ratcliff 1988,

167, 254). The right-wing parties fiercely defended property rights and private enterprise and vehemently opposed the expansion of union rights in the rural sector, an issue that became particularly contentious because of the high degree of concentration in land ownership. At the same time, since the early part of the twentieth century, there had been an important indigenous Marxist movement in the labor movement. Although willing to collaborate with centrist parties, it called for an end to capitalism and a fundamental alteration in property relations. Moreover, by the 1960s, important elements within the centrist Christian Democratic Party also appeared to favor alterations in property relations as reflected in that party's support for land redistribution and for the "Chileanization" (state takeover) of the American-owned copper mines. Such positions represented a threat to the business class in general, but in particular to the country's integrated industrial/financial/landed elite.[5] Nevertheless, the strategy of the Chilean elite was to attempt to absorb political opponents into the electoral process, a strategy that worked fairly well until the 1960s but then began to break down.

Chile differs from Mexico and Argentina in the development of an independent trade union movement, a feature rooted in a variety of institutional and other arrangements that had the effect of decentralizing and weakening the labor movement and inhibited it from developing a strong and wealthy national leadership.[6] Meanwhile, geographic isolation in northern mining communities, foreign ownership, bouts of unemployment caused by sudden drops in commodity prices, and government repression fed worker militancy. Until 1970, the trade union movement was isolated from the centers of decision making, its few representatives on state bodies being appointed and removed by the state (Angell 1972, 79). Given its weak union structure and exclusion from political power, the Chilean trade union movement sought support from political parties so as to take its battles to arenas where there was greater likelihood of success (Drake 1978, 30). And the political parties, particularly the leftist ones, soon saw the trade union movement as an important ally and potential basis of political support. At its establishment in 1933, the Socialist Party began to compete with the Communist Party for worker support. The Radical Party was successful in gaining support from white-collar workers, especially in the public sector, while the Christian Democratic Party sought support from public sector white-collar workers, railway workers, postal employees, teachers, and industrial plant workers (Angell 1972, 207). The trade unions were the mainstay of support for the left-wing parties (the Communists and Socialists). The link established between the trade unions and the leftist political parties politicized the trade unions and reinforced the militancy and solidarity of both trade unions and parties. In areas such as the coal mining town of Lota, where one party was dominant, there was a close identity between party and union; indeed, people's daily lives often went on within a network of party loyalties (Constable and Valenzuela 1991, 21).

The growth in support for the left was reflected in the 1938 victory of the Popular Front over the rightist alliance of Conservatives and Liberals that had governed the country for over a century. This was Chile's populist episode, and its failure to meet popular expectations for reform combined with growing political repression, especially of the Communist Party, fed leftist party solidarity, worker militancy, and social unrest. The antilabor stance of President Carlos Ibañez produced a calamitous decline in workers' income and in economic growth (Mamalakis 1976, 197) and solidified labor solidarity and leftist party unity. In 1953, labor came together to form a nationwide organization, the CUT (Single Workers' Central), and before the 1958 election, the leftist parties united to form the FRAP (Popular Action Front), which ran in the 1958 election with Salvador Allende as its presidential candidate. By 1958, Chile's political center was beginning to crumble as the Christian Democrats and Radicals moved leftward. In the 1958 election attention turned to the countryside, where the FRAP and the Christian Democrats campaigned among and organized rural workers and made important inroads into the Conservative and Liberal Parties' bases of support. By the early 1960s, the Radical Party, pushed by electoral pressures, supported agrarian reform, but it was quickly being replaced by the Christian Democratic Party as the important centrist party.

The Christian Democratic government of Eduardo Frei, backed by a political right fearful of the FRAP Marxists (the Conservatives and Liberals), won the 1964 presidential election with 41.3 percent of the popular vote. The Christian Democrats had promised a variety of measures—agrarian reform, rural unionization, and the enforcement of labor laws—that were intolerable not only to the party's right-wing allies but also to many of its own members. Nevertheless, the party carried through on its rhetoric, mobilizing women, students, workers, and peasants into unions and cooperative and community organizations and provided these new organizations with both funding and official encouragement. The administration also initiated agrarian reform, a program that took three years to get through Congress, expropriating large tracts of land to form peasant co-ops. Its 1967 legislation making possible rural unions, combined with the mobilization activities of both it and the Marxist left, produced a rapid rise in rural unionism (Grayson 1969, 59). The number of strikes in the rural areas shot up, as did rural land invasions and factory takeovers. As political action became more and more conflictive involving a direct threat to property interests, the political right withdrew support from the Christian Democrats. With the Liberals and Conservatives united in the National Party, the MIR (Movement of the Revolutionary Left), a group formerly within the FRAP, began to operate clandestinely, inciting subversion, and MAPU (Movement for United Popular Action), led by Christian Democrat Jacques Chonchol, encouraged peasant activism. But political polarization and the growing threat of violence would reach their apogee only with the administration of Popular Unity president Salvador Allende (1970–73).

The election of Salvador Allende, leader of a coalition of socialists and communists known as Popular Unity, with 36.2 percent of the popular vote, sent alarm signals throughout the private sector. Between 1970 and 1973 fear and violence on both sides and a deteriorating economic situation set the stage for the military coup of 1973.[7] President Allende's attempt to carry out a major transformation of the economy without the support of Congress and a substantial majority of the public was important in deepening right-wing animosities. His use of the little-known decree/law 520, along with other legal loopholes, to requisition, intervene, or expropriate a wide array of private enterprises seemed to represent clear evidence to the private sector that there was no room for it in the UP scheme of things. Land occupations and factory takeovers accelerated, often under the leadership of leftist elements within the UP, while right-wing vigilante groups, such as Patria y Libertad, engaged in armed confrontation (Roxborough, O'Brien, and Roddick 1977, 132). The MIR was demanding full-scale insurrection. The CUT called for mass demonstrations in support of the government and for workers and peasants to occupy factories and agricultural lands. In a single day, the number of companies taken over by the government doubled (Sigmund 1977, 215). Strikes against government policy carried out by shopkeepers, various professional associations, and later the truckers wreaked havoc on the economy and eroded political support while the hostility of the United States to the regime made the economic deterioration greater than it would otherwise have been (Petras and Morley 1975, 92, 95). Shortages of many products were widespread and inflation exceeded 500 percent. On the eve of the military coup, not only had Chile's political center evaporated, but both rhetoric and actions had destroyed the trust and goodwill necessary for compromise. Chile's elites had by now abandoned their reliance on the incorporative capacity of the electoral process; indeed, civilians from many quarters, including housewives and members of the House of Deputies, now clamored for a military coup (Constable and Valenzuela 1991, 29).

The Chilean military had intervened only twice in the country's history: in 1924, when it had remained in power for four months, and in 1931, when, again, its stay in power was a matter of a few months. By all accounts, the armed forces had a fairly strong nationalist and statist predisposition. But it was isolated from society at large, despised parliamentary practices, and was resentful of the country's political elites, whom it viewed as corrupt and incompetent (Loveman 1988, 193; Constable and Valenzuela 1991, 40). Moreover, the Chilean military had little contact with civilians and was banned from voting in elections. Its disgust of parliamentary politics, parties, and politicians predisposed it to eliminating them once it achieved power, while the military's relatively high degree of isolation from societal pressures meant that factions within it would not act as advocates for societal allies.

Chilean history from the turn of the century until 1973 is to a considerable extent the history of popular mobilization and radicalization. This radicalization was carried forward by a Marxist left with the support of a weak but relatively independent and unusually militant trade union movement. Chile's electoral politics allowed demands for change to be played out to their ultimate conclusion—to the acquisition of political power by a Marxist regime. But the process engendered unprecedented political and ideological polarization, political violence, and economic chaos, a situation that disgusted the country's insulated military establishment. Moreover, the strength and independence of the Chilean left and the country's general lack of faith in market mechanisms had not gone unnoticed by market proponents in the United States. As we will see in Chapter 4, Chile's deep political and economic crisis would open the way for a new ruling alliance.

ARGENTINA: POLITICAL CYCLES AND THE PERSISTENCE OF ECONOMIC LIBERALISM

If Chile before 1973 stood out for its liberal pluralist electoral stability, Argentina was marked by chronic political instability, with cycles of democracy and authoritarianism of ever-increasing intensity. Since 1930, six constitutionally elected governments have been overthrown by military coups in Argentina, there have been six countercoups, and between 1952 and 1994 no democratically elected president had served out his term of office (Manzetti 1993, 163; Wynia 1986, 86). Susan Calvert and Peter Calvert (1989) have argued that in Argentina, the conflict between liberal and Iberian strains has been by far the greatest of any Latin American country. While this is certainly true, it is important to recognize what those traditions stand for in the Argentine context: liberalism refers to economic liberalism, not the pluralism and legality of liberal democracy that were features of the Chilean political landscape. The Argentine historical experience gave the country's Iberian patterns enormous strength and resiliency. Moreover, in contrast with Chile, political struggle in Argentina was waged outside of the institutional framework of liberal competitive political parties and in the sphere of corporate interests with recourse to military intervention to decide the outcome. Indeed, Argentina has a long history of politicians, union bosses, entrepreneurs, and landed interests maintaining close links with the military.

Economic liberalization was a recurring feature of a bitterly contested political agenda. Although economic liberalism had strong domestic supporters, it had just as powerful opponents. Despite appearances to the contrary, market reforms in Argentina (again, unlike Chile) did not occur suddenly but had been on the back burner for a very long time. And, unlike Chile, such reforms would be blocked by the military, which had a long history of political involvement and was an important presence in state industry. The strongest and most consistent support for economic liberalism was found in Argentina's "oligarchy" of beef producers and commercial import-export interests, who from the last quarter of the nineteenth century strongly opposed government protection of "false" industries — industries that were not viable because they were not based on domestic primary products. The country's most powerful industrial interests took a softer stand on the free market issues but were also highly critical of state intervention and criticized state enterprises as inefficient (Freels 1970, 62). By the mid-1950s, support for economic liberalization in the military was on the rise. The liberal economic perspective prevailed before 1930 and reemerged at every economic crisis thereafter.[8]

Unlike the Chilean mining/landholding elite, the Argentine counterpart was unable to forge a viable conservative party capable of winning elections and gaining significant parliamentary representation to protect those interests and therefore resorted to military intervention when threatened (Cavarozzi 1997, 28; Peralta Ramos 1992a, 46). The Saenz Pena Law of 1912, making the franchise secret, universal, and compulsory, allowed the Radical

Party to win the 1916 national election and wrest power from the country's conservative landholding and business elite. Argentine landed and business interests soon lost patience with the Radical Party's nationalist, statist, and mildly reformist predisposition and with its general incompetence in the face of the Great Depression. The landed/business elite's return to power through the military coup of 1930 marked the beginning of a thirteen-year period (1930–43) known as *la década infame* (the infamous decade) during which electoral fraud and political repression kept opposition political parties out of the political game and social reform off the political agenda. The infamous decade eroded the legitimacy of Argentina's liberal democratic institutional framework as elections and political parties came to be viewed as sources of political and economic exclusion (Ciria 1974, 74).

While the public was becoming increasingly disillusioned with the exclusionary and fraudulent nature of politics, rapid social changes soon gave rise to a new political movement that forced open the political system. After an initial economic slide, the Great Depression triggered a more vigorous phase of import-substitution industrialization than occurred elsewhere in Latin America, producing a dramatic rise in the number of industrial workers, most of them migrants from the interior (James 1988, 7–8; Fuchs 1965, 262). Although the Communists had some success in organizing workers in certain sectors, in general this new urban proletariat lacked an organizational leadership to articulate its very pressing demands for housing, urban services, and better wages and working conditions. As a consequence, the Argentine working class was ripe for the appeal of Peronism, a political movement that gave voice to workers' collective humiliation and offered plausible and immediate remedies. Described as a "modern culture derived from the Iberian legacy" (Calvert and Calvert 1989, 119), Peronism is probably the most notable manifestation of Argentina's Iberian strain, owing much of its resiliency to the manipulation and degradation of liberal democratic political institutions by the country's conservative elite. Besides its heavy emphasis on personal leadership, it displayed a tendency toward monism, hierarchy, nationalism, statism, clientelism, and corporatism. Peronism rejected liberal democratic politics as corrupt and proposed corporative representation in the state of society's major social groups.

The military officers carrying out the coup of 1943, among them Juan Domingo Perón, shared a widespread disgust for the operation of the political system. Under Perón's auspices the Argentine labor movement acquired unparalleled political power, becoming the strongest labor movement in Latin America. With the elections of 1946, which brought Perón to the presidency, labor leaders entered Congress, and from then on, union leaders were routinely consulted on matters of national importance (James 1988, 11). Indeed, the Peronist leadership was never capable of fully controlling the labor movement, which experienced its most important growth during the years of Perón's presidency.[9] In direct contrast with the Chilean case, legal and institutional arrangements gave the labor leadership centralized power and great wealth.[10] The compulsory deduction of union dues, and especially the legal requirement for employers to contribute to social welfare funds (*obras sociales*), provided the basis for a wide range of social services (hotels, hospitals). With a centralized union structure, these funds became a source of patronage and pressure in the hands of union leaders and were used to reward loyal followers. At the same time, the requirement for legal recognition from the state (without which a union could not negotiate or receive union dues) facilitated control of the country's labor movement through the Ministry of Labor. Perón used this structure to consolidate his base of support in the trade union movement, intervening and withdrawing legal recognition from uncooperative unions and establishing parallel ones to which he extended recognition. Over time, wealthy and corrupt union leaders, considerably distanced from the rank and file, came to dominate most unions in Argentina. Nevertheless, worker support for the movement was grounded in real gains made during the first period of Peronist rule. Working conditions improved when legislation was passed providing for the eight-hour day and the forty-eight-hour week. Between 1946 and 1948, real wages were raised almost 50 percent (Wynia 1986, 66), and the share of wages in national income increased from 40 percent to 49 percent (James 1988, 11). A new statute introduced collective bargaining for farm workers and provided for a minimum wage and restricted child labor.

The Perón regime's nationalism, concern for industrialization, and commitment to redistributive issues led to a dramatic increase in the role of the state. Until that time, state involvement in the economy had been sporadic. Much of the earliest state investment responded to the military's desire to become self-sufficient in weaponry and in heavy industrial sectors deemed to be strategic. By 1941, when fourteen military factories were consolidated into a holding company called Fabricaciones Militares, the military complex had expanded beyond munitions production into liquid gas piping, agricultural equipment, and oil drilling machinery (Lewis 1990, 149). Military men were in charge of these companies from the beginning.

Between 1943 and 1955 (Perón held the presidency between 1946 and 1955), the functions of the state increased dramatically as a consequence of nationalizations and the expansion of the state into a wide variety of activities, including trade, banking, and industrial promotion. Between 1945 and 1952, the state acquired most of its largest and most important companies.[11] The explicit bias of the regime in favor of state-led industrialization is illustrated by the role of the Argentine Institute for the Promotion of Trade (IAPI), which appropriated a sizable portion of the agricultural surplus, which it funneled in the form of credit to national industry through the Banco Industrial de la República Argentina.[12] By 1950, total state spending adjusted for inflation was 87 percent over the 1940–44 level, and between 1943 and 1952, government employment increased by 144 percent (Smith 1989, 45; Most 1991, 111). While state enterprise provided the private sector with cheap inputs, heavy industrial protection shielded domestic business from foreign competition. In addition to increased protection granted in 1948, in 1950 importation was totally prohibited in sectors in which local production was deemed sufficient. Numerous other industries received such benefits as quota protection (in which quantitative limits are placed on the importation of a product), and additional protection was made available under the "national interest" designation (Kenworthy 1970, 76, 82).

The overthrow of Perón by a military coup in 1955 signaled the division of Argentine society into Peronists and anti-Peronists. Big business and landed interests had been intensely threatened by Peronist economic policy, especially by the transfer of the wealth produced by the agricultural sector to support what was believed to be an inefficient industrial sector and the expansion of benefits and privileges to workers, which cut into profits. Although Peronism claimed a commitment to class conciliation, the so-called third way, it was a working-class movement based in the trade unions, and it had developed a "political culture of opposition" rooted in the lived experience of its mass base (James 1988, 34). Like Chile, Argentina became a deeply divided society.

Between 1955 and 1965 the explicit aim of the various military and civilian governments and their landed and big business allies was the elimination of the Peronist movement. The Peronist Party was not allowed to run candidates in the elections of 1957, 1958, 1960, and 1963; in 1958, no one who had held office under Perón could run for public office; and between 1962 and 1965, the Peronist Party could run only under tough restrictions (Lewis 1990, 232). Despite legal restrictions on its activities, Peronism, now more than ever embodied in the trade union movement, remained a major political force. It carried out its political struggle not through the party system but by means of direct action — strikes, demonstrations, and marches against the state.

The focus of the Peronist trade union movement's opposition was the various attempts by regimes, after 1955, to move economic policy away from its expansionary interventionist course toward a more orthodox approach. The Peronist episode had triggered a renewed antistatism among powerful landed and business interests and in the military. Indeed, the coup overthrowing Perón had been backed by the economic liberals in the military (McSherry 1997, 44). But efforts at economic liberalization were constantly blocked by strong popular opposition. Economic policy between 1955 and 1973 did not move decisively in any direction for long; indeed, in response to shifting political coalitions, it swung between expansionary populism and orthodox stabilization with the occasional attempt at compromise through heterodoxy.[13] Although Arturo Frondizi (1958–62) began with an expansionary, populist program, by the end of 1958 his government had embarked on a stabilization program that made some attempt at structural change. That program removed government subsidies and price controls, removed direct controls on trade, reduced tariffs from 300 to 150 percent, and carried out some privatizations (Goldwert 1972, 171; Ferrer et al. 1974, 191). But Frondizi's program generated growing opposition from the labor movement manifested in a rise in strike activity. When the elections of 1962 produced Peronist victories in the governorships of four provinces and in the Chamber of Deputies, the economic liberals in the military overthrew Frondizi. Between 1961 and 1976, this scenario would be repeated as each attempt at stabilization was followed by expansionary episodes. During this period, two additional attempts were made to improve the efficiency of the railway sector under President Arturo Illia (1962), and under President Juan Carlos Onganía (1966) shares in the state-owned steel company, Mixed Argentine Steel Corporation, or SOMISA, were put up for sale. In 1966–68, the military closed down eleven sugar mills in Tucumán and announced its intent to privatize various public companies (McSherry 1997, 67; Fuchs 1965, 372, 358).

The state's role, however, remained central; indeed, despite the best efforts of liberal reformers, its role had expanded. As a consequence of legislation passed in 1970, the state was empowered to take over failing private sector companies and soon took over fifteen more companies (Ugalde 1984, 22). The civilian Peronist government elected in 1973 initially embarked on yet another expansionary program increasing subsidies, granting wage increases, and taking over five television stations. By 1975, total public expenditure as a percentage of GDP reached almost 40 percent, while the public deficit as a percentage of GDP stood at 15 percent (Appendix 2, Table A.2). The second Peronist regime ended its days with a tough stabilization program in the face of rising inflation (Smith 1989, 230). As usual, such an austerity program was met with widespread opposition.

By the early 1970s Argentina, like Chile, was facing both an economic and a political crisis. The experience of military rule had split the labor movement between those choosing to negotiate and those favoring outright opposition. The growing bureaucratization of the labor movement, a function of its centralized structure and economic wealth and its collaboration with military regimes, had produced a conservative stratum of corrupt labor leaders increasingly opposed by their rank and file and by the idealistic youth of the Peronist movement.[14] From 1969 on, violent mass confrontations gathered momentum beginning with the uprising in Córdoba (the *Cordobazo*) and continuing with wildcat strikes and increased guerrilla operations conducted by four guerrilla organizations including that of the Peronist left (the Montoneros). Meanwhile, assassinations and bombings were carried out by paramilitary groups linked to the Peronist right and to the authoritarian nationalist current in the army (McSherry 1997, 72). By 1975, the liberal wing of the military was deeply concerned about the growing division in its ranks, the extent of political unrest, and the worsening economy. Landowners and big business now saw an authoritarian solution as the only feasible way out, and in the midst of this political and economic chaos much of the public came to agree with them. The stage was set for the economic liberals in the military to take power—but strangely enough, that group would prove far less successful than the more solidly nationalist Chilean military regime in reducing the role of the state.

Argentine history, from the turn of the century, has been marked by the struggle for access to the political process by a working class excluded by repression and by the manipulation of liberal democratic institutions. In this process, the construction of a powerful working-class identity with Peronism, a movement that is both statist and nonliberal with features from the Iberian strain, vies for power with an economic elite whose liberalism extends only to the economic sphere. Unlike the Chilean military, the Argentine one is characterized by strong ties with a wide spectrum of social groups and political parties; like the Chilean one, it now moves in to fill the breach created by the country's political and economic crises, but it makes only small inroads into the realm of market reform, as we will see in Chapter 5.

MEXICO: CORPORATIST AUTHORITARIANISM
AND STATE-LED INDUSTRIALIZATION

In Mexico, as in Chile, the private sector expanded under the aegis of a highly interventionist state; like Chile, the liberal economic impulse was considerably weaker than in Argentina. Even more so than in the Argentine case, corporatist political controls and clientelism became key in containing political unrest. Politically, the Iberian strain has predominated in Mexico. By the late 1980s, however, the old corporatist/clientelist mechanisms of control were weakening (Teichman 1997b), while elections and democratic institutions increased in importance. Further, the Mexican case stands out from the southern cone and from Latin America generally for the absence of military intervention in its politics and for the longevity of its political stability, only recently threatened by the impact of repeated economic crisis and rural insurgency. Compared with Chile and Argentina, Mexico's pre–market reform phase was marked by a relatively high sustained growth rate (Appendix 2, Table A.1), while Mexico remained one of the most inequitable countries in Latin America (Hansen 1980, 1, 71). Political stability and one-party rule allowed for the development of bureaucratic/technocratic enclaves within the state from which the country's most ardent market reformers would expand their control. Further, the country's corporatist and clientelist arrangements played a critical role in the ability of the country's elite to contain dissent during the market reform process.

Mexico has a revolutionary past. The Mexican Revolution (1911–17) was fought not just against the political brutality of the rule of Porfirio Díaz (1876–1911) but also against an economic liberalism that divested peasants of land and reduced the living standards of workers. Victory for the popular participants (workers and peasants) of the Mexican Revolution signified the defeat of the paramountcy of property rights and foreign investment. But when the dust settled and the country's old landed elite was removed from power, Mexican workers and peasants were subordinate to the middle-class professional and bourgeoisie who had largely led the revolution and who now took over the reins of political power and established the country's postrevolutionary political arrangements. The rigid authoritarian rule of the Porfiriato would soon be replaced by more flexible and highly effective authoritarian arrangements.

Indeed, a proficient system of political control that inhibited the emergence of unified and politically independent organizations of workers and peasants emerged. The key institution involved in this process was the Institutional Revolutionary Party (PRI). Created by President Plutarco Elías Calles in 1929, the party centralized power in the presidency and used patronage in the form of roads, schools, and agricultural credit to incorporate state political machines and to co-opt and control rebellious regional caudillos (Cline 1961, 199). It was not until the 1930s, however, that it became closely identified with a mythology of revolutionary nationalism involving nationalist aspirations and popular desires for land and social justice. Mexico's revolutionary mythology, a powerful source of regime legitimacy for years to come, arose with the presidency of Lázaro Cárdenas (1934–40), as did the corporatist/clientelist institutional framework, a set of arrangements that contributed to regime stability through containing dissent and potential dissent.

The Great Depression had produced a drastic decline in Mexican exports (by 1932, they were one-third their 1929 level); between 1929 and 1932, GDP declined 6.3 percent annually (Solís 1981, 87). The resultant social and political unrest gave rise to a growing radical movement within the PRI and to the ascent of reformer Lázaro Cárdenas to the presidency. The identification of peasants with the PRI was intimately tied to the benefits from land reform they received during these years. A little over 44 million acres of land were distributed, more land than had been distributed by any administration before or since. Spending on education was doubled in rural areas, agricultural credit was increased, and spending on social welfare in general reached the highest point in Mexican history (Wilkie 1967, 136, 157, 159). Cárdenas supported the formation of trade unions, strikes, and the negotiation of collective agreements, and under his administration state arbitration decisions consistently favored labor over capital (Berins Collier 1991, 25; Middlebrook 1995, 95–101).

Labor and peasants were organized at the national level and incorporated into the PRI. The administration sponsored the formation of the Confederation of Mexican Workers (CTM), the National Confederation of Peasants (CNC), and the National Confederation of Popular Organizations (CNOP). Each of these organizations was incorporated into a reorganized party replacing the former regional representation.[15] After 1940, however, power came to be heavily concentrated in the presidency, as the leaderships of sectoral organizations, if not handpicked by the president, had to meet with his approval; the loyalty of sectoral leaders was to the party and the goals of the president, not to rank-and-file trade unionists.

The 1931 Labor Code, which required labor unions to obtain legal recognition from the state as a condition of engaging in strike activity, gave the state the wherewithal to favor cooperative unions and punish the unco-operative. The code also set up the legal requirements of strike activity, in effect making it impossible without state support (Grayson 1989, 57). More-over, centralized control within unions gave the top leadership the power to discipline union locals or individual members (Bizberg 1990, 123). Hence labor organizations in Mexico, as in Argentina, were hierarchically orga-nized and centralized. Unlike Argentina, however, their autonomy of action was heavily circumscribed by control from the top down exercised through the state and through the PRI.

By the 1950s, corporatist arrangements in the official labor organiza-tions were reinforced by *charrismo*,[16] a particularly nefarious form of patron clientelism involving state imposition (usually by violent means) of cor-rupt union leaders. Union leadership control of union dues, access to spe-cial funds provided by the company for "social works," and rights to gov-ernment contracts often provided in collective agreements allowed it to amass considerable wealth (Teichman 1995, 65; Córtes 1984, 93). In exchange, *charros* remained loyal to the political leadership, quelled dissent, and en-sured that their rank and file voted for the PRI at election time. Collective agreements that provided labor leaders with the ability to dispense such re-wards as housing, scholarships, and loans greatly facilitated their ability to keep rank-and-file workers generally loyal to the union leadership and to the PRI. The peasant organization, the CNC, performed a similar role in co-opting peasant leaders and ensuring support for the PRI until the late 1960s. After that date, this role was taken over by agencies of the state agricul-tural bureaucracy such as marketing boards and state farm banks, especially the National Bank of Rural Credit (BANRURAL), which provided support for *ejidos* (communal landholding cooperatives). While corporatist/clientelist control of worker and peasant organizations was generally effective in con-taining political unrest, it was not always sufficient. When it was not, the political leadership did not hesitate to use violent repression.

Because the economic liberalism of the Porfiriato had brought such severe hardships to so many Mexican peasants and workers, a new role for the state in the economy was enshrined in the constitution of 1917. At the behest of radical revolutionaries, articles were inserted that declared private property subordinate to the public interest, declared the nation to be the owner of all minerals and deposits beneath the soil and all waters, and empowered the state to solve disputes between capital and labor (Witaker and Eslava 1988, 336; Ayala Espino 1988, 77). The Great Depression triggered the initial ex-pansion of the state; between 1934 and 1938 the country's most important state enterprises were established. Under the powers provided by the 1936 Expropriation Law, President Cárdenas fulfilled the nationalist dreams of Mexican workers by nationalizing enterprises in foreign enclaves. The most important of the new state companies established during this period was the state petroleum company, Petróleos Mexicanos (PEMEX). State expenditure on infrastructure and social programs shot up and state investment accelerated (Ayala Espino 1988, 373). By 1936, government finances were in deficit (Ayala Espino 1988, 188).

Between 1940 and the early 1980s, the expansion of the Mexican state was relentless. Public enterprise moved into important sectors such as the production of steel, copper, and fertilizer, the manufacture of railway cars and trucks, telecommunications, and the operation of airlines. By 1961, National Financiera (NAFINSA), the state development bank, was creditor, investor, or guarantor of 533 business enterprises (Blair 1964, 196). This state expansion continued to be reflected in dramatic increases in the level of investment and expenditure: by 1965, total public expenditure was at 24 percent of GDP (Appendix 2, Table A.2). As in the other two cases, there were strong protectionist measures. Quota protection was the preferred instrument, administered discretionally on a case-by-case basis by committees of officials and businessmen, although tariffs were also used. By 1956, 25 percent of imports were controlled; by 1970, 80 percent of imports required a license (Villareal 1977, 71; Izqueirdo 1964, 268).

Unlike Argentina and Chile, Mexico's statist import-substitution model did not begin to run into trouble until the late 1960s. To a large extent, Mexico's early reformist measures and the mechanisms of political incorporation and control laid the groundwork for sustained growth until the late 1960s. By the late 1950s, Mexico's import-substitution model was experiencing difficulties; high levels of government spending sustained through increasing the money supply were generating inflation. Using the mechanisms of authoritarian corporatism to contain political dissent, Mexico made a relatively smooth transition to a new strategy known as "stabilizing development," which abandoned this inflationary source of financing and turned instead to high reserve requirements, foreign investment, and, increasingly, foreign borrowing (Green 1981, 106). Strong labor unrest in the railway, petroleum, and mining sectors springing from the decline in real wages in the late 1950s was dealt with through a combination of charrismo and state repression (Alonso 1986, 153).[17]

By the mid-1960s, however, the economy began to stagnate, and by the late 1960s it was in crisis. As agricultural production slowed, the balance-of-payments deficit shot up. Unemployment and underemployment stood at between 50 and 60 percent (Tello 1979, 76). At the same time, the country's authoritarian political arrangements began to show serious signs of strain. Political unrest climaxed in 1968 with the student strike and massacre of an estimated two hundred striking students by government troops at Tlatelolco. The legitimacy of its rule sorely damaged, the PRI scrambled to recoup its image. It began to open the way for a greater role for political opposition: political reforms in 1973 made it easier for small parties to gain seats in the Chamber of Deputies and government censorship was loosened. Further reform in 1977 eased registration requirements, allowing more political parties legal status and guaranteed at least one-quarter of the Chamber of Deputies seats for opposition parties (Story 1986a, 47–49). While these reforms are usually characterized as part of the ruling elite's strategy to contain and channel dissent, there is no question that they raised the importance of electoral politics, a change that would be further accelerated after 1982 with the combined impact of economic crises, the growth of political opposition, and additional political reforms.

Meanwhile, Mexico's rulers were acutely aware of the pressing need to spur economic growth. Belt-tightening measures were initially implemented under President Luis Echeverría (1970–76) but were soon abandoned in favor of an expansionary program under which total government spending increased from 25 percent of GDP to 36 percent between 1969 and 1973 (Appendix 2, Table A.2). The state acquired more than seven hundred companies during the Echeverría years, spanning a wide variety of sectors, many rescued by the state to protect employment. The international economic downturn of the early 1970s caused by the world petroleum crisis of 1973–74 hit Mexico hard and was made worse by U.S. protectionist measures. Hence the Echeverría administration closed with the signing of a stabilization agreement with the International Monetary Fund which limited borrowing and public spending.

The discovery of vast petroleum reserves in Tabasco and Chiapas, however, allowed Mexico to escape the cutback in state activity that was occurring in Chile at the time and that was attempted and fiercely resisted in Argentina. With capital flowing in, International Monetary Fund loans were paid off in advance and the country embarked on a period of state-led expansion that saw growth rates averaging 8.5 percent per year between 1978 and 1981. In 1981, petroleum prices began to slide in the international market, however, and international interest rates increased, while international banks resisted providing new loans. The Mexican economy crashed:

GDP declined by −1.5 percent in 1982. Between the mid-1970s and 1982, the participation of public enterprises in GDP had more than doubled (Villareal 1986, 32) and the number of firms in which the state participated increased from 845 in 1976 to 1,115 by 1982 (Teichman 1995, 29). The economic crisis itself had triggered an unprecedented expansion of the state. In the face of massive capital flight, the administration of President José López Portillo nationalized eighteen private banks in 1982.

The steady growth of the Mexican economy through the 1960s and the boom of the 1976–81 years had created an environment in which it was not possible to question the expansion of the state. Officials in the Mexican Central Bank and in the Finance Ministry, however, had long been critical of the extensive nature of the state's roles, particularly the high level of state expenditure and the role of the state enterprise sector (Bennett and Sharpe 1982, 175, 177; Purcell and Purcell 1980; Teichman 1988, 99). But as concerned as these public officials were for the expansion of the state, they did not advocate reduction of industrial protection, nor did they call for the state to divest itself of any its many enterprises. The other locus of anti-statism—although not economic liberalism in general—was found among powerful members of the private sector. The most powerful business interests, originating in prerevolutionary Mexico, are a group of financial industrial conglomerates based in the city of Monterrey. The "Monterrey Group" has been characterized by fierce resistance to state intervention in the economy (Haber 1989, 84–104; Saragoza 1988, 116, 151). The most notable periods of conflict with the state occurred during the last years of the Echeverría administration and the final months of López Portillo's term and were a consequence of the 1982 bank nationalization.[18] Although big business was a strong supporter of state withdrawal from the public enterprise sector, streamlining the state, and reducing state spending, its free market propensities, like those of its allies in the public finance sector, did not encompass trade liberalization. Reducing Mexico's strong statist propensities sufficiently to allow market reform to move forward would require another economic crisis and the political triumph of radical reform technocrats. It would also be a process in which the country's corporatist clientelist political arrangements would play a key role.

CONCLUSIONS

All three countries pursued highly statist economic models, especially from the 1940s onward. By the late 1960s, all three began to experience increasing economic difficulties. By the 1970s both Chile and Argentina faced serious economic and political crises. Only Chile, however, was on the threshold of a radical market reform program. Chile, where worker militancy was not contained through mechanisms of corporatist/clientelist political control, had developed an institutionalized competitive party system. By the late 1960s this system was no longer capable of containing the ideological polarization that had been building over past decades. In 1973, Chile's competitive democracy was replaced by military rule—by this time fully and enthusiastically endorsed by a propertied middle class fearful of the socialist experiment. Chile in many ways seemed to be an unlikely candidate for market reform, however: ideas of economic liberalism generally lacked support either in society or in the military, well known for its nationalist orientation. But market reform ideas were taking root among a small segment of society by means of an educational aid program supported by the United States, whose interest in Chile had been triggered in part by the overwhelming presence of statist, including Marxist, ideas. Other historical factors would give market reformers the edge: the weakness of the labor movement and its heavy dependence on political parties would facilitate the political exclusion of labor; the military's historical lack of political involvement and its relative absence of ties to outside civilian groups that could provide channels for political lobbying against market reform would also prove important. The intensity with which the postcoup economic program would be pursued was a reaction to the intensity of change in the brief period of UP rule. The new ruling alliance, involving the military, the traditional right, and technocrats, would mark the reemergence of Chile's Iberian strain.

Argentina, too, was a highly polarized society by the mid-1970s—polarized between Peronists and anti-Peronists and between statism and anti-statism. There was a strong indigenous base of support for economic liberalism, and steps had been taken on numerous occasions in this direction. Indeed, much of Argentine politics has revolved around the question of economic liberalization versus statism, as the country oscillated back and forth between the two. Further, a great deal of this struggle occurred outside of the institutions of electoral democracy. Indeed, manipulation of the institutions of electoral democracy had strengthened the country's Iberian strain, which continued as a major feature of its politics into the twentieth century. Neither corporatism nor clientelism could contain Argentina's powerful labor movement. An ardent opponent of economic liberalism, the Argentine labor movement became the most powerful in Latin America. It was capable of gaining access to the highest reaches of power and blocking policies it did not like. Argentina's military establishment had a long history of political involvement. It had vested interests in state industry, and its ties with civilian groups opened it to outside lobbying. Despite the presence of an important faction supportive of economic liberalism, Argentina therefore would not be a good candidate for leading market reform, as we will see in Chapter 5. The strength of Argentine civil society meant that the road to market reform would be tortuous and protracted, and it would be one in which the country's two political strains would continue to interact.

Unlike the other two cases, Mexico experienced a revolution and the opportunity to establish a set of political arrangements that proved highly successful at containing dissent and potential dissent. Largely based on the hierarchical principles of corporatism and patron clientelism, the Mexican political process has been characterized by the predominance of its Iberian strain. It is largely as a consequence of its corporatist/clientelist political arrangements that Mexico avoided the extreme political polarization that characterized the other two cases during the 1960s and 1970s, while a highly centralized presidentialist system was able to impose fairly coherent economic programs. These features would operate during the market reform process.

Until the mid-1980s, Mexico was characterized by a strong national consensus favoring an activist state, a consensus rooted in the country's revolutionary past. Many years of political stability, however, had allowed for the development of a state bureaucracy in which enclaves of support for economic liberalism emerged. Meanwhile, powerful private sector interests, alienated by the 1982 bank nationalization, became increasingly antistatist. The discovery of petroleum reserves enabled Mexico to postpone the serious consideration of policy reform; it continued to borrow and spend right up until 1981. But when recurrent economic crises forced a rethinking of economic policy, the market reform process bore the dual imprint of the country's antistatist bureaucratic enclaves and powerful private sector groups and its corporatist/clientelist authoritarian political history.

chapter three

THE INTERNATIONAL CONTEXT
Policy-Based Lending, Policy Dialogue, and International Policy Networks

The economic policy reforms carried out in the three countries covered in this book can be fully understood only in the context of the international financial system. It is this broader context that defined the parameters of policy choice, particularly as the debt crisis of the early 1980s became increasingly intractable. Indeed, international factors were operative even in Chile (in 1983–85), the country seen as the independent Latin leader in market reform. Hence this chapter sketches the broad outlines of that international context, highlighting the direction and nature of pressures on Latin American policy elites. I do not argue that international financial institutions imposed reform policies but rather that the interaction of external pressures and actors with domestic policy elites was important in driving the process forward and in keeping it on track—indeed, in some cases it was essential to reform momentum. The pressures of debt negotiations, however, were not the same for all countries, nor were the responses of policy elites.

THE INTERNATIONAL FINANCIAL SYSTEM AND THE INSTRUMENTS OF POLICY-BASED LENDING

The international financial system includes the commercial banks and the network of official banks, known as multilateral lending institutions: the International Monetary Fund, the World Bank (the International Bank for Reconstruction and Development), and the various regional banks. The Bretton Woods Agreement between the major Western powers in 1944 established the IMF and the World Bank to prevent a relapse into the competitive devaluation, protectionism, massive unemployment, and general economic chaos of the Great Depression. Originally, the World Bank was to provide long-term project-oriented money for the rebuilding of infrastructure in war-torn Europe, while the IMF was to provide short-term financing for countries with transitory balance-of-payments problems. Neither institution was set up to solve the enormous economic problems of developing countries in general or of Latin American countries in particular.

Both institutions were to become intimately involved in the debt crisis faced by Latin American countries in the early 1980s and in the formulation and implementation of market reforms thereafter. In fact, both the IMF and the World Bank have long histories of involvement in Latin America beginning in the mid-1950s, a history that has involved what is known as conditional lending practices. Conditional lending, requiring the recipient country to agree to prescribed economic measures as a condition for loans, evolved as standard procedure in the IMF between 1948 and 1952 (Biersteker 1993, 3). In 1952, the IMF introduced the standby agreement, a twelve-to-eighteen-month agreement in which the disbursement of each tranche (installment) is contingent on the achievement of economic performance targets (Dale 1983, 14). In the late 1950s, standby agreements were signed between several Latin American countries, including Chile and Argentina, and the IMF. As country after country in the region faced balance-of-payments difficulties through the 1950s and 1960s, such agreements between Latin American countries and the IMF proliferated. The stabilization programs embodied in standby agreements included a variety of targets involving restrictions on the expansion of money and credit, on public sector expenditures, and on wages and salaries (Marshall S., Mardones S., and Marshall L. 1983, 279–84). Some of these early programs sought the elimination of trade protection, devaluations of national currencies, and measures to encourage the entry of foreign capital. Although the IMF's commitment to state streamlining and the opening up of markets would become considerably more marked following the 1982 debt crisis, its support for such policy prescriptions predates that crisis and is rooted in its belief that such policies will reduce inflation and the balance-of-payments deficit (Lichtensztejn 1983, 212–16). Such sound economic policies, the IMF believed, would improve economic performance so as to "maximize the probability that the loan will be repaid" (Mosley 1987, 1). For the most part, the Latin American countries signing such agreements with the IMF did not comply with the policy conditions (Marshall S., Mardones S., and Marshall L. 1983, 297–98). With the rise of regimes espousing expansionary spending policies in the region during the 1970s (Echeverría in Mexico, Allende in Chile, Perón in Argentina), the influence of the IMF declined even further (Marshall S., Mardones S., and Marshall L. 1983, 216).

In 1974, the IMF made its first foray into stimulating longer-term reform when it established the Extended Fund Facility (EFF) to help correct "structural maladjustments in production and trade" (Azizali 1991, 246). EFFs provide credits for up to three years and in larger amounts than under standby arrangements, and repayments are stretched out to four and one-half to ten years. To be eligible, a country must be in balance-of-payments difficulties and have structural imbalances in production, trade, and prices. Brazil, Chile, Mexico, and Venezuela have been the greatest borrowers under the EFF program, which calls for trade liberalization, decontrol of prices, and restructuring of public sector enterprises (Griffith-Jones 1992, 69; Rodríguez 1991, 35). By 1992, EFF loans had replaced standby loans in importance, with Mexico and Venezuela taking the lion's share of these loans (Bird 1995, 110, 102). Other IMF policy-based programs important for Latin America have been Enhanced Surveillance and Compensatory and Contingency Financing Facilities (CCFF).[1] IMF facilities all involve a high degree of conditionality. Among the IMF's most important policy requirements are the elimination of foreign exchange controls and trade restrictions and the reduction in various forms of subsidies, especially to loss-making public enterprises (Finch 1983, 83; Biersteker 1993, 13). While the main mandate of the World Bank was project lending, it was also concerned that sound macroeconomic policies be in place and increasingly took macro policy into consideration before agreeing to or disbursing loans (Kapur, Lewis, and Webb 1997, 458). The specific origin of World Bank structural adjustment lending is found in the 1963–64 program lending the bank made available to India in support of that country's balance of payments (Mosley, Harrigan, and Toye 1995, 28), although lending for broader policy change would not be officially inaugurated until 1979.

Both the bank and the IMF have shared similar concerns although the bank's views, for a variety of reasons, have been considerably more heterogeneous. Both have supported trade liberalization and incentives to increase exports. During the 1960s, however, the bank supported protection for infant industries, economic planning, and state enterprise (Kapur, Lewis, and Webb 1997, 450–51). Indeed, during those years, the bank financed directly state-owned enterprises, and the 1970s witnessed a massive shift in lending to them (Babai 1988, 259). The IMF, in contrast, had a historically more hostile stance to public enterprises because of its greater concern for their wider economic impact on inflation and the public deficit (Babai 1988, 266). Two interrelated developments—changes in the world economy initiated by the 1973–74 petroleum crisis and the concomitant change in the international policy culture—were key in strengthening the commitment to market forces among both the economists of these multilaterals and policy makers of borrowing countries. The increase in petroleum prices, the consequent decline in U.S. competitiveness, and the decline in international trade gave rise to a questioning of Keynesian economic assumptions. The rise of the new orthodoxy in economic thinking was echoed in the increasing commitment of the multilaterals to policy reform to increase the role of the market.

At the same time, the first oil shock in 1973–74 and the second one of 1979 forced the World Bank to face the pressing need to make available quick disbursing loans for countries with sudden gaps in trade balances. Increasingly imbued with a belief in the efficacy of market forces, its staff wanted to use this opportunity to provide financial support in such a way as to encourage the adjustment process (policy reform) and reduce the deficit in the current account (Fortin 1988, 310). In 1979, therefore, the bank officially initiated structural adjustment loans (SALS) to support programs of specific policy changes and institutional reforms with the objective of reducing the current account deficit (Stern 1983, 89). Policy-based loans of three to five years' duration, SALS were given for trade liberalization, reform of the pricing structures of public enterprises, the removal of subsidies, revision of public investment priorities, tighter financial discipline in public enterprises, and measures to increase nontraditional exports (Babai 1988, 268; Stern 1983, 95–98). By 1987, the bank had granted forty-three SALS to thirty-one countries, for a total of $6.5 billion (U.S.) (Epstein 1989, 134). SALS were followed by sectoral adjustment loans (SECALS), which came to replace SALS in many Latin American countries because it was easier to implement sectoral-specific reform measures (Rodríguez 1991, 30; Epstein 1989, 134). Designed for those occasions in which the bank perceived "a readiness for a more concentrated adjustment exercise" (Kapur, Lewis, and Webb 1997, 516), SECALS were important in supporting reforms in agriculture and the restructuring of specific public enterprises.

THE FIRST PHASE OF THE DEBT CRISIS: THE CRISIS OF LIQUIDITY, 1981–1985

Although the instruments of structural adjustment lending were largely in place before 1980, the debt crisis of 1981–82 was instrumental in triggering an increase in this type of lending and opened up the opportunity for influence on client countries' economic policies. In 1979, the price of international crude oil began to rise and the United States responded with an increase in interest rates that hit hard those countries (mainly Latin American) that had borrowed at floating rates from commercial banks. From 1980, prices for Latin American commodities began to slide (James 1996, 356). The Mexican announcement in August 1982 that its foreign debt would not be serviced and the consequent reluctance of commercial banks to extend further lending to Mexico and other highly indebted Latin American countries thrust the International Monetary Fund to center stage as global manager of the crisis. The role of the U.S. government, particularly the actions of the chair of the Federal Reserve System, Paul Volcker, however, was even more important. The primary goal of the IMF and of American policy makers during this initial phase of the debt crisis was to prevent individual commercial banks from going under. This meant the crisis had to be treated as a short-term liquidity problem rather than one of insolvency; as such, debtors had to maintain interest payments in full in order to maintain creditworthiness, whereas a recognition of insolvency would have dictated debt reduction, anathema to the commercial banks that refused to take losses (Kapur, Lewis, and Webb 1997, 607).

The IMF coordinated the response to what appeared to be the imminent collapse of the global financial system in 1982. In the most important case, the then IMF managing director, Jacques de Larosière, by threatening to withhold new loans from the IMF to Mexico, successfully pressured reluctant commercial banks to lend more money to that country, a practice that became known as "concerted lending" (Aggarwal 1996, 342; James 1996, 370).[2] Concerted lending meant that all members of a bank syndicate had to provide new money in proportion to amounts directly lent out. Such loans were accompanied by and were dependent on an agreement with the IMF involving a commitment to policies to "facilitate the adjustment process" (Lehman 1993, 35). Commitment to IMF conditions was seen by creditors as a demonstration of debtor countries' resolve to improve economic viability. Hence Larosière advised Mexican government officials to adopt a severe adjustment program "to convince the outside world, particularly the banks, that the Mexican economy would indeed soon be set on the path of return to order and stability" (James 1966, 366). But though "adjustment" was an accepted concept by this time, it did not have the depth of connotations it would have in later years, especially in areas of privatization and deregulation. Indeed, during these early years of the debt crisis, stabilization (designed to reduce inflation and the balance-of-payments deficit) through demand management was the primary policy goal.[3]

For each indebted country, a separate banking committee (banks advisory committee) was set up consisting of from twelve to fourteen of the most important banks holding that country's debt. It was this committee's responsibility to negotiate a new schedule of payments. Commercial banks have had an indirect impact on the economic policies of indebted countries insofar as their desire for a profitable business climate creates informal conditionality in which borrowers must try to impress lenders with their creditworthiness. Borrowers therefore send officials to explain government policies to creditors. The need to impress lenders favorably may induce borrowers to formulate policies they know will garner private sector confidence while bankers may infer or explicitly state changes deemed desirable (Friedman 1983, 117). Between 1983 and 1988 Latin American countries engaged in twenty-nine debt restructuring operations with private banks by means of this process (Edwards 1995, 73). Of relevance here is that commercial banks pressured to have the public sectors of debtor countries socialize large private sector debts, a development that, along with heavy interest payments on existent public debt, was to have severe budget implications (Kapur, Lewis, and Webb 1997, 610).

The rescheduling of official bilateral loans and, beginning in 1985, multi-year rescheduling agreements (MYRAs) with the private commercial banks were often contingent on the successful implementation of IMF-sponsored programs and the observance of World Bank conditionality (Kearney 1993, 63; Mosley, Harrigan, and Toye 1995, 54). MYRAs were precipitated by the recognition that medium-term debts contracted in the early 1980s would be coming due in the mid-1980s, producing a "debt lump" that borrowers would be unable to handle. Spreading repayment over a longer period of time, MYRAs instigated appeals from the private banking sector for longer periods of IMF surveillance (James 1996, 394). Furthermore, the convention became that for new lending from the World Bank and the multilateral development banks, there must be agreement with the IMF.[4] Indeed, between 1982 and 1990, the IMF became involved in almost every significant rescue package and the establishment of the various facilities linked to adjustment enhanced its role as "an agent of surveillance" (Oliveri 1989, 66).

The debt crisis also accelerated World Bank lending to Latin American countries, and the crisis coincided with important changes in the bank's attitude toward policy reform. By the late 1970s, the bank was already taking a firmer trade liberalization stance and had begun to reduce its support for public enterprises (Kapur, Lewis, and Webb 1997, 483). As long as recycled petrodollars were available through syndicated bank loans from the commercial banking sector, the World Bank had little ability to influence policy, at least for those countries, such as the ones in Latin America, that had access to loans from such sources (Kapur, Lewis, and Webb 1997, 476). But the debt crisis gave the bank an opportunity to use financial leverage to attempt to influence the macro policies of countries with pressing needs for financial support. Meanwhile, W. A. Clausen, a strong believer in the virtue of markets, replaced Robert McNamara as president of the World Bank. From then on, the bank became increasingly committed to influencing economic policy in the direction of market reform. The numbers of conditions on SALS multiplied during the first half of the 1980s but declined thereafter when the difficulties in monitoring became apparent. Even so, the bank's role, in the new context of the debt crisis, did not become really important until the mid-1980s.

The clout wielded by a united private commercial banking sector and the generalized fear among the international financial community (and among borrowers as well) that financial collapse was imminent produced a commitment to ensure the stability of the international financial system as a first priority. This commitment, in turn, patterned a preference for no-slow-growth austerity as the stabilization program of choice during the 1982–85 period. The commercial banks, during these early years, developed a united bargaining front, but debtors did not. Moreover, the process of debt negotiation came to be dominated by a small number of the most highly indebted banks with the largest stakes (Aggarwal 1987, 17). During the first phase of the crisis, these commercial bankers were fiercely and unalterably opposed to any consideration of debt relief and remained adamantly committed to collect as much as possible and to write off as little as possible. Hence options of some debt forgiveness or some agreed interest forgiveness were not considered (Griffith-Jones 1983, 20). Since the amount of new money involved in involuntary lending was to be less than debt service payments, negative net transfers were inevitable. At this stage, the parameters of policy choice for Latin American debtors facing financial crisis excluded the option of economic growth. In the face of a powerful united front of creditors, the priority remained debt service payments (Griffith-Jones 1983, 28).

The implications of all of this for the evolution of economic policy in highly indebted countries was profound. But despite the apparent leverage provided by conditional lending and the seriousness of the threat being faced, structural adjustment did not come quickly. On the surface, conditionality and particularly cross conditionality would appear to represent a powerful impetus for policy reform. Certainly the paramount importance

of debt negotiations shifts political power within the state in the direction of those domestic officials heading up such negotiations. But the depth
of the adjustment required to ensure continued payments on the debt was
extremely difficult, and often impossible, for countries to achieve. Moreover, even in those situations most favorable to reform, unforeseen circumstances, such as declines in commodity prices, had the ability to wreak havoc
on hitherto successful stabilization programs. Between 1982 and 1985, net
transfers of resources from Latin America had amounted to 5.3 percent of
GDP and per capita national income had declined by 10 percent since 1981
(Kapur, Lewis, and Webb 1997, 627). A new formula had to be found—one
that allowed a modicum of economic growth.

By the mid-1980s, early assumptions regarding the debt crisis and its solution were beginning to break down. By 1984, thirty countries had fallen
into arrears and began to negotiate commercial banking debts (James 1996,
388). Moreover, by mid-1985, it became apparent that voluntary lending was
not returning. Debtors were abundantly aware of the disproportionate costs
being imposed on them by the short-term strategy of debt adjustment and
began to take a political stance against such a burden. The threat of a debtors'
cartel raised by the meetings of Latin debtors in Quito and in Cartagena in
1984 was likely an important stimulus to reassessment on the part of the U.S.
government and creditors, as was the fact that the world economy began to
run into further difficulties by the mid-1980s. By 1985, Mexico had fallen
out of compliance with the IMF, and in that same year, President Alan García
announced that Peru's payments on its debt service would be limited to 10
percent of export earnings. Debtors now became committed to ensuring a
minimum of economic growth. With the World Bank in the lead, by mid-
1985, creditors too had come to the recognition that adjustment without
growth was not working and that an alternative had to be found.

FROM BAKER TO BRADY: THE ROAD TO DEBT RELIEF, 1985–1988

The Baker Plan, announced by U.S. treasury secretary James Baker at the
World Bank/IMF meetings at Seoul in October 1985, set targets for bank
and official lending and called for structural reform in debtor economies.
Its objective was to provide $20 billion (U.S.) to fifteen (later seventeen)
major debtors over the following three years; the World Bank and the Inter-
american Development Bank (IDB) would increase their total lending by
$10 billion (U.S.). In return, borrowers would carry out a variety of eco-
nomic reforms, including trade liberalization, the liberalization of invest-

ment regimes, and privatization. The Baker Plan marked an important departure in several respects. First, it gave increased vigor to market reform, implying an increase in conditionality. Second, it recognized that belt tightening by itself was not the solution and that there was a need for economic growth in debtor countries. Therefore, lending was to strengthen exports, stimulate growth, and thereby help countries emerge from the debt crisis. Last, it signaled an expansion in World Bank disbursements to debtor countries and a consequent increase in structural adjustment lending (Kapur, Lewis, and Webb 1997, 629). This latter development signaled an increase in policy dialogue. In 1986, the World Bank's adjustment lending to Latin America tripled to $2 billion, representing about 40 percent of its loan commitments to the region that year. SALS and SECALS together reached 30 percent of total World Bank/Interamerican Development Bank disbursements between 1987 and 1990 (Kapur, Lewis, and Webb 1997, 521, 630). But the core intellectual assumption of the Baker Plan remained the notion that the crisis was one of liquidity and that the solution was increased lending rather than debt relief. Mexico cut a deal under Baker, as did Argentina and Brazil in 1988.

As the IMF moved into longer-term facilities and the World Bank moved into structural adjustment program lending, relations between the bank and the IMF grew increasingly tense as the division of labor between the two organizations became blurred. Indeed, the IMF and the bank overlap in a wide variety of policy concerns: export incentives, agricultural pricing, public enterprise performance, external borrowing, and debt. This tension was no doubt deepened by the different analytical perspectives of the two organizations, with the IMF maintaining a more uniform and harder form of policy conditionality than the bank (Mosley, Harrigan, and Toye 1995, 54). The distinct orientations of these two banking institutions stem from their different responsibilities and the consequent dissimilar experiences of their staffs. The IMF's involvement is focused on a singular concern (support of balance of payments) and its staff make relatively infrequent and limited visits to a country, whereas the bank has many missions relating to a wide range of operations from project loans to structural adjustment program loans (Stern 1983, 100–104). In general, the bank was inclined to be more flexible in performance assessments and to support the need for economic growth, a difference with the IMF that was at least partly responsible for a turf struggle over Argentina (Polak 1997, 499, 506).[5]

The crisis of the early 1980s forced Mexico, Argentina, and Chile along with other countries of the region to avail themselves of the various lending facilities provided by the IMF and the bank. In addition, all of these countries renegotiated their debts with both bilateral creditors and the private banking sectors. Chile started its negotiations with the IMF in 1982 and with its international creditors in 1983. Between 1982 and 1987, Chile negotiated two standby loans, one compensatory facility, one extended fund facility with the IMF, and three SALS with the World Bank. In 1983, Mexico signed a standby agreement with the IMF and had IMF standbys covering the end of 1985, 1987, and the beginning of 1988. It also had EFF arrangements covering 1984–85 and 1989–92. Its multiyear rescheduling agreement in 1984 involved securing the IMF as a monitor. The bank provided a "Special Action Program" loan to Mexico in 1983 for export development and between 1984 and 1990 provided a variety of SECALS in such areas as agriculture, trade, export promotion, and privatization, in addition to numerous project loans. Mexico was constantly involved with the IMF and the World Bank throughout the period. Argentina's relationship with the IMF, involving an ongoing process of negotiation and renegotiation as Argentina fell repeatedly out of compliance with the terms of its agreements, was continuous until the complete breakdown of relations in 1988. Between 1982 and 1988, Argentina signed four standby agreements with the IMF and in 1985 reached a rescheduling accord with its commercial creditors. Between 1983 and 1988 the World Bank increased its structural adjustment lending to Argentina (especially for export promotion) while continuing to make a variety of project loans. Like Mexico, Argentina's relations with the IMF were continuous with the exception of the latter part of 1988 and the first half of 1989, when relations between Argentina and the IMF collapsed.

As the almost continuous negotiation and renegotiation with the IMF suggests, attempts at policy leverage through conditional lending, especially under the early conditions that precluded economic growth, were largely a failure. After 1985, the Baker Plan did not generate the lending necessary to stimulate growth. Moreover, there was little incentive to make structural reforms if the benefits went to creditors in the form of the continuation of debt payments. For these and other reasons, attempts to impose policy reform directly through policy conditionality have in general not worked. IMF conditionality has been described as a "toothless tiger" (Killick 1995, 121), a perspective borne out by a study showing that a high proportion of standbys have failed (Remmer 1996). Debtor countries, believing that any open objection to such conditions might block approval of loans at the IMF, often agreed to packages of conditions that they had no intention of fulfilling so as to ensure the flow of necessary loans (Sachs 1989, 261).

The World Bank does not even have a credible threat to breaches of conditionality. The results of SALS cannot be assessed until three or four years after the fact, giving the borrower time to study the reform in the abstract and avoid compliance (Mosley 1987, 11). Indeed, relative bargaining strength rather than economic criteria appears to have been key in influencing World Bank conditional aid packages (Mosley 1987, 22). Further, since bank conditionality runs the spectrum from quantitative to highly qualitative (as opposed to IMF conditionality, which is quantitative and therefore precisely measurable and nonnegotiable), compliance is not always easy to judge and is negotiable. As a consequence, about one-half of the bank's conditions have not been complied with (Mosley, Harrigan, and Toye 1995, 68).[6]

In a few short years the Baker Plan had run out of steam. The collapse of oil prices by 1986 caused a major change in the system's model debtor, Mexico, which refused to continue adjusting without the opportunity for growth. By 1986, as well, debt had increased in sixteen of the seventeen Baker Plan countries, raising disturbing questions regarding the plan's viability (Kapur, Lewis, and Webb 1997, 643). The rising incidence of interest arrears, led by Brazil in early 1987, was further evidence that the established formula was not working. Negotiations frequently broke down, and there were extended periods during which some of the biggest debtors (such as Argentina, Mexico, and Brazil) were not in compliance with the IMF. Compliance with conditionality was weak and debt overhang made it less and less likely that conditionality would be successful because there was little incentive to adjust if adjustment produced income for foreign banks rather than for the debtor's own citizens (Sachs 1989, 257; Edwards 1995, 73). Most important, perhaps, was the distinct reluctance on the part of the banks to lend new money (Cline 1995, 209; Lehman 1993, 38). Commercial banks provided only $4 billion of the $20 billion target during 1986–88 (Kapur, Lewis, and Webb 1997, 635).

The turning point occurred in May 1987, when Citicorp created a $3 billion (U.S.) provision against its $14.8 billion (U.S.) sovereign debt exposure (of which $10.4 billion was to Latin America) (Luke 1991, 61). Loan loss provisioning (setting aside funds to balance off future losses) by banks set the stage for the shift away from the new money strategy to debt forgiveness — a risky endeavor before the banks had set aside large loan loss provisions (Cline 1995, 20). The new debt relief scheme, the Brady Plan, which called for debt relief in exchange for market reform, had roots going back to the initial stages of the debt crisis. Certainly, highly indebted countries had been pressing for debt relief for some time, beginning with the meeting of Latin debtors in 1984 in Cartagena, where radicals demanded concerted default to pressure for writing down the debt, and continuing with Mexican president Carlos Salinas's decision to establish debt reduction as the core of his debt policy (James 1996, 393; Cline 1995, 26).[7] Some officials in the Latin American and Caribbean Regional Division (LAC) section of the World Bank recognized as early as 1984 that debt reduction would be necessary when an internal study argued that the situations of Argentina and Chile could not be resolved without it (interviews with two senior LAC officials). By 1985, the beginning of a shift in the bank's attitude became perceptible in a study to identify countries with solvency problems that would require debt reduction (Kapur, Lewis, and Webb 1997, 620). There were even some murmurings of sympathy for debt relief in the IMF (James 1996, 390). But the private banking sector and the U.S. government had been vehemently opposed to debt reduction so that it remained on the back burner until the Baker Plan proved incapable of solving the Latin debt problem.

The change of administration in Washington (the election of President George Bush) and the appointment of a new Federal Reserve Board chairman made possible a departure in debt policy. According to a March 1989 speech delivered by U.S. treasury secretary Nicolas Brady, official support would now be forthcoming for debt reduction for countries with records of consistent economic reform (Aggarwal 1996, 36–37). Under Brady, one-quarter of IMF and World Bank policy-based lending was to be used for discounted debt buybacks (James 1996, 401). Brady represented a breakthrough as it was an explicit recognition that the debt overhang required reduction. Just as Mexico had been the first country to reach an agreement under Baker, once again, Mexico was the first to reach an agreement under Brady in 1989.[8] By May 1994, Brady Plan agreements were in place or tentatively agreed on for eighteen countries, representing about $109 billion (U.S.) in long-term bank claims (Cline 1995, 17).

Brady has been associated with the marked spread of structural adjustment programs throughout Latin America after 1989 (Ramamurti 1992, 164–65). In providing for debt relief, it offered an enormous incentive to policy reform in that it insisted that such reform be well under way before an agreement could be reached. Indeed, the Brady conception of structural adjustment and the commitment of its designers to market reform had become, by the late 1980s, far deeper than ever. In the area of privatization, for example, Brady moved into the promotion of privatization in core areas such as petroleum and minerals. Although Brady was important in keeping the reform process on track, it was the ongoing influence of international policy culture and networks that really helped get the reform process under way and sustained it in times of crisis.

POLICY CULTURE, POLICY DIALOGUE, AND INTERNATIONAL POLICY NETWORKS

Consideration of policy conditionality per se contributes little to our understanding of how the multilaterals helped to drive market reform forward in Latin America. The debt crisis and debt negotiations were important in that they facilitated the expansion of what has come to be known as the "international policy culture" favoring market reform and thereby contributing to the emergence of a new Latin American consensus on the need for market reform (Edwards 1995, 41). The diffusion of this international policy culture by international financial institutions has been described as a process of "social learning" (Ikenberry 1990, 103). The negotiations required by these institutions created a "cycle of influence" that, sustained over time, was able to alter attitudes and perceptions and build commitment to reform (Kahler 1992, 123; Nelson 1992, 314).

Indeed, both the World Bank and the IMF, although the latter somewhat more reluctantly and later, came to recognize that policy conditionality would not be sufficient without domestic commitment (Nelson 1992, 314; Qureschi 1992, 11). Indeed, for the bank "policy dialogue," discussions with the borrowing country "about various aspects of development policy and policy reform," was to be one of the key components of structural adjustment lending at the time it was conceived (Kapur, Lewis, and Webb 1997, 510). The priorities of the bank in adjustment lending, however, changed over time, as it underwent its own ideological transformation in the early 1980s. This change, involving a strengthened commitment to the market, was reflected in the policy dialogue it carried out with borrowers. Initially, structural adjustment policy priority was in the area of trade policy, particularly export promotion. Hence trade liberalization, incentives, and marketing measures to promote exports and export diversification were key concerns. For public enterprises, the emphasis before 1985 tended to be on restructuring. As the 1980s progressed, however, ownership came increasingly to the fore as an issue and privatization became a major theme in the policy dialogue. Similarly, the content and emphasis in negotiations held between the IMF and its Latin borrowers also evolved over time. Whereas early EFF agreements (during the first half of the 1980s) focused on achieving balance in macroeconomic indicators, with deficit reduction and inflation being key, by the end of the 1980s the IMF was pushing hard for structural adjustment measures such as trade liberalization. Although the IMF was supportive of privatization, this issue has been less central to its policy dialogue than to the bank's (interviews with senior IMF official). Insofar as the IMF required substantial reductions in public deficits, however, it encouraged privatization because officials tended to see privatization as the quickest means (sometimes the only one) to reach such targets (interviews with senior officials in Mexico and Argentina).

The onset of the 1982 debt crisis triggered the expansion of policy dialogue between multilaterals and Latin borrowers and established the conditions for the emergence of international policy networks of domestic and multilateral officials whose policy development activities would become a crucial component of the market reform process. The debt crisis immediately thrust the top finance officials of highly indebted countries into negotiations with the IMF for standby and EFF agreements and with the World Bank for discussions leading to SALS and SECALS. Although IMF officials did become actors in international policy networks, for reasons discussed below, the impact of the bank on structural adjustment through policy dialogue and international policy networks appears to have been considerably more far-reaching and all-pervasive than the IMF's. Senior bank officials, particularly then vice president for operations Ernest Stern, began the push for policy reform in the region in 1983.[9] But commitment to policy reform on the part of bank officials working specifically on Latin America was stalled until the mid-1980s.

Important organizational and personnel changes in the World Bank appear to have been instrumental in the ability of its officials to develop close working relationships with client countries in Latin America. Before 1972, in addition to area administrative units that contained country specialists or "desks," there were also administrative units organized along project lines. A reorganization in 1972 strengthened the area units and area chiefs by distributing project personnel among them. This was particularly pertinent for the Latin American and Caribbean Region section as its officials had maintained a strong interest in macroeconomic issues (because of the inflation in the region) and were particularly supportive of SALS as mechanisms to bring financial relief to cash-strapped countries (Kapur, Lewis, and Webb 1997, 461). But when the debt crisis broke in 1982, the LAC section lacked a clear policy vision and was divided ideologically with some of the senior-level figures, including the division chief, still supportive of state intervention and expansionary policies.[10] Because the bank failed to foresee or forestall the Mexican crisis of 1982, however, a major shakeup of the LAC section resulted in a clearing out of prostatists and the emergence of a consensus in LAC on the importance and necessity of policy reform in Latin America (interviews with three senior LAC officials). Further personnel changes in the early 1980s altered the traditional modus operandi of the LAC section. The replacement of David Knox by Shahid Husain as vice president of LAC in 1985 signaled both a commitment to policy reform and an important change in the way LAC officials would pursue reform in the region. A conscious decision was made to move away from the arms-length formalism that had characterized the relations between LAC and officials of the Latin countries to a new strategy that would involve the cultivation of relationships of trust between bank and client country officials in the region. In this way, it was hoped that ongoing policy dialogue in a context of personal trust would nudge Latin American countries toward policy reform (interviews with one senior and three middle-ranking officials of LAC). Indeed, in some cases, particularly in the area of public enterprise reform and privatization, LAC officials were already building on a legacy of personal friendship and trust that had been initiated by bank project officers even earlier (interview with middle-ranking LAC official). Indeed, LAC officials during the 1980s were probably unique even for the freewheeling modus operandi of the bank: they spoke the language of their client countries, had a strong esprit de corps, and developed a strong attachment both to their reform agendas and to the personalities and countries they dealt with. Appendix 3 lists the most important officials in the LAC section during the years when the bank's influence on market reform was the greatest. Some among the participants present during almost the entire reform period (Vice President Shahid Husain, Rainer B. Steckhan, Paul M. Meo, Pieter P. Bottlelier, Peter R. Scherer, Myrna Alexander, Hans Binswanger, and Ricardo Halperin, for example) held a variety of different positions in LAC. This continuity gave LAC officials both the time and the opportunity to develop close personal relationships with the officials of client countries.

LAC officials had a leeway in cultivating policy dialogue and close collaborative relationships with officials of client countries that the IMF did not have. Bank officials deal with a much wider array of government officials and therefore often have the opportunity to gain access to a much broader range of channels through which they can influence the direction of policy. While SALS brought LAC officials into contact with top government finance officials, SECALS could bring them into contact with sectoral officials in ministries of industry and housing or with top officials of public companies. IMF officials, in contrast, deal with a relatively small number of officials in the Ministry of Finance and Central Bank of a client country. Furthermore, the World Bank sends many more missions to Latin countries than does the IMF and the latter's missions occur in situations of extreme crisis when agreements must be arrived at quickly and confrontation is more likely. The potential for conflict is considerably greater than for the bank, whose negotiations are lower profile, less intense, have opportunity for partial agreement, and have less severe consequences when no agreement is reached (Stern 1983, 100–104).

Indeed, the peculiar circumstances of the World Bank, as opposed to the IMF, enabled policy dialogue to go on continuously for years even in areas where there was little likelihood, even no intention, of a loan from the bank.[11] Since it is more difficult to judge adherence to performance targets when conditionality is qualitative, career interests of bank officials are not so closely linked to nonfulfillment of conditions by a client country. The objective of the bank therefore became not so much the fulfillment of conditions but keeping the dialogue going in the belief that eventually reforms would occur and be maintained. IMF officials, in contrast, had to face the criticism of their superiors when an agreement, involving easily interpretable quantitative criteria, was not fulfilled. Indeed, developing close ties with a client country and becoming its advocate within the IMF is generally frowned on by senior administrators of the IMF (interviews with two senior-level IMF officials). Under these circumstances, trust and close personal relationships were less likely to develop between IMF and client government officials. Such relationships as did develop generally occurred in cases of a very tightly integrated domestic policy elite that firmly excluded domestic opponents of tough austerity from policy discussions. Nevertheless, despite the distinct institutional interests governing the attitudes and behavior of IMF and World Bank officials and the turf disputes that increased in intensity during the 1980s, bank and IMF officials have often cooperated in the formulation of structural adjustment programs and missions have frequently involved officials from both institutions (Rodríguez 1991, 29).

Additional factors facilitated the emergence of policy networks of multilateral and borrower country officials. By the mid-1980s, officials at the helm of the most powerful ministries (the ministries in charge of macroeconomic policies) in Latin American countries were increasingly people with graduate degrees in economics from American universities, particularly from Harvard, Yale, and the University of Chicago (the technocrats). Some had gone to graduate school with the very multilateral officials with whom they were now negotiating.[12] Moreover, the fact that Finance Ministry officials had worked in the IMF or the World Bank before assuming a position in their home governments or moved into positions in multilateral institutions later contributed further to the homogenization of policy culture, to trust and close collaboration, and to the emergence and cohesiveness of policy networks.[13] In the words of one senior IMF official, when referring to IMF, World Bank, and the finance/economy officials of Latin American countries: "We are all the same—people who come and go through the Bank, the Fund, and Finance Ministries and Central Banks of Latin American countries. We all studied at the same universities; we all attend the same seminars, conferences . . . we all know each other very well. We keep in touch with each other on a daily basis. There are some differences, such as between those who studied at Harvard and those who studied at the University of Chicago, but these are minor things." Indeed, the technocratic pedigrees of top Latin government officials have been important in engendering relationships of trust.[14]

The dialogue between bank LAC officials and client countries took two basic forms, both usually occurring concurrently. In one, often at the beginning, bank officials served as lobbyists, engaged in a concerted campaign to convince officials of the client country of the necessity of policy reform. This lobbying effort involved discussions, often informal. But it also entailed the presentation of studies, with technical data backing up arguments in favor of reform and thematic conferences in which international experts were invited to speak in support of specific policy reforms. These attempts were usually tense and could produce a hostile reaction from the client country. Simultaneously, however, World Bank officials would also seek out discussions with those in client governments who were sympathetic to reforms and would try to provide these individuals with technical and other support to enable them to expand support for reform within the state. It was from this latter process that international policy networks usually developed, although they occasionally also developed from the former.[15]

As the 1980s progressed and as more and more officials of client governments became open to the market reform process, networks of multilateral and client government officials began to work out detailed policy reform plans. In general, these international policy networks were composed of multilateral and client government officials who shared the same policy culture and a broad agreement on a particular policy goal, if not a more general program of reform. The international policy network is composed of anywhere from three to twenty people. While trust and often friendship were key ingredients, these networks contained an inherent tension because although officials shared a common policy culture, they answered to distinct institutional pressures: client country officials had to answer to political pressures and domestic vested interests but multilaterals did not and were generally, although not always, more concerned that reforms go forward and that the political risks be taken. Multilaterals, however, especially the bank LAC region group, wanted to keep conflict to a minimum. The unwritten rule for the bank became to avoid, if possible, policy areas that would meet a brick wall of resistance, such as pushing for privatization in sacrosanct areas. The LAC's strategy in building policy networks was to develop reform policies in collaboration with client officials in those areas where there was the least resistance. While senior officials of LAC took an active role in this process, especially at the beginning, over time middle-ranking officials became very actively involved as well. Such a development was less true of the IMF, where hierarchy and discipline gave mission officers considerably less leeway. Hence there were many more policy networks involving World Bank officials, and these, as we will see, would become essential components of the market reform process.

GEOPOLITICAL FACTORS IN POLICY REFORM

Clearly, this general policy environment played out differently with different debtors. A country's geopolitical/strategic importance influenced the amount of latitude in policy choice available. While Mexico received consistent support from the United States, enabling it to wring concessions not available to other debtors, Argentina received less consistent support and Chile none at all. Different opportunity structures played into the debt and adjustment strategies of domestic policy makers and, as we will see in later chapters, had implications for the depth and timing of reform.

Mexico had unparalleled importance for the United States because Washington wanted a solution to that country's economic difficulties that would not produce political instability and trigger greater migration to the United States (Oliveri 1989, 76; Aggarwal 1987, 30). Hence policy toward Mexico was consistently more generous than toward any other Latin American country. In the 1982 crisis, a bridge loan from the United States stabilized the bargaining process (Aggarwal 1996, 344). In negotiations with commercial bankers in 1983, Paul Volcker, chairman of the Federal Reserve, sided with Mexican negotiators and pressed U.S. banks for concessions (Aggarwal 1996, 47). The United States continued to be heavily involved in the negotiations between Mexico and its commercial bank creditors in 1986 with the result that Mexico came away with contingency (extra) financing should its income from exports deteriorate—a concession that other Latin American countries were unable to duplicate. The U.S. treasury exerted strong pressure on commercial bankers in the 1989 negotiations to assure an agreement under Brady and new loans for Mexico (Hughes 1991, 20; Cline 1995, 220). Moreover, the U.S. executive played a key role in helping Mexico out of its 1995 financial crisis, even in the face of stiff resistance from Congress, which refused to approve loan guarantees requested by the U.S. president to help Mexico out of that most recent economic predicament.[16] The importance of Mexico to the United States gave Mexico greater leeway in policy reform and allowed it to go forward at a more leisurely pace. Mexico's importance to the United States was also reflected in the nature and operation of policy networks, as we will see in Chapter 6.

Although the U.S. attitude toward Argentina was to harden over time, in the early 1980s, Washington did wish to improve relations with Argentina, particularly in light of concern that Argentine default might lead to a more generalized moratorium by Latin debtors. Hence in 1984, the Federal Reserve Board stepped in to pressure commercial banks to lend to Argentina, coercing new bank lending even before a solid IMF agreement was in place and certainly before any economic reform. Moreover, the United States wanted emergency funds provided to Argentina so as to mitigate harsh social conditions that might trigger upheaval and thereby threaten the country's fragile democracy. By 1985, however, the United States began to take a tougher stand toward Argentina, refusing to release a bridge loan until Argentina and the IMF had resolved their differences. The American attitude toward Argentina softened once again in 1987, when another bridge loan was offered, but hardened by 1988 (Aggarwal 1996, 43, 414, 425, 438). When negotiations between Argentina and the IMF broke down in 1988, however, the United States, once again concerned about the fragile political situation in that country, pushed the World Bank to step in to provide the necessary financial support. This involvement, as we will see in Chapter 5, was key in triggering the development of a plethora of international policy networks involving the bank and Argentine officials.

If the United States had a special interest in alleviating the situation faced by Mexico and a moderate interest in helping Argentina avoid the harshness of an immediate and deep adjustment, its attitude toward Chile reinforced a tough stabilization and adjustment program. During the socialist regime of Salvador Allende, the United States had pressured the bank not to lend to

Chile. And indeed, virtually no new loans were forthcoming during those years.[17] By the early 1980s, the United States was reluctant to be seen as in any way involved in the Chilean case because of the widespread international condemnation of the military regime's human rights record. Washington pressured the bank (and the bank resisted) to have human rights considerations injected into loan considerations (Kapur, Lewis, and Webb 1997, 477). The harsh repression carried out by the military regime put the 1985 World Bank's loan guarantee, a vital part of the rescheduling and new money package, in jeopardy with the consequence that the state of emergency (in which civil rights were suspended) was lifted in order to receive the loan and then reimposed in September 1986 (Griffith-Jones 1992, 51). International enmity toward the Pinochet regime was so strong that the 1986 structural adjustment loan was approved by only 51 percent of the board of governors (Ffrench Davis 1992, 104). This situation, combined with the reluctance of bankers to lend and the pressing need to encourage international confidence, encouraged tough measures. The Chilean government pursued a model debtor strategy, readily adopting the harsh policies then being advocated by multilateral officials.[18] Not only did Chile carry out policy reforms to the letter, but it frequently went beyond loan requirements. Chile faithfully serviced its debt and generally cultivated harmonious relations with creditors. The strategy worked: the economic policies of the regime encouraged the flow of loans to Chile (Ffrench Davis 1992, 104). As we will see in the following chapter, Chile's image problems gave IMF and World Bank officials who wanted to see Chile's market reform program stay on track the leverage to demand orthodoxy.

CONCLUSIONS

Policy conditionality per se has not been effective in inducing policy reform. International developments and pressures, however, did play an important role in market reform in winning over domestic policy makers to policy change and in reinforcing their commitment to reform. Two key international developments helped to push Latin American countries along the road of market reform. First, the international policy environment from the mid-1970s onward changed toward a belief in the efficacy of reliance on market forces. Second, the international debt crisis created extreme financial exigencies and increased contact between the multilaterals and the officials of cash-strapped creditor countries. Both of these developments acted in concert and reinforced each other. The negotiations involved in policy-based lending and the more diffuse process of "policy dialogue" reinforced a common policy culture, the groundwork for which had often already been laid by the shared educational and career experiences of multilateral and domestic government officials.

The sheer number of loans negotiated during the period meant that multilateral and borrower country officials would have constant interchange, encouraging the spread of "social learning" about the efficacy of market reforms. At the same time, a fundamental change in the thinking on the debt problem helped to reinforce commitment to policy reform— policy elites were less likely to remain committed to difficult reforms if the only or major beneficiaries were foreign creditors. Under the Brady Plan, debt relief was offered in exchange for market reforms. But the groundwork for agreements under Brady was laid by the work done by international policy networks and policy dialogue. Through this means, the World Bank, more than the IMF, given the nature of its lending practices, was able to campaign continuously and effectively for reform in areas where it saw opportunity and avoid areas that might lead to irreconcilable tension and conflict. For the most part, the bank used a "soft-sell" approach, building policy networks based on personal trust, within which it was able to influence and sometimes even guide the specific direction and nature of reform. But the most important international actor was, by far, the United States, whose top officials established the general parameters of debt strategy and privileged some debtors more than others.

chapter four

MARKET REFORM IN CHILE
From Military Rule to Concertación

By the early 1970s, Chile's economy was in crisis and its political system on the verge of collapse. The country had lost its political center; political violence by both the extreme right and the extreme left was on the rise. The left saw its dream of social transformation threatened by entrenched propertied interests while the right feared social chaos and the loss of political and property rights. In addition, the economic situation was the worst it had been since the Great Depression. In the midst of such political and economic turmoil, the military coup of 1973 ushered in the opportunity for drastic economic restructuring. But the depth and rapidity of Chile's economic transformation awaited the interplay of opportunity and politics.

Chile's market reform under military rule, carried out in two phases interrupted by the 1981–82 economic collapse, was domestically driven. With the return to electoral democracy in 1989, market liberalizing reforms, privatization, and further trade liberalization continued under the coalition Concertación government. Once again, reform in this most recent phase has been led by domestic policy makers. However, international actors have not been totally absent from the Chilean reform process. As we will see in this chapter, following the crisis of the early 1980s the World Bank and the International Monetary Fund, through an international policy network, became important actors in restoring the reform process.

Under military rule, particularly between 1975 and 1982, domestic policy networks were highly integrated, cohesive, hierarchical, and fiercely resistant to penetration—the closest fit to the ideal type construction of any of the policy networks dealt with in this book. During the post-1982 period of reform under military rule, networks opened up to a wider array of private sector interests. Under the civilian Concertación government, policy networks are more numerous still, but their openness to extrastate penetration remains largely confined to the private sector. Partly as a consequence of institutional arrangements inherited from military rule, economic policy remains a highly concentrated activity, involving a dedicated policy core and a dominant intrastate policy network bound by personal loyalty and programmatic commitment. The private sector has by far been the most successful in gaining direct and personalized access to economic policy networks.

The initial crusading force behind Chile's economic transformation was a group of technocratic reformers, known as the "Chicago boys," young economists who had been trained at the University of Chicago's Department of Economics. Although these technocrats were the most important group of actors in the formulation of the market reform program, they had important domestic partners: key personalities in the military, in a restricted world of business conglomerates, and among the gremialistas. The highly integrated and personal nature of the alliance among these individuals produced what has been described as a combination of liberal economic principles with "a revival of Portalian authoritarian forms, having its roots in Spain and monarchy" (Fontaine Aldunate 1988, 102). Indeed, Chile's Iberian strain, with its concentration of almost total power, monism, and heavy emphasis on personal power, would play an integral part in the technocratically inspired market reform process.

The rise of a group of technocrats to predominance in policy making during the period of military rule marked the culmination of a development begun decades earlier. The incorporation of highly trained personnel (especially engineers) into the public bureaucracy accelerated from the 1930s on as the state expanded (Montecinos 1998, 5). During the presidency of Eduardo Frei (1964–70), economists began to be appointed to important positions in the state bureaucracy, a trend that was continued under Socialist president Salvador Allende (1970–73). But technocrats' ability to influence policy was heavily mitigated by party pressure and by the specialized interests that permeated the state (Montecinos 1998, 20, 46, 50–55; Velasco 1994). Policy shifts in the pre-1973 period were usually explained by the impact of shifting coalitions of societal groups pressuring the state rather than by the action of a cohesive state bureaucracy (Cleaves 1974, 89; Stallings 1978).

Much of the scholarly work has emphasized the central role of the Chicago technocrats in Chile's market reform under military rule (O'Brien and Roddick 1983; Fontaine Aldunate 1988; Délano and Traslaviña 1989; Valdés 1995; Hira 1998). Eduardo Silva, however, has taken issue with the importance accorded to the role of technocrats in the process. He explains market reform during the 1975–81 period as the result of the rise to predominance of a radical neoliberal coalition of technocrats and internationalized businessmen and sees the following 1985–89 period as characterized by the replacement of this coalition by technocrats and a wider cross section of big businessmen (Silva 1996, 107, 156). The notion of policy network used in this analysis draws attention to features of the process downplayed by the coalition approach *and* by an exclusive focus on technocratic actors. It draws attention to the extremely high degree of integration between technocratic and nontechnocratic key actors during the initial reform period, a feature that reduces the usefulness of the coalition idea. The policy network concept, however, retains the assumption that vested interests will affect policy. At the same time, the policy network concept acknowledges the role of policy ideas and emphasizes the importance of personal trust and loyalty in policy development. The concept allows us to pinpoint the entry of international actors in the 1983–85 period and to more closely chart their role in policy development. With the return to civilian rule, the notion of policy network affords an explanation of policy choices (such as privatization) resisted by larger constituencies within the broader support coalition.

Military rule enabled technocratic policy makers to isolate themselves from party and public pressures as never before. Nevertheless, the Chicago boys faced considerable obstacles to achieving deep and immediate reduction in industrial protection, deregulation, and divestiture of state enterprises. Nationalists in the military opposed privatization. Industrialists, even those of large firms, opposed a rapid drop in protection, while elements in the military and in the right of Christian Democrats were concerned about the impact on labor and favored more incorporative forms of labor control. Finally, many technocrats in the state wanted a much more gradual approach to policy reform.

THE CURIOUS NETWORK: TECHNOCRATS AND THE TRADITIONAL RIGHT

Table 4.1 lists key actors in the network (in fact, two subnetworks) responsible for Chile's radical market reform program from 1975 to 1981.[1] Members of these networks shared a variety of links, including personal friendships, common educational and professional experiences, and other historical contacts, in addition to a strongly felt policy commitment. Many individuals occupied simultaneously the technocratic, conglomerate, and traditional right categories. When friendships were not preexistent, strong personal relationships were cultivated after individuals obtained positions in the state. The nature and intensity of the personal ties binding individuals prompted one insider interviewed to describe those responsible for this

TABLE 4.1. KEY ACTORS IN CHILE'S FIRST PHASE OF MARKET REFORM

NAME	LINKS
MILITARY, TECHNOCRATIC, CONGLOMERATE LINKS (NAVAL BROTHERHOOD OF THE SOUTH PACIFIC, MONDAY CLUB NETWORK)	
Adm. José Toribio Merino*	Naval Brotherhood, Military Junta, responsible for economic matters
Hernán Cubillos*	Former navy officer, Naval Brotherhood, Monday Club, El Mercurio, Edwards group, gremialista
Augustín Edwards	Naval Brotherhood Club, Edwards group, research group, CESEC
Javier Vial	Monday Club, head of BHC conglomerate
Manuel Cruzat	Monday Club, Cruzat-Larraín conglomerate, Chicago economist, courses to entrepreneurs at SEFOFA, "El Ladrillo" technical team
Orlando Saenz*	Monday Club, Edwards group, president of SEFOFA, "El Ladrillo" technical team
Roberto Kelly*	Former navy officer, Monday Club, personal links with Toribio Merino
Emilio Sanfuentes*	Edwards group, CESEC, Chicago economist, "El Ladrillo" technical team, brother to Andrés Sanfuentes, close to Kelly, Cubillos's right-hand man
TECHNOCRATIC, CONGLOMERATE, GREMIALISTA LINKS (CHICAGO, CATHOLIC UNIVERSITY NETWORK) (Extrastate links of key state policy actors, radical reform group)	
Sergio de Castro	Chicago economist, director of the Faculty of Economics, Catholic University, member of "El Ladrillo" technical team, Edwards group, as a student especially close to Manuel Cruzat, close links to gremialista Guzmán
Andrés Sanfuentes	Chicago economist, "El Ladrillo" technical team, brother of Emilio
Sergio Undurraga	Chicago economist, "El Ladrillo" technical team, courses at SEFOFA, childhood friend of Manuel Cruzat
Jorge Cauas	"El Ladrillo" technical team, director of the Faculty of Economics, Catholic University, where he linked up with de Castro

TABLE 4.1. CONTINUED

NAME	LINKS
Sergio de la Cuadra	Chicago economist, Vial group, SEFOFA, CESEC, Edwards group
Pablo Baraona	Chicago economist, Cruzat-Larraín, SEFOFA, CESEC, Edwards group
Sergio Fernández	Close friendships with Kast, Guzmán
Jaime Guzmán	Gremialista leader, close to de Castro, Fernández
Miguel Kast**	Second-generation Chicago economist, gremialista, links to Kelly, Fernández
Rolf Lüders	Chicago economist, BHC executive
José Piñera	Taught at the Catholic University, executive of Cruzat-Larraín
Hernán Büchi	Worked closely with Chicago technocratic team from 1975

Sources: O'Brien and Roddick 1983, 34, 39; Délano and Traslaviña 1989, 32–35, 37, 73, 204–9; Valdés 1995, 18, 165, 277, 247; Fontaine Aldunate 1988, 16–17, 31, 117, 170–71, 183; Osorio and Cabezas 1995, 48, 233, 256, 282; Silva 1996, 49, 141; and interviews by author.
*Indicates individuals in the naval/Monday network who went on to hold formal positions in the government.
**Other second-generation Chicago technocrats in ODEPLAN with gremialista links included Juan Carlos Méndez and Felice Lamarca.

phase of the reform as "a very closely knit *camarilla* bound together by personal loyalty and ideology."

The Chicago boys were Chilean market reform proponents who, as a consequence of an agreement signed between the University of Chicago and the Catholic University of Santiago in 1955, were among the 150 Chileans who went to the University of Chicago to do graduate work in economics. The arrangement has been described as "an organized transfer of ideology from the United States" prompted by growing U.S. concern about the increasing public support in Chile for left-wing parties and the desire to promote a belief in free enterprise and discourage communism (Valdés 1995, 15–16, 107). Training in the United States involved a strong socialization process that produced fervent supporters of the basic ideological tenets of the Chicago school: support for the market and the belief that the economist must be a teacher and crusader winning over converts to the scientific truth of economics (Valdés 1995, 53, 61). Throughout the 1950s and the 1960s, the Chicago graduates in Chile remained an isolated, beleaguered minority in a sea of accelerating political and social changes that were diametrically opposed to their most fundamental beliefs.

Nevertheless, the Chicago economists, based at the Catholic University, were anxious to imbue the private sector with their belief in market forces and took a variety of steps, largely unsuccessful, to win private sector converts. The Chicago economist Sergio de Castro began to cultivate the private sector, particularly the powerful Edwards group, from the mid-1960s. He and other Chicago graduates gave courses for entrepreneurs at SEFOFA, or Society to Promote Manufacturing, the peak industrial trade association. Manuel Cruzat decided upon graduation from the University of Chicago to devote his career to business rather than to academia, on the premise that this was the most effective way to reform the business sector (Valdés 1995, 229). Sergio de Castro and other Chicago boys were asked to participate in the formulation of Jorge Alessandri's election platform in 1969 but withdrew when the private sector resisted rapid trade liberalization. Unable to win much support for their ideas in the private sector generally, the technocrats developed highly integrated links with three powerful conglomerates: the Edwards group, BHC (Mortgage Bank of Chile), and Cruzat-Larraín. The Edwards group responded to the technocrats' outreach efforts by employing Chicago-trained economists as executives and in the economics section of its newspaper *El Mercurio*. It also created the Center for Social and Economic Studies (CESEC), which brought in many Chicago economists. In the years to come, many technocrats shifted between top-level positions in the state and executive-level positions in these conglomerates, effectively blurring the distinction between government technocrat and conglomerate executive.

In addition, some key participants in the market reform network were active in the gremialista movement, a combination of business and professional associations that adhered to a corporatist ideology inherited from Hispanic authoritarian values. The gremialista movement had been a chief opponent of the Popular Unity government, a strong supporter of the right-wing National Party, and, with the coup, ardently Pinochetista. It would become, in the words of one observer, "the dominant cultural and political expression of the military regime" (Pollack 1995, 22). A tightly interwoven network evolved, and some gremialista Chicago technocrats eventually obtained positions in the state bureaucracy. The most important figure among the gremialistas was its leader, a young lawyer at the Catholic University named Jaime Guzmán.

One might have expected considerable tension to arise between the "scientific" U.S.-oriented free market position of the Chicago boys and the Hispanic, corporatist position of the gremialista and traditional right. But their mutual contempt for parliamentary politics and political parties and their strong anticommunism offered common ground. The 1967 student rebellion at the Catholic University, an institution devoted to the education of the traditional right, brought Chicago boy Sergio de Castro and gremialista leader Jaime Guzmán together. Repulsed by the attitudes of student rebels, together they led the antireform movement at the university (Osorio and Cabezas 1995, 38). In their disgust for politics and fear of communism, the economists and the gremialistas were joined by the military.

The story of the origins of Chile's economic reform program begins with a policy initiative that was formulated outside of the state. In the highly polarized atmosphere of the Allende years, members of an informally organized boating club, the Naval Brotherhood of the South Pacific, concluded that in view of the country's growing economic and political crisis it was crucial to develop an economic program to have ready for the next government. At their initiation, a discussion group, named for its Monday meetings, began to meet in 1971 in the office of Hernán Cubillos, the president of the *El Mercurio* newspaper. This group included the Chicago economists Manuel Cruzat and Javier Vial, each head of a conglomerate that would benefit inordinately from the market reform program, while the Edwards group, whose head was heavily involved in these early discussions, was closely linked to Cruzat-Larraín through investment companies (Dahse 1979, 68). Roberto Kelly, a close friend of Emilio Sanfuentes, provided the names of economists for a technical team to draw up an economic program. Many who were part of this team would later hold positions in the government, and most would, at one time or another, hold positions in one of the conglomerates; they were all trained economists and, if they did not have Chicago training, had taught at the Catholic University. The policy document produced by this early technical group, "El Ladrillo" ("the brick"), with its emphasis on the opening of international trade and privatization and belief that inflation was caused by the collusion between trade unions, politicians, and business, provided the basis for the reform program that was to follow after 1975. When the coup occurred in 1973, this document was passed on to the military through the network's navy connection.

Following the military coup, several of the Chicago boys who advocated a rapid and deep policy reform were able to secure advisory positions in the new government.[2] Sergio de Castro, the leader among these radical reform technocrats, took up a position as adviser to the minister of the economy. Roberto Kelly was appointed minister-director of ODEPLAN, the National Planning Office. Kelly immediately recruited like-minded technocrats, thereby creating a base from which technocrats were able to expand throughout the state and spread their views of economic reform. During 1974, members of an emerging radical reform policy clique (Kelly, de Castro, Pablo Baraona, and Sergio Undurraga) met to formulate strategies to persuade the junta to adopt their radical approach (interviews with two senior government officials). Throughout 1974, policy clique members spent long hours explaining and persuading the military leaders, particularly Pinochet, of the efficacy of their economic program. That radical reform technocrats were united, more numerous than other bureaucratic factions in the state, and had a policy solution backed up by detailed studies were all no doubt important factors in their ability to persuade Pinochet that reform was necessary. At the same time, it was through the personal relationships that Sergio de Castro and Roberto Kelly cultivated with General Pinochet that they were able to persuade the general of the need for market reform. Indeed, the absolutely central importance of the relationship of trust and loyalty that developed between de Castro and Pinochet and the consequent key role of Pinochet in policy reform distinguish this interpretation from other versions of the process. De Castro cultivated a relationship of personal trust and loyalty with Pinochet that would endure even the economic collapse of the early 1980s and became important in ensuring the survival of market reform after 1983 (interviews with three senior officials). Furthermore, the technocrats' alliance with Pinochet was more than just a marriage of convenience—Pinochet became an active adherent of economic policy reform. Economic deterioration in 1974 opened the way for the new radical program.[3] With Pinochet on their side and with the pressing need for an effective policy response, the technocratic radical reformers now had the edge, and the influence of those bureaucrats and military men who were advocating a more gradualist approach quickly waned.[4]

Just as important as Pinochet's active support for market reform, however, was his control and management of the armed forces, which inhibited the Chilean military from blocking reform as the Argentine military did. Once he had established a position of dominance within the four-man military junta, Pinochet focused his attention on the establishment of personal rule, especially important in securing the acquiescence of the army, the branch of the armed forces that was not only dominant within Chile's military establishment but also the most resistant to the Chicago boys' economic project (O'Brien and Roddick 1983, 34, 40). Pinochet quickly cleared out the old guard, and within three years of the coup Pinochet loyalists monopolized all the command positions (Angell 1988, 96). Loyalty was rewarded with appointments to boards of public enterprises and public commissions, and defense spending soared by 30 percent in 1974 and by 44 percent in the second semester of 1975 alone (Constable and Valenzuela 1991, 60–61; Varas 1995, 55).

Once de Castro had secured Pinochet's agreement to a law giving the Ministry of Finance power over all decisions with economic implications, radical reform went rapidly forward. A small, cohesive policy clique consisting of the newly installed top economic managers (all involved in the market reform policy network before entering the state)—Minister of Finance Jorge Cauas, Central Bank president Pablo Baraona, Minister of the Economy Sergio de Castro—and Roberto Kelly, head of ODEPLAN since 1973, produced the Plan for Economic Recovery, more commonly known as the "shock treatment." The plan, which drew heavily from "El Ladrillo," called for a variety of liberalizing measures (see Table 4.2). While Cauas took over the most powerful ministry, the Ministry of Finance, de Castro remained the de facto leader of the group (interviews with three senior-level officials); indeed, de Castro remained the predominant policy reform figure until 1982, and continued to play an important role thereafter. ODEPLAN produced the technical studies upon which the forthcoming reforms would be based and was especially important in the development of labor reform, social security reform, and health reform, all of which followed later in the decade (see Table 4.2).

The impact of the 1975 shock program was profound. Inflation abated, and the fiscal deficit, at nearly 25 percent in 1973, was reduced to 2.6 percent by 1975 (Appendix 2, Table A.2). But GDP dropped 16.5 percent in 1975 and unemployment climbed to more than 15 percent despite the government's employment programs (Appendix 2, Table A.3). While considerable progress was made on the privatization front, the companies that remained in state hands were the largest and most important ones, such as copper, oil exploration, and steel. Even though their economic program met resistance from within the state (from nationalists in the military and gradualist bureaucrats) and from outside of it, especially from the labor movement, the radical reformers steadily expanded their influence and pushed the program forward.

Once market reformers inside the state had won over General Pinochet, market reform until 1982 was driven by two highly integrated subnetworks,

TABLE 4.2. ECONOMIC POLICIES UNDER MILITARY RULE, 1973–1982

FINANCE MINISTER	POLICIES
General Lorenzo Gotuzzo (1973–74)	Price controls on 3,000 items removed Tariff reduction begun Privatization of companies taken over by previous regime
Jorge Cauas (1974–76) • Plan of Economic Recovery • "Shock Treatment"	Steep trade liberalization; maximum nominal tariff set at 35 percent with minimum of 10 percent by 1978 Drastic cut in government expenditure and investment Deregulation of financial markets, including removal of interest rate restrictions and restrictions on foreign banking; no requirement for minimum reserves; privatization continues
Sergio de Castro (1976–82)	1979: removal of all restrictions on foreign borrowing by banks 1979: reform of the labor code; right to bargain and strike with restrictions 1981: social security reform: system of private savings to be administered by private capital; health reform Law prohibits fiscal deficit Market reform institutionalized in 1980 constitution Number of public companies reduced to 48 from over 500 by 1982 but most important companies remain in state hands

Source: Privatization figures from Lüders 1993, 151.

one economic and one political. Policy development in the various reform areas occurred over several years and generally went on for some time before the individuals involved in policy development assumed formal positions of power. Discussion of labor policy, for example, was well under way by 1974, as was social security and health reform, both the subject of ODEPLAN studies. A nontechnocratic political subnetwork, also linked by personal loyalty to all of the key actors involved in the formulation of economic policy and to Pinochet, became instrumental in the political management of the reform process and was closely involved in all major policy discussions. The appointment of Sergio Fernández, the main figure in the political subnetwork, as labor minister in 1976 was essential in enabling reform to move forward. Fernández's predecessor, Nicanor Díaz Estrada, opposed radical economic adjustment in general and the Chicago boys' wishes in the area in labor policy in particular (interview with senior official).[5] Before he entered the government, Fernández's connection to the Chicago boys had come through his close friend Miguel Kast. Fernández developed probably the closest relationship of support and trust with General Pinochet of any of the civilians involved in market reform, a relationship that would see him appointed first civilian interior minister in 1978, giving him the title of "cabinet chief" and the extraordinary privilege of naming other cabinet appointments (Osorio and Cabezas 1995, 237; interview with senior official).

Fernández became closely involved in discussions on labor policy once he assumed the Labor Ministry, and he worked with José Piñera, who would take over the Labor Ministry in December 1978, to complete the 1979 labor plan. As minister of the interior (1978–82), he was in charge of the implementation of all policy reform measures. He met on a daily basis with de Castro, and under Fernández's auspices, the Political Advisory Committee, consisting of the ministers of external relations, justice, defense, the interior, and labor, mapped out the implementation of the privatization of the social security system, the 1979 labor code, and reforms to the health care system (interviews with two senior officials). Fernández joins de Castro at the pinnacle of the economic and political policy subnetworks, as a member of the market reform policy core, of which Pinochet remained an active participant and the predominant and decisive force.

Important also was Fernández's close relationship with gremialista leader Jaime Guzmán (Osorio and Cabezas 1995, 232), with whom he would work on the 1980 constitution. In formulating that constitution, both liaised closely with the radical reform technocrats, particularly de Castro (Osorio and Cabezas 1995, 283–84; Fontaine Aldunate 1988, 117). The 1980 constitution provided the essential institutional framework for market reform: it established the inviolability of private property, required that owners of expropriated property be compensated, provided for the creation of an independent central bank, and set up a variety of institutional arrangements that gave inordinate political weight to the military and political right once the country returned to civilian rule—measures that would become key in preventing alterations in economic policy. The 1980 constitution also provided the carefully paced institutionalized return to a restricted democracy that de Castro felt was essential to the continuity of this economic model (Osorio and Cabezas 1995, 284; interview with senior government official).

The outcome of reform policy reflected the confluence of policy ideas, vested interests, actors' perceptions of political feasibility, and responsiveness to larger constituencies—all played out within the highly integrated economic policy/political network described above. The Labor Plan, for example, contrary to the wishes of the Chicago boys, established the obligatory adjustment of salaries in accordance with inflation and stipulated that the minimum offer that employers were allowed to make was the salary level of the previous period (Ramos 1986, 21). This stipulation occurred in response to demands made by the members of the military (including Pinochet himself), who were concerned about the reaction of labor (interviews with two senior officials). The limited nature of the privatization program before 1982 also sprang from both resistance from the military in general and from Pinochet. Whereas economists favoring radical reform wished to privatize all public enterprises, including the state copper company, Pinochet blocked privatization beyond those companies confiscated by the Allende regime and strongly resisted privatization in such areas as telecommunications and steel. He and most military officers at the time believed it was important to maintain such activities in state hands for reasons of national security (interviews with senior officials). It was only after 1985 that the radical reformers' persistent proselytizing persuaded Pinochet to begin privatization in these "strategic" areas.

Despite having to make such compromises with their reformist vision, by 1981 the Chicago boys appeared to have achieved the impossible: the deepest and the earliest market reform program in Latin America, in a country with an independent and militant labor movement and a long history of a highly interventionist state. General Pinochet remained an active member of the policy core, and his close involvement in policy development had a decisive impact on both the extent and the limits of reform, in particular in wage indexing and in the exclusion of the largest and most important public companies from privatization. Market reforms would soon be placed in jeopardy by the 1981–82 economic collapse, however. And it would be a different policy network that would help ensure the recovery of the market reform model, albeit in a more pragmatic and flexible form.

COLLAPSE AND RECOVERY: THE RADICAL POLICY
NETWORK IS INTERNATIONALIZED

As illustrated in Table 4.1, the Chicago boys were closely integrated with a few large conglomerates, precisely the ones that expanded most rapidly during the first phase of economic reform. By 1978, Cruzat-Larraín controlled thirty-seven of Chile's largest companies, while BHC controlled twenty-five. After the privatization of the social security system, these two conglomerates controlled 70 percent of the insurance market (O'Brien and Roddick 1983, 73). The top three conglomerates (Cruzat-Larraín, BHC, and the Edwards group) came to control 53 percent of the banking sector and seventy-one of the country's largest firms in activities such as forestry, financial services, export agriculture, and mining (Silva 1995, 98).

Vested interests interacted with policy ideas within a tightly integrated network of senior government officials and conglomerate executives/owners to produce policy outcome. In response both to the preferences of the owners of these conglomerates and to their own ideological predilections, economic policy makers removed restrictions on capital flows and on banks' foreign liabilities (Edwards and Cox Edwards 1987, 55), measures that precipitated a binge of borrowing on the part of the conglomerates' financial institutions.[6] In addition to purchasing public companies, banks of holding companies lent heavily to companies in their own group, a maneuver they were legally able to do given lax regulatory policies (Hastings 1993, 218).[7] The bubble burst in 1981 in response to a variety of external factors. Between 1980 and 1982 the terms of trade fell, interest rates skyrocketed, and the Mexican crisis brought a halt to the inflow of funds from abroad. The overvalued exchange rate exacerbated the situation by making exports uncompetitive.[8] De Castro steadfastly refused to take action, arguing that the situation would correct itself ("automatic adjustment"). But clearly export competitiveness required either devaluation or the deindexing of wages. Because the navy (through Pinochet) blocked the latter policy choice, the only apparently prudent course was the former.

De Castro and a small coterie of collaborators, supported by the highly indebted economic conglomerates for whom devaluation would spell certain economic disaster, stood firmly against devaluation.[9] Meanwhile, the majority of state technocrats, along with industrialists and agricultural exporters, called for devaluation (Silva 1996, 155). In the face of mounting opposition to his policy position, de Castro departed from office—still on good terms with General Pinochet and still convinced of the correctness of his position—but believing that his departure would alleviate the growing antagonism against the market reforms (interview with senior government official). De Castro helped select his successor, close collaborator and Chicago boy Sergio de la Cuadra, who now took the helm of the Finance Ministry.[10] The long-anticipated devaluation was carried out three months later. The financial system, thrust into crisis in 1981, was now shaken to its very core as its major institutions teetered on the brink of collapse. By 1982 production and investment had plummeted, real wages dropped, and unemployment reached 22 percent (Appendix 2, Tables A.3, A.4).

It was in this context, following the appointment of Rolf Lüders as minister of finance and economy, that the state intervened in the banking system. Pressure for the state to step in had been mounting since 1981, from the private sector in general (but particularly from the conglomerates, who wanted to be rescued) and from technocrats in the Central Bank, who took the position that an economic collapse of this magnitude would place all of the economic reforms in jeopardy (interviews with three senior officials). In January 1983, the government intervened in five banks, including the two largest, the Banco de Chile (BHC, Vial) and the Banco de Santiago of Cruzat-Larraín. Three banks were closed, one belonging to BHC, the other to Cruzat-Larraín. The banking intervention brought an end to the close and cozy relationship between the Chicago boys and the conglomerates.[11] In 1983, the state assumed responsibility for the external debt of the private intervened banks, a condition of the debt rescheduling and new money agreement with creditor banks (Larrañaga J. and Marshall R. 1990, 17).

Meanwhile, pressure for basic changes in the economic model mounted. The private sector demanded debt relief, lower interest rates, public works projects, protection, and a realistic exchange rate, and it demanded greater access to the economic policy process (Silva 1995, 110–12). Some big agriculturalists, construction businessmen, and industrialists mobilized openly for a change of the model and attacked the Chicago boys (Marín and Rozas 1988, 77). Nationalists in the military demanded increased tariff protection and other measures demonstrating that the state would not abandon private enterprise (Délano and Traslaviña 1989, 95). The regime responded by appointing entrepreneurs with expansionary tendencies to key economic positions in the government in 1983 and 1984. Manuel Martín, an industrialist, became minister of the economy in 1983 and was replaced by Modesto Collados, a construction entrepreneur, in 1984. Import tariffs were raised to 20 percent in 1983 and to 35 percent the following year. Luis Escobar Cerda, appointed minister of finance in 1984, called for an expansive fiscal policy and further increases in tariffs (Fontaine Aldunate 1988, 171–74). Expansionary measures were taken to stimulate the economy, resulting in a rise in the fiscal deficit (Appendix 2, Table A.2).

Key members of the radical reform policy network began to fear for the survival of their economic model. That the model survived in the face of economic collapse, mounting social unrest, the vociferous disaffection of most of the private sector, criticism from the military, and the demise of previous strong adherents (i.e., the biggest conglomerates) merits careful consideration. The most commonly held explanation points to the impact on the private sector and the middle class of rising political unrest—a development that raised the specter of a return to the chaos of the Popular Unity period. The interviews I conducted bore out this explanation with regard to the private sector, for which anything was preferable to a return to the chaotic days of the UP. Silva has pointed to the regime's capacity to incorporate a wider spectrum of entrepreneurial interests as a key factor (Silva 1996). But in addition, the dogged persistence of the radical policy network, facilitated by its highly personalist integration, combined with its reinforcement by World Bank and IMF personnel (in effect, the construction of an international policy network), is integral to a full explanation of the survival and recovery of Chile's market reform model.

Both the IMF and the World Bank—the latter formally reentered Chile in 1984—strongly opposed the expansionary propensities of Finance Minister Escobar Cerda (1984–85). Agreement with the IMF proved impossible in 1984 and formal discussions were suspended, precluding a structural adjustment loan from the World Bank. Nevertheless, informal discussions, which had begun in late 1982, continued through 1984 in what became a cohesive and highly effective international policy network involving World Bank and IMF officials and radical market reformers both inside and outside the state.[12] The most important participants in the Chilean state were Hernán Büchi (then superintendent of banks), Juan Andrés Fontaine (a senior official in the Central Bank), and Brig. Gen. Enrique Seguel, an economist, who would take over the Finance Ministry in 1989. Büchi, although not formally a Chicago boy, had begun his career with the Chicago technocracy as an adviser to de Castro in 1975 and had worked on a wide variety of reform programs, including the municipalization of education, the Labor Plan, and the Pension Plan (Fontaine Aldunate 1988, 183). The discussions, involving one World Bank and one IMF official, formed the basis of a three-year economic plan that would result in an IMF EFF loan and three World

Bank SALS in 1985, 1986, and 1987. The economic plan also formed the basis for Büchi's 1985 economic program, which would return Chile to the path of market reform in the following years. Participants, both multilateral and Chilean, were concerned about the possibility that the military and other groups would push for a markedly more expansionary and interventionist model. As discussions went on, "an excellent relationship of trust" was built up among all participants, not only between multilateral and Chilean officials but also between the World Bank and IMF officials. The policy network, however, extended beyond this immediate intrastate group to involve Pinochet and even actors no longer within the state. Indeed, some of the original policy network members were still very much in the picture. Every Wednesday, General Pinochet had lunch with former finance ministers Sergio de Castro, Jorge Cauas, and Carlos Cáceres. Before each lunch meeting, the World Bank official involved in the policy discussions with Büchi briefed de Castro so he, in turn, could inform Pinochet of the latest developments in the emerging economic program.

A wide-ranging policy discussion occurred. Tariff reduction and privatization were apparently not contentious issues, and there was easy agreement that these programs should go forward. The rescue of the private banking sector, however, was of concern to the World Bank, which took a strong position against a blanket rescue operation in the face of the enormous pressure from the private sector, especially the highly exposed conglomerates, for such a move. The bank insisted on a case-by-case treatment so as to exclude the bailout of the worst cases, a demand that was eventually agreed to by the Chileans and was probably the most important condition of bank involvement with Chile at the time.[13] Considerable tension occurred over the extent of the austerity Chile was required to bear. Büchi apparently regarded the 3 percent growth rate recommended by the IMF and World Bank officials as not sufficient. The multilaterals demanded that wages be allowed to fall to stimulate competitiveness and that expenditures on health care and on the emergency employment program be contained. The military, which wanted a viable employment program, bristled under this latter requirement. The multilaterals' demand for a drastic reduction of the fiscal deficit was agreed to by the Chileans reluctantly even though they initially feared that the public deficit target was unachievable.

Büchi and his international policy network had time on their side. The expansionary economic policy of 1983–84 quickly ran into trouble: throughout 1984 imports grew faster than exports and the deficit in the current account worsened (Aguilera Reyes 1994, 46). In 1984, the country could not cover the interest on its foreign debt (Griffith-Jones 1987, 32). The exit of Interior Minister Sergio Onofre Jarpa, a strong supporter of the expansionary policy in 1983, followed by Escobar Cerda's departure in 1984, paved the way for the Chicago boys' return by 1985. The reluctance of some members of the World Bank's executive board to lend to Chile because of its problematic human rights situation strengthened the bank's and the IMF's ability to ensure orthodoxy. Officials at senior levels in the bank were willing to risk the opprobrium that involvement with Chile might bring only if the agreement with Chile was flawless on economic policy grounds (interview with senior bank official).[14] Although Büchi's own policy predilections predisposed him to a strict program, the program that emerged appears to have been more rigorous, in some respects, than what he originally may have had in mind.

Hernán Büchi took over the Finance Ministry in February 1985, and within a month of his taking office, the program developed with the participation of the international policy network was complete. In 1985, Chile signed formal agreements for a $2 billion (U.S.) financial package, which included a $750 million extended fund facility agreement from the IMF, a $250 million World Bank structural adjustment loan (SAL I, one of three), and $1.1 billion (U.S.) of new financing from the private sector.[15] But these formal agreements did not reflect the key role played by multilateral officials in the many months, indeed, years, of discussions preceding the agreements that largely bypassed ministers in official positions of power, particularly the ministers of finance and the economy at the time who were resisting harsh adjustment. The role of the multilaterals was crucial here; they participated in the development of a new economic program that returned Chile squarely to market reform. True, the officials with whom the multilaterals held discussions were already committed market reformers who believed that Chile's most feasible "negotiating" strategy was cooperation and exemplary behavior (interview with senior government official). But by supporting those technocrats who were the strongest supporters of market reform, multilateral officials helped to strengthen the hand of that group in the state. The plan developed by the international policy network came complete with the financial support that Chile so desperately needed at the time. Indeed, in the words of one World Bank official, Chile's structural adjustment program "would not have been the same without support from the international financial institutions" (interview). The World Bank and IMF had followed a strategy of "biding their time," of holding "a permanent dialogue" to develop an optimal economic plan while waiting for political events to open the way for implementation. The same strategy was followed in both the Mexican and Argentine cases.

Hence by early 1985 Büchi came forward with a clear economic plan that had international support. The persistence of Pinochet's Wednesday luncheon companions and the economic deterioration of late 1984 ensured strong support from Pinochet and propelled Büchi and his program forward. When Büchi was appointed finance minister, some key members of the old policy network returned to predominant positions: Pablo Baraona was appointed minister of mining in 1988 (to spur privatization in an area trade unions were likely to give trouble) and minister of the economy in 1987, and Sergio Fernández returned as interior minister. Büchi brought with him a team of dedicated technocratic reformers. Like de Castro before him, Büchi now became the fulcrum of the economic policy network with his own dedicated technocratic followers in the state.[16] Although economic policy formulation remained firmly with the minister of finance (always, of course, with close consultation with General Pinochet), the economic policy network now extended much more broadly into the private sector, providing a variety of avenues of consultation, both personal and institutionalized.

The major exception to consultation of the private sector was tariff reduction. Büchi believed that this reform had to be accomplished quickly without discussion with those affected who would have reasons to stall change (interviews with senior and two middle-ranking Finance Ministry officials). Export promotion measures won the favor of businessmen, however, and restrictive banking regulations ensured financial stability. The peak entrepreneurial associations in the Confederation of Production and Commerce (CPC) were now able to make their views known through the Ministry of the Economy's Commission for Commerce and Industry, the junta's legislative commissions, and the Economic and Social Council (Silva 1995, 117). Moreover, the minister and other government officials were personally accessible to private sector leaders to an extent unheard of before 1983 (interviews with three members of the private sector). In addition, business representatives remained in charge of sectoral portfolios such as agriculture, economy, and mining, thereby providing a direct channel for members of the private sector to make their views known (Silva 1996, 204). And Büchi's privatization program won the strong support of the private sector—indeed, winning the confidence of the private sector was one of the main motivations behind privatization during this phase (interviews with senior government official).[17]

The military, through Pinochet, continued to exercise enormous influence over the resurrected market reform process, particularly in privatization. The privatization of the firms intervened by the government as a consequence of the financial crisis was carried out in 1985–86. The post-1986 period saw a move into the sale of shares of a substantial number of the "strategic" companies owned by CORFO—energy, communications, airlines, and mining.[18] Büchi, pressing for the privatization of all state companies, like his predecessors met resistance from the military with its old national security arguments and from the bureaucrats in the public enterprises. Eventually, however, Büchi succeeded in persuading Pinochet to privatize everything except CODELCO (the state copper company) and ENAP (the state petroleum company) (interviews with two senior-level officials). Even with Pinochet's assistance, however, resistance was still strong and the task was not an easy one. Hence there was never a ranking of firms to be privatized. The strategy was to move loyalists into the management of public enterprises to prepare them for sale and to move most quickly with privatizations in areas where there was the least resistance (interviews with two senior-level officials). Hence between 1983 (before the state banking intervention) and 1989, the number of public companies was reduced by only three. Although the share of public enterprise production of GDP dropped from 28 percent in 1981 to 16 percent by 1988 (Hachette and Lüders 1994, 17), Chile's public enterprise sector still remained substantial by Latin American standards.[19] Often privatization was carried out over several years, with only small amounts of shares sold at first, at very low prices, to small investors. Only later were larger packages of shares sold on the stock exchange (Hojman 1993, 133).[20] Although an effort was made to ensure a greater dispersal in asset ownership of privatized companies, the country's biggest companies, now with foreign partners, gained control of privatized companies (Délano and Traslaviña 1989, 126; Marín and Rozas 1988, 104).

Export earnings more than doubled between 1985 and 1989 (Aguilera Reyes 1994, 55), and the resumption of economic growth helped to mitigate political tensions. Pinochet's conversion to the privatization of major public companies, combined with private sector pressure for privatization, was reflected in the move to privatize important public companies, although the process continued to be resisted and slowed down by opposition within the military. The return to civilian rule in 1990 would, however, result in further progress in this policy area. In that year, the reins of power were handed over to the elected Concertación government of Patricio Alywin, an alliance of left and center parties, the most important being the Christian Democratic Party (PDC) and the two socialist parties, the Socialist Party (PS) and the Popular Party for Democracy (PPD). Concertación was reelected in 1994 under the leadership of another Christian Democrat, Eduardo Frei, and again in 2000 with Socialist Ricardo Lagos as its presidential candidate. Concertación has continued to maintain the major features of the economic model combined with a concern for social justice.

CONSOLIDATING MARKET REFORM:
THE NEW TECHNOCRATS AND CONCERTACIÓN

The legacy of the 1973–89 period of military rule was reflected in the development of public policy in the postmilitary era. Under civilian rule, Chile remains heavily presidentialist with macroeconomic policy lodged in the hands of a committed elite bound together by both policy commitment and personal loyalty. The state retains its technocratic character; the Finance Ministry remains hegemonic within the state; and the Finance Ministry's priorities rule public policy development. Of course, under civilian rule there are far more policy networks. Policy networks based in the state extend into the private sector even more than during the post-1985 phase of military rule, although the most cohesive, integrated, and homogeneous network is based in the Finance Ministry. The cohesion of the policy elite, strong at the beginning of the period, now appears more fragile as it confronts an increasingly restive opposition within its ranks. Policy networks do not extend into the international sphere.

Table 4.3 sets out the major policy reforms under Concertación. In general, Concertación has pursued a policy thrust that has involved an effort to address poverty through increased government spending on social welfare, a careful watch over public spending, privatization, trade liberalization, and the negotiation of regional and bilateral trade agreements. Only relatively minor changes have been made to the extremely flexible labor code in order to afford workers greater bargaining power.[21] Three adjustment programs were implemented during the period: one in 1990 to counteract the expansionary policies of the last year of the military regime and to strengthen business confidence, another in 1995 in response to the Mexican crisis, and a harsher adjustment in 1998 in response to the Asian crisis.

What is most striking about this policy direction is its consistency and coherence in a democratizing context in which popular expectations might be predicted to slow down if not halt further market reform measures and to trigger a destabilizing increase in public expenditures. The commitment of

TABLE 4.3. ECONOMIC POLICIES UNDER CONCERTACIÓN

PRESIDENT/ FINANCE MINISTER	POLICIES
President Patricio Alywin (1990–94) Alejandro Foxley (1990–94)	1990: tax reform to raise revenue for social programs 1990–94: increased spending on social welfare, especially health and education 1991: tariff reduction from 15 to 11 percent; labor reform 1991: privatization of remaining 40 percent of LAN Chile (airline) 1992: foreign investment rules loosened; law allowing CODELCO (copper) to enter into joint ventures with private capital 1993: announcement that thirty-nine remaining state companies (excluding CODELCO), including zinc mining and electricity, to be privatized 1994: bill to break up CODELCO into four divisions; nonmining divisions to be privatized 1990–94: bilateral trade agreements with United States and Mexico
President Eduardo Frei (1994–99) Eduardo Aninat (1994–99)	1995: adjustment involving fiscal austerity and tight credit policy; social spending continues as top priority accounting for 70 percent of the budget in 1995, from 63 percent in 1994, 40 percent in 1996 1995: privatization of state sanitation companies announced; ports given out to private concessions; concessions to private sector for highway, airport construction, and railway passenger service, repair, and maintenance; state railway passenger service to be privatized 1997: partial privatization of ENAP (oil) and ENAMI (mining) announced 1997: bill lowering tariffs from 11 to 6 percent over the next five years 1996–98: trade agreement with Canada, Peru, the European Union, and MERCOSUR 1998: adjustment involving increased interest rates and cuts in public spending and social programs

the Concertación leadership to avoid an Argentine scenario of expansionary policies and consequent hyperinflation was certainly important in encouraging restraint (interviews with two senior officials). The institutional legacy of military rule was also a factor. The 1980 constitution (amended by plebescite in 1989) not only bolstered the government's ability to maintain the new economic model but also enabled it to carry market reform even further. At the same time, these political arrangements were instrumental in frustrating attempts at reform in other policy areas. In particular, the nine designated (appointed) senators have been key in giving the right wing disproportionate clout in setting policy. In accordance with the 1980 constitution, Pinochet appointed nine loyal supporters to that body in 1988, including one from each branch of the armed forces and the Carabineros (the national police). The alliance between the right-wing elected senators and the nine designated ones made the Concertación two votes short of a simple majority and six votes short of the twenty-eight votes needed for a major constitutional change (Linz and Stepan 1996, 208). These Senate appointees and the elected senators of the right-wing political coalition were in general staunch supporters of the market and were less concerned with issues of poverty and inequality. The tenure of the Pinochet-appointed senators ended in 1997, and the administration was unable to secure a constitutional reform to obtain their elimination and remained without assured support to carry out constitutional reform.[22] The importance of the appointed senators in influencing policy emerged in the case of the 1991 tax reform. Concertación had to negotiate its tax reform bill required to raise funds to increase social spending with the right-wing National Renovation Party in Congress while its own parties participated very little in policy development (Boylan 1996, 27). Similarly, Concertación saw its attempt at labor reform in 1995 frustrated in the Senate because of right-wing opposition.[23] It is fair to say that the institutional legacy of the military regime facilitated the continuation of market reform while presenting obstacles to measures such as labor and tax reform seen as important in alleviating poverty and inequality.

Although the executive's maneuverability in policy was constrained in important ways by the ability of the right wing in the Senate to frustrate its policy initiatives, the Chilean political system nevertheless concentrates enormous power in the hands of the presidency. One observer has described the Chilean presidency as "one of the most powerful in Latin America and in the world" (Siavelis 1997, 324). The role of Congress is particularly restricted in fiscal matters; for example, it can only approve or reduce expenditures; it cannot increase or redistribute them (Siavelis 1997, 328). The law requested by the Chicago boys in 1975, empowering the finance minister with ultimate authority over all decisions having financial implications, remains in effect. It facilitates the concentration of economic authority in the Finance Ministry and determines the relative strength of intrastate policy networks.

Chile's policy makers under Concertación are technocrats—another legacy of military rule. During the years of military government, academic think tanks played an important role in the socialization of both intellectuals and politicians in scientific methods of social science research and in the new ideas of market economics. In addition, academic think tanks, among the few opposition institutions that were able to operate during the Pinochet years, brought together socialists and Christian Democrats who honed their technocratic skills in a deluge of studies critical of the military regime's economic policies. Both Christian Democrats and socialists, influenced by the intellectual climate and the upturn of the Chilean economy after 1985, began to accept the major tenets of the neoliberal model (Silva 1991, 400; Petras and Leiva 1994, 63–64; Kinney Giraldo 1997, 250). By 1989, the interchange of ideas in workshops produced a firm commitment to the maintenance of the neoliberal economic model and a blurring of the distinction between politician and technocrat. Highly trained social scientists headed up a wide array of ministries in both the Alywin and Frei administrations, including ones with noneconomic responsibilities.[24] As was also true in the Argentine and Mexican cases, technocrats in charge of macroeconomic policy in Chile were recruited from a common source, largely from the think tank CIEPLAN (Corporation for Economic Research on Latin America) (Silva 1991, 406), and formed a cohesive policy clique and support base.

Notably absent from policy development after the return to civilian rule were international policy networks. By 1989, Chile had completed the most socially costly aspect of market reform and the civilians who now came to power apparently feared that negotiations for debt reduction under the Brady Plan might oblige them to pursue market reforms regarded by the public as involving additional social costs (*Latin American Weekly Report*, October 5, 1989, 2).[25] Moreover, reforms already carried out by 1990 made Chile ineligible for structural adjustment loans from the World Bank. A dialogue did continue with bank officials, but relations were strained, lacking the trust and close working relationships that are the key features of international policy networks. The bank's close working relationship with officials of the military regime after the crash of the early 1980s was deeply resented by many Concertación officials, and officials of the bank reluctantly came to accept that this situation constrained their influence (interview with senior LAC official).

The policy elite, those who initiate and define the direction of economic policy, has consisted of a cohesive group of powerful Concertación ministers. Under Alywin, this group included the president, the secretary of the presidency, the minister of finance, the head of the Central Bank, the minister of the economy, the minister of public works, and the minister of labor. These ministers met frequently as the Interministerial Committee on the Economy to discuss macroeconomic policy issues. While then minister of finance Alejandro Foxley was the recognized leader in economic policy, he collaborated closely with Carlos Ominami, minister of the economy from 1990 to 1992 (interviews with two senior officials in the Economy and Finance Ministries). Macroeconomic policy making under the Alywin administration has been described as a process involving cooperation and compromise (Kinney Giraldo 1997, 265–66). Under the subsequent presidency of Eduardo Frei, however, the power of the finance minister increased and the role of the minister of the economy diminished as the process became less one of negotiation, particularly in areas in which the Finance Ministry had exclusive jurisdiction.[26] The Interministerial Committee on the Economy met only occasionally. Neither macroeconomic policy nor the nation's budget was discussed at the full cabinet level—a conscious decision designed to insulate economic policy makers from pressures to increase public spending. Macroeconomic policy rested in the hands of the minister of finance, the head of the Central Bank, and their respective technocratic teams.

Table 4.4 outlines the policy networks under Concertación. Policy networks, rooted in the state and dominated by technocrats, replace the truncated, more informal, highly integrated, and exclusionary networks of the period of military rule. In their bureaucratic character and institutional bases, these networks resemble the more standard concept of policy network found in developed countries. The overwhelming importance of the Finance Ministry became even more marked under President Frei. Highly trained individuals are found at the helm of virtually all the ministries, and these people (the first one or two strata below ministerial rank, numbering approximately fifty or so in total) meet together on a regular basis and hammer out economic policy.[27] The largest and most cohesive set of technocrats, however, is found in the Ministry of Finance. Here there is a strong esprit de corps, a common educational background (usually a graduate degree in economics), a common source of recruitment (CIEPLAN), often previous friend-

TABLE 4.4. POLICY NETWORKS UNDER CONCERTACIÓN (MINISTRIES AND
GROUPS FROM WHICH NETWORK PARTICIPANTS ARE DRAWN)

POLICY AREA	MINISTRIES	EXTRASTATE GROUPS
Public expenditure/ budget	Finance* vs. other ministries	Private sector** pressure to restrict expenditure (periphery)
Monetary policy	Central Bank, Finance	Private sector informed (periphery)
Trade liberalization	Finance	Private sector informed (periphery)
Taxation policy	Finance	Private sector consulted (periphery)
Bilateral trade agreements	External Relations, Labor, Finance	Private sector involved (support base)
Privatization	Presidency, Finance, CORFO	Private sector influence (periphery/support base)
Social policy	Finance, sectoral ministries, especially Health, Education	None
Labor policy	Labor, Presidency, Finance	Labor claims consultation insufficient, private sector pressure; 1995: private sector refuses participation***

Source: Interviews by author.
*Since the same top Finance Ministry officials are involved in these various policy areas, we cannot speak of distinct policy networks within Finance.
**Excludes small and medium nonexporting firms and the banking sector. Members of the private sector participate in policy through both institutionalized and noninstitutionalized means.
***See Chapter 7 for details.

ships, ongoing interaction outside of the state, a strong institutional identity, and powerful loyalty to the finance minister and to the state (interviews with three Finance Ministry officials).[28] In the importance of trust, loyalty, and interaction outside of the institutional setting, the Finance Ministry's networks resemble the more typical Latin American pattern.

Intense conflicts occur between the Finance Ministry technocrats and the technocrats of other ministries over public budget allocations. Such conflicts over policy priorities normally, however, do not become public knowledge.[29] Highly trained technocrats at the helm of the Finance Ministry, many of them with expertise in particular sectors, scrutinize the budget of other ministries each year and turn down programs they believe are expendable.[30] Despite the intensely conflictive nature of these interchanges during budget time, the constant interaction among all technocrats at the upper echelons of the state, their relatively small number, and broad commonalities in their training have (thus far at least) been conducive to their reaching agreement.[31]

Finance Ministry officials play a leading role in policy areas outside of the finance sector. The ministry has, for example, become heavily involved in the development of social policy, linking up directly with officials of sectoral areas such as health and education in which it wishes to see policy developed. Indeed, the Finance Ministry was widely seen as having the leading role in the development of social policy. There is an Interministerial Social Policy Committee with representation from the Social Planning Ministry and the sectoral ministries such as health and education, but it was not the driving force behind social policy development, and its role diminished markedly once Eduardo Aninat became minister of finance (interviews with two Finance Ministry officials and one Planning Ministry official).

Although the country's policy elite is supported by a technocratic base committed to the market and to the maintenance of macroeconomic stability, the policy consensus among the policy elite has probably been even more important in maintaining consistency in policy direction. Indeed, Chile's policy elite's cohesiveness on macroeconomic issues is particularly remarkable given that Concertación is an alliance of political parties. At the ministerial level, both Concertación presidents have divided up cabinet portfolios so as to achieve a balance of sorts among the parties.[32] Personal loyalty, especially to the president, has been an important supplement to the policy consensus brought about by common exposure to academic training and the international policy environment. It was especially important when the fear of military intervention began to recede and rumblings began from the base of Concertación (more will be said about this in Chapter 7). Those interviewed stressed that loyalty was a critical requirement for cabinet appointments and that personal loyalty to the president and his policy goals (in particular, the goals of macroeconomic equilibrium) must unequivocally predominate over loyalty to one's particular party and certainly over one's own personal policy preferences. At the top bureaucratic levels of ministries, among the technocratic policy networks that work out the details of policy, personal loyalty to the minister is similarly operative. Personal loyalty and policy commitment were, therefore, mutually reinforcing tendencies. In the words of one senior-level official interviewed: "My first loyalty is to the president and to the government and only secondarily to my party." For the loyal technocratic teams at the helm of each ministry and those surrounding the president himself, loyalty to the president, respect for training and education, and loyalty to the state predominate over party loyalty.

The presence of a binding loyalty at the policy elite levels contravening party loyalty clearly distinguishes postmilitary Chilean politics from the sharp party polarization of the pre-1973 years, when compromise became virtually impossible. At the same time, however, there are tensions within the policy elite and certainly within the cabinet more generally over the specifics of economic policy. Several ministers and highly placed officials outside of the Finance Ministry were resentful of the ministry's inordinate power. Comments tinged with animosity toward the Ministry of Finance were especially marked among senior-level officials concerned with social welfare and poverty reduction who felt that the ministry's power over the budget gave it the opportunity to interfere in the priorities of other ministries. Alienation was particularly marked among officials in the Social Planning Ministry (MIDEPLAN) who felt bypassed even in their own policy area (see Table 4.4). Several acknowledged a tension in the cabinet and certainly at high levels in the public bureaucracy between maintenance of economic indicators (the overwhelming concern of Finance Ministry officials) and reduction of poverty and inequality.[33] In these circumstances, personal loyalty insofar as it induces the quiescence of intrastate actors excluded from important policy networks has been key in maintaining policy coherence. The 1998 resignation of Social Planning Minister Roberto Pizarro (a socialist) in protest against President Frei's decision to have the Finance Ministry draw up the country's social action plan for the next two years and the decision to close a debate on fiscal reform that would have generated funds for his social program suggest, however, that tension arising from technocrats outside the Finance Ministry who feel excluded from important policy discussions is becoming more serious. Subsequent events—the arrest of Pinochet and the struggle over the presidential candidacy of Concertación—also tested the policy elite's unity.[34]

Under Concertación, the private sector has had a wide array of channels through which it can influence policy. One of the regime's major concerns upon assuming power in 1990 was the maintenance of business confidence, faced as it was with a private sector fearful of a return to the statist policies of the premilitary years (Estrategia 1994, 130). The strategy for maintaining that confidence has been to ensure the private sector ready access to the policy process, to pledge the maintenance of the key features of the neo-liberal model, to heed business concerns about avoiding increases in public spending, and to afford the private sector increased investment opportunities through privatization (interviews with two senior Finance Ministry officials and three business leaders). Private sector actors have privileged access to the state and are clearly within the policy network periphery on most economic issues (see Table 4.4). They are integral actors in bilateral trade agreements and have had heavy input into privatization policy. The private sector has two important avenues of policy input. One is through lobbying sympathetic members of Congress, a strategy employed when support of the right is required to defeat legislation business does not like. A forceful lobbying effort was made against the 1995 proposal to reform the labor code, for example. At the same time, the private sector has privileged access to the policy elite through both institutional and personal channels. Working commissions on economic policy (Muñoz and Celedon 1993, 128, 131), the Foro de Producción,[35] a yearly conference during which ideas on economic policy are exchanged, and monthly meetings with the head of the Central Bank all provide the private sector with regular opportunities to press its point of view. When CORFO was reorganized the private sector was given representation on its board of directors (*El Mercurio Internacional*, January 18–24, 1996, 5). The government has always involved representatives of the private sector, generally potential exporters, when negotiating trade agreements.[36] But equally important for members of the private sector is the direct and personal access they enjoy to top policy makers. The following comment by one businessman was generally reflective of the way business/Concertación relations were described: "If I want to talk to the minister of finance or the minister of the economy I just call them. The minister of finance returns my calls in half an hour, the minister of the economy in five minutes. The situation is a vast improvement over the military government, whose officials were impossible to talk to." Indeed, the cordiality of business-government relations was reflected in the claim that business involvement in economic policy was greater under Concertación than it had ever been under military rule (interviews with two business leaders). Business generally had high praise for economic policy under Concertación.[37]

Business leaders, with the exception of those in the banking sector and nonexporting small and medium firms, not only believed that senior government officials were easily accessible but also maintained that their involvement had an impact on policy in at least two areas: privatization and bilateral trade agreements. Evidence from both the print media and interviews makes it clear that the private sector strongly favors privatization and has been lobbying intensely for it. All business leaders interviewed believed that their persistent lobbying had been responsible for the government's decision to privatize ports and sanitary works and that they had also been instrumental in new arrangements whereby the state copper company could now form associations with private capital.[38] The private sector's overriding concern for the public deficit served to bolster policy makers' cautiousness in public spending. Indeed, technocratic policy makers readily acknowledged their openness to business leaders on all issues except generalized tariff reduction where consultation with "affected business interests" would have blocked policy implementation. Indeed, openness to business was seen by policy makers as key to the maintenance of business confidence (interviews with two senior Finance Ministry officials).

The relationship between the private sector and top policy makers is not without tension, however, and there are clearly differences within the private sector with regard to their access to the state. There continues to be a great deal of tension between policy makers and the country's big banks— a legacy of the crash of the early 1980s and the bank rescue operation that resulted in increased state indebtedness because of the so-called subordinated debt, a debt subsequently transferred to the Central Bank. The private sector, in general, has opposed tax hikes, interest rate increases, and labor reform (however minimal), which it says will make Chile uncompetitive (interviews with all business leaders; *El Mercurio Internacional*, July 15–21, 1995, 3, July 13–19, 1995, 4). What is key, however, is that the policy core remains accessible and open to penetration and influence by the private sector. Members of the private sector are certainly well within the periphery of policy networks insofar as they are regularly and carefully consulted and listened to on a wide variety of economic policies.

CONCLUSIONS

The fear and economic chaos of the Popular Unity years engendered an extreme political reaction: the rise to power of a highly repressive military regime that embarked on a profound transformation of the old economic order. Policy networks, involving the military, Chicago-trained technocrats, the executives and owners of powerful conglomerates, and members of the traditional right, were hierarchical and tightly integrated. Features of Chile's Iberian strain—personal power, centralism, and the exercise of wide discretion—came to define the character of the policy-making process; indeed, Pinochet's personal rule proved highly miscible with the technocratic style of constant personal contact and discussions. The personal power of General Pinochet and his authoritarian control over the army, combined with the tight personalistic relationships among technocratic and nontechnocratic members of the policy core, were key factors propelling reform forward. In this initial period of market reform under military rule (1975–82), two integrated subnetworks, an economic and a political one, were absolutely essential to the reform process.

The highly personalistic network leading policy change arose outside of the state, entered the state, and carried policy reform forward. Economic policy reflected the confluence of ideas, interests, and perceptions articulated by key members of the policy elite. Market liberalizing ideas, particularly privatization, were tempered by the military's perception of national security interests. Moreover, the political calculations of both Pinochet and factions in the military, especially the navy, had an impact on wage policy, once again tempering the policy preferences of technocrats, at least until 1982. At the same time, the highly personalistic integration of technocrats and a very small number of conglomerate owners and executives in a tightly integrated policy network provided the context for a lax regulatory framework, a binge of foreign borrowing, and a reluctance to devalue, all of which made the crash of the early 1980s worse than it otherwise would have been.

An international policy network, containing some members of the original radical policy core, played an important role in keeping Chile's market reform process on track once the crisis of the early 1980s hit. Again, personal trust and loyalty played a key role in binding participants together and in ensuring agreement on an invigorated reform program that would have multilateral financial support. Orthodoxy was reinforced by the leverage wielded by the World Bank in view of Chile's poor human rights record under Pinochet. In addition, the World Bank's role appears to have been key in inhibiting generalized rescue of the banks. Once the new program was in place, private sector input into policy was broadened to include that sector more generally, and access to policy was afforded to the private sector through both personalistic and institutional means.

Chile's return to civilian rule has seen important changes in the policy process and therefore in the market reform process but also significant continuities. The Concertación was elected on a platform that promised to maintain the basic features of the neoliberal model but with a clear commitment to social justice. The political arrangements developed by the military government's political subnetwork have left an institutional legacy that has constrained policy change, precisely in those areas where members of the elected Concertación's broader constituency have been pressuring for alteration: labor legislation and stronger measures to alleviate poverty and reduce inequality.[39] The Senate's opposition to proposed changes in labor legislation and its resistance to tax increases to allow for increased social spending are evidence of this.

While on the one hand, under civilian rule policy networks are more numerous, on the other hand, they remain selective. At the executive and bureaucratic levels, it is clear that access to the state and top state managers remains the privilege of the private sector, largely because of the regime's concern for maintaining the confidence of business. Business influence has been especially important in certain privatizations and in ensuring tight control of public expenditure. The most important policy network is based in the Finance Ministry, monopolizing several policy areas and dominating the networks in others. It is characterized by most of the standard features of Latin American technocratic policy networks: personal friendship, trust, loyalty, common sources of recruitment, and common policy objectives. It is hegemonic within the state and is predominant in policy development, including social policy. In addition, a new, albeit fragile, element appears to have entered the Chilean political scene: the loyalty technocrats profess to the leadership, especially to the president and to the goal of macroeconomic stability, a loyalty its adherents claim transcends particularistic party or policy preferences.

In many respects, the situation is a vast improvement over that before 1973, when the state lacked central coordination and responded to the push and pull of competing vested interests that had succeeded in colonizing various parts of the state. Undoubtedly, the new arrangements have been key in keeping inflation low and the fiscal situation under control, certainly a prerequisite to political stability and ultimately to democracy. In important respects, policy development is far superior to that in the other two cases dealt with in this book. The use of personal channels for business to the policy elite has seemingly not resulted in the rampant corruption that has come to characterize the cases of Argentina and Mexico, while institutional channels for private sector input are highly developed. It is probably useful to recall, however, that pre-1973 Chilean political history was characterized by institutionalized politics and a relative lack of features such as patron clientelism and patrimonialism considered to be related to corruption (see Chapter 2). While a healthy fiscal balance and low inflation are important to political stability, political stability is also contingent on the perception that electoral democracy has the capacity to change what needs to be changed. While Concertación is an electoral coalition backed by two socialist parties and working-class supporters, policy networks have provided the private sector with privileged access for policy input that has enabled it effectively to influence policy development. In addition, many technocrats with social policy concerns as their number one priority have been excluded from major economic policy decisions. Under these circumstances, the policy elite must balance the need to maintain business confidence with the pressure to open the channels of policy access to a wider cross section of state and society.

chapter five

MARKET REFORM AND POLITICAL TRANSITION IN ARGENTINA
From Military Rule to *Menemismo*

Looked at historically, Argentina's market reform process, a case of "liber-alization in a country born liberal" (Halperín Donghi 1988), has followed a long, circuitous path. The military regime that took power in 1976 ini-tially appeared to be strongly committed to the market, but unlike in Chile, the reform process became stalled and ultimately collapsed during the eco-nomic crisis of the early 1980s. Radical market reform would not get under way for another decade. Only after the return to civilian rule and the failure of the heterodox economic program of President Raúl Alfonsín did Peron-ist president Carlos Menem move decisively toward policy reform. But he did so in record time; by the end of Menem's first term of office, the state had divested itself of virtually all of the national government's major public firms. While hyperinflationary episodes in 1989 and 1990 propelled market reform forward, developments during the period of military rule (1976–83) and the Afonsín years (1983–89) laid the groundwork for Menem's policy reform.

Explaining the delay of market reform in Argentina involves a careful consideration of both international circumstances and domestic political factors. The military was the key obstacle to reform for many years. But the labor movement probably proved to be the most formidable opponent of market reform, defining the limits of reform even under radical market reformer President Carlos Menem. From 1989, policy reform was driven forward by a policy elite that, although linked by personal bonds, would experience increasing tension within its ranks. Argentina's market reform policy core has been the most porous of the three cases. Policy networks flowed from it into society, incorporating powerful members of the pri-vate sector, and into the international sphere, where it included officials of the World Bank. Unlike the other two cases, collaborationist labor leaders penetrated policy networks, a phenomenon I will explore in depth in Chapter 7. Of the three cases, Argentine policy networks were the least hierarchical, the least technocratic, the most numerous, and the most personalistic. Moreover, in comparison with the other two cases, international actors and members of the private sector had the most active role in policy reform. The character of Argentine policy networks stems from the fact that although Peronism's base and platform were transformed in the years between 1976 and 1989, the predominant Iberian features of the movement were not. Clientelism, wide discretion, and personalism not only remained but, because of the nature of the political leadership, became the defining features of the Argentine policy reform process.

Most observers have seen the Argentine state as weak and have attributed economic policy change, even during military rule, to shifts in the coalition backing the state (O'Donnell 1977b; Epstein 1989, 66). Although trained individuals began to enter the Argentine state during the 1960s, technocrats failed to remain within the state and had little influence on policy because the turbulence of Argentine politics forced their exit with each regime change (Teichman 1997a, 34). Nevertheless, there is evidence that after 1970 pressures from public employees and their clienteles gained in importance (Most 1991, 57). By 1987, state managers were having some success in isolating themselves from societal policy pressures (particularly labor), and by the early 1990s there had developed a technocratic cadre of economic policy makers able to obtain a greater degree of autonomy from societal pressures than in the past. Nevertheless, observers continue to speak of a coalition backing the Menem regime, although the nature of that backing depends not only on the policy issue but also on whether one is talking about an anti-inflation electoral coalition (Starr 1999a) or corporate group backing, involving big business and excluding small and medium business and labor (McGuire 1997, 259). Insofar as my analysis demonstrates the inordinate role of big business in market reform, it lends support to the latter interpretation. But the coalition approach overlooks some important elements of the picture, namely, the driving force of policy ideas and the deep penetration of the Argentine state by international actors. In this context, actual policy came to reflect the interplay among policy ideas, increasingly defined by technocratic participants both international and domestic, political considerations arising from coalition and interest pressure, and personalistic political ties. We now turn to a consideration of the thirteen-year period leading up to reform, a period of stiff resistance but ultimately one in which the basis for the important changes to come was laid.

STRUGGLING WITH MARKET REFORM: FROM THE
PROCESO TO ALFONSÍN, 1976-1989

Features of the Argentine military that distinguish it from its Chilean counterpart help to explain the failure of the Argentine military regime to push
ahead more consistently with a market reform agenda during the period
of highly repressive military rule, known as the *proceso.* Unlike the Chilean
military, the Argentine military was severely divided and lacked the firm
hierarchical control from the top needed to overcome military resistance
to policies it did not like. Moreover, the Argentine military had a history
of links with civilian political groups that were accustomed to lobbying
its various factions in the direction of their particular concerns. Labor, although severely repressed by the military regime, did not disappear as a
power factor. Its collaborationist faction maintained access to public policy.
Finally, long before the 1976 coup, the Argentine military had colonized the
state, with military men heading up many public enterprises and thereby
forming vested interests resistant to privatization.

The period of the proceso was marked by deepening conflicts within
the armed forces. Economic liberals, the largest group linked to the country's most important landed, commercial, and industrial interests, feared
the power and influence of Peronism and sought its elimination (McSherry
1997, 79–89). But the military also contained ardent economic nationalists,
who favored an alliance with the labor movement in order to confront the
communist threat. This group opposed privatization, arguing that it threatened national security because state companies in strategic sectors would
fall into the hands of foreigners (Manzetti 1993, 185, 187; Lewis 1990, 455).
Divisions within the military were further exacerbated by its extensive responsibilities in the state apparatus. The military had always operated Fabricaciones Militares, a group of industries that alone produced 2.5 percent
of national production. Over the years, the management of these public
companies had created a friendly interdependence between public firms and
their private sector clients such that upon retirement military officers often
went to work for private sector firms that had contracts with Fabricaciones
Militares (Wynia 1986, 114). After the military coup of 1976, military officers came to run almost all state institutions: the army, navy, and air force
divided up ministries and public enterprises and most other government
positions (McSherry 1997, 91; Manzetti 1991, 125).[1] This situation fostered
divided loyalties and contributed to the breakdown of the chain of command (Manzetti 1993, 185). Moreover, the economic liberalism of Argen-

tina's military men was heavily qualified: privatization was intended only for those activities that the private sector was willing and able to carry out, and privatization of the Fabricaciones Militares group was categorically rejected (Schvarzer 1981, 135–36).

The military-appointed civilian minister of the economy,[2] José Martínez de Hoz, was a representative of the country's most powerful landed and business interests and an adherent of economic orthodoxy and had excellent personal connections with international financial institutions. De Hoz worked hard to convince military officers of the efficacy of market reform and succeeded in convincing the junta to grant him wide powers over economic decision making. But he could not overcome the enormous resistance to reform from within the military, especially from the statist/nationalist faction, which opposed privatization and loss of protection for military industries.[3] Nor was he able to eliminate labor influence in the state, as the Chilean market reformers had. The military's strategy for dealing with labor, which included, in addition to repression, collaboration with cooperative labor leaders, gave labor the contacts and the space to lobby against certain aspects of market reform.[4] Many military intervenors in trade unions, for example, kept on old trade union leaders as advisers (Gaudio and Thompson 1990, 76). Hence union leaders joined forces with the nationalist wing of the military, lobbying General Diego Urricarriet, head of Fabricaciones Militaries, to vigorously oppose de Hoz's plans to sell some of the group's companies (Manzetti 1991, 131).

Hence de Hoz's economic program was a heterodox and often contradictory blend of price and exchange controls, selective tariff reduction, privatization, and state expansion. The growth of the Argentine state in the decades before the military coup of 1976 had produced a chaotic public enterprise sector, the extent of which was far from certain. One study lists a total of 747 companies controlled totally or partially by the state; in 347 of them, the state had a controlling interest (Ugalde 1984, 27). But the core of the Argentine public enterprise sector consisted of a relatively small number of state firms: 14 enterprises represented between 61 and 77 percent of total public enterprise activity whether measured by sales or total employment (Schvarzer 1981, 32–34). The public enterprise sector dominated a few economic activities and held a legal monopoly over the exploitation of hydrocarbons, control of the largest copper deposits, exclusive control of air and railway transportation, and control over one-half of all radio and TV programming and over almost half of the steel produced (Ugalde 1984, 47–49).

With the 1976–82 privatization program not only did the extent and nature of activities covered by the public enterprise sector not change but government policy created vested interests that would oppose further reform. The state divested itself of a few companies and sold state-owned shares in others (Ugalde 1984, 23), but it also took on new responsibilities with the 1979 purchase of La Compañía Italo de Electricidad for a dollar value greater than that received for the sale of all public enterprise shares sold during the period (Schvarzer 1981, 57). In addition, the state took over a variety of other companies, including the airline, Austral Líneas, and its three subsidiaries (Orlansky 1994, 11). Meanwhile, the reforms that had been carried out in the core public enterprise sector generated the emergence of powerful private sector vested interests in support of the continued existence of public enterprises. "Peripheral" privatization involved the contracting out of a wide variety of auxiliary functions of public enterprises such as maintenance, transportation, consulting, and petroleum exploitation. Contracting out benefited a small number of large industrial companies that provided the required materials and services. These government contractors were afforded assured markets, tax privileges, guaranteed payment, and easy credit from the state Banco de la Nación (Schvarzer 1981, 79, 113; Canitrot and Sigal 1994, 99). By the return to civilian rule, total expenditure and the public deficit as a proportion of GDP remained virtually unchanged (Appendix 2, Table A.2).

Other aspects of the reform program were uneven. While many subsidies for industry were removed, such as those for nontraditional exports and subsidized credit, selected activities were targeted for new subsidies.[5] Nor was tariff reform applied evenly. While between 1976 and 1982, the average tariff rate on imports declined from 55 to 22 percent (Dornbusch and de Pablo 1990, 123), a nucleus of branches producing intermediate goods considered to be "strategic" retained high tariff protection. These industries were in the sectors controlled by the military: petroleum and derivatives, transport material, cement, and steel (Peralta Ramos 1992a, 76).

In any case, these uneven steps in the direction of reform fell victim to the economic crisis that hit Argentina in 1979 before the increase in international interest rates or the Mexican crisis. The sharp deterioration in the current account and the balance of payments and the consequent loss of confidence and capital flight were distinguishing features of the Argentine crisis. In 1980, the Argentine growth rate had dropped to 0.7 percent, and the banking crisis also hit that year (James 1996, 374). As in Chile, the Argentine government intervened in the private banking sector, which was on the verge of collapse, auditing and liquidating sixty-two financial institutions.[6] The remaining two years of military rule have been referred to as a period of "chaotic adjustment" (Damel and Frenkel 1996, 59) involving strong devaluations, price controls, heavy restrictions on lending, and the bailout of the highly indebted private sector.

Despite its economic failures, however, the years of military rule were an important prelude to market reform. Military rule had weakened one of market reform's most ardent opponents, the labor movement. Unions had been targets of political repression; labor leaders had been jailed or "disappeared," and noncooperative union activity had been curtailed. The union financial basis had been seriously eroded when workers' contributions to the obras sociales (social welfare funds providing health care), a key source of union financial power, were made voluntary and union control eliminated by requiring that all union funds be deposited in state banks under the control of the minister of labor, an army general (Grassi, Hintz, and Neufeld 1994, 128). Union wealth was further undermined when compulsory union membership and dues from nonunion members were abolished. The decline in industry also weakened labor. As the number of bankruptcies rose, the size of the industrial labor force dropped.[7]

The labor movement and much of the Argentine public believed that the return of democracy would alleviate economic hardship. But the economy was to deteriorate even further before the final swing in economy policy and improvement. In the next phase, an interplay between international pressures and domestic events would transform the Argentine economy. Argentina's transition to democratic rule in 1983 was probably the most obvious and most important factor in the country's resistance to market reform. In the public mind, orthodox stabilization and market reforms were associated with the loathed military regime that had blocked the expression of popular demands for improvements in wages and social welfare. Hence newly elected president Raúl Alfonsín, whose campaign promises had included measures to stimulate growth and increase wages and salaries, resisted strict austerity and market liberalizing measures. He pursued a confrontational position vis-à-vis private creditors and the International Monetary Fund on the premise that a democratic government did not have to honor the debt acquired by an illegitimate military regime, and he sought U.S. support for a lenient treatment of the country's debt problem (Aggarwal 1996, 417; interviews with two senior Radical government officials). U.S. support for the Argentine position gave breathing space for the experiment with heterodoxy (thereby delaying reform) but also produced a close integration with the World Bank — a relationship that would help spur sudden and complete change when the opportunity arose in 1989.

Table 5.1 summarizes the economic programs of the Alfonsín administration and the conflictive relationship with the World Bank and the IMF. A series of economic programs moved from expansionary, to heterodox, to increasingly orthodox solutions to the country's growing economic difficulties. These policies were pursued in a context of incessant labor unrest, recurring military uprisings, and a deteriorating economic situation (particularly rising inflation), combined with stiff resistance from private creditors. As each plan failed, Argentina's economic situation deteriorated further.

Upon assuming power, the Radical government was faced with 600 percent inflation and a public treasury in shambles. Its first economy minister, Keynesian economist and member of the Radical traditional wing Bernardo Grinspun, adopted an expansionary program that involved, among other things, increased wages (Appendix 2, Table A.4) and the printing of money to meet government payrolls. The expansionary policy exacerbated an already dire situation: inflation hit 1500 percent, and the IMF suspended disbursements and creditor banks suspended financing (di Tella 1987, 181). The Austral Plan was next. As the economy deteriorated, Alfonsín placed hope for improvement in a new technical team of economists from the subsecretary of planning in the Ministry of the Economy, headed up by Juan Sourrouille. The viewpoint shared by the new economic team, although far from orthodox, marked an important change in attitude. All agreed that a new economic program, including policy reform, was necessary, that Argentina had to abandon the notion of the debt as illegitimate, and that the government must negotiate with the multilaterals (the IMF and the World Bank).

Although the Austral Plan was initially successful (inflation was reduced to 3 percent per month by the end of 1985), by early 1987 the country was experiencing a renewed inflationary leap and rise in the fiscal deficit (Appendix 2, Table A.2). Like so many economic plans before it, this one faced rising opposition from business and especially from labor. The latter, having succeeded in having one of its own (Carlos Alderete) appointed labor minister, obtained wage increases despite the strong opposition of the economic team.[8] But the Austral Plan did put trade liberalization and public enterprise restructuring on the agenda, while the Australito kept it there by calling for an intensification of tariff reduction, the restructuring of public enterprises, and, for the first time, the privatization of public enterprises. Presi-

TABLE 5.1. ECONOMIC PROGRAMS UNDER RAÚL ALFONSÍN, 1983–1989

ECONOMY MINISTER AND PLAN	POLICIES
Bernardo Grinspun *Expansionary program* January 1984	Salary increases (12 percent) Tariff protection Credit for small and medium businesses Increased money supply
Juan Sourrouille *Austral Plan* June 1985	15 percent devaluation New currency (austral) Wage and price freeze Restructuring of public firms Trade liberalization Increase public utility rates Reduce fiscal deficit to 1.5 percent
Juan Sourrouille *Plan Australito* February 1987	New wage and price freeze Intensified tariff reductions Restructuring and privatization of public enterprises Monetary and fiscal policy as in Austral
Juan Sourrouille *Plan Primavera* August 1988	12 percent devaluation Temporary price truce Increase in public tariffs Three-tiered exchange market Privatization Target fiscal deficit: 2.4 percent

dent Alfonsín announced the sale of 40 percent of the shares of ENTEL, the National Telecommunications Company, and of Aerolíneas Argentinas, the state airline (Editors 1993a, 85). These initial attempts at privatization failed in the face of stiff congressional opposition. But there was progress in trade liberalization: by late 1988 the number of products subject to prohibition or quantitative restrictions had been reduced from four thousand to three thousand, and the average tariff rate was reduced from 51 to 36 percent (de la Balze 1995, 115). As inflation accelerated, the Primavera Plan was the final attempt by the Radical government to bring the economy under control. Although it was not any more successful than its predecessors, all three economic plans reflected important changes in policy ideas that were closely linked to the growing interaction with international actors.

RELATIONSHIP WITH INTERNATIONAL FINANCIAL INSTITUTIONS

Tense: moratorium on debt payments
Negotiations under way; unilateral letter of intent; agreement September 1984; falls
   out of compliance within three months

New letter of intent with IMF supporting Austral targets; IMF accepts heterodoxy
World Bank initiates increased lending program: SECALS to increase export
   competitiveness
Rescheduling accord with creditors, August 1985

Rigorous standby agreement with IMF
Argentina falls out of compliance; new agreement July 1987; again out of compliance;
   disbursement of funds stopped
World Bank SALS for trade, banking reform, plus SECALS

Discussions with IMF for three-year EFF; fourth revision of letter of intent approved
Disagreement between World Bank and IMF over targets
In April 1988, ceases to make interest payments to foreign banks; arrears build up
Fails to reach agreement with IMF, which refuses request for standby; World Bank
   steps in, making $1.25 billion loan; disbursement of much of loan blocked because
   of noncompliance

Before 1987, Argentina's opposition to policy reform was paralleled by its hard line on the debt issue. Argentina was described as "the single most resistant debtor in international finance" (Oliveri 1989, 163). Its leadership's debt strategy was the opposite of Chile's at the time and distinct from the generally pliant position taken by Mexican negotiators. In 1984 and 1985, Argentina led the Latin debtors in discussions held in Cartagena, Colombia, and Mar del Plata, Argentina, demanding greater equity in the distribution of adjustment costs between debtors and creditors (Tussie 1988, 290–91, 293). Shortly after assuming power, Alfonsín declared a moratorium on debt payments and allowed arrears to build up through 1988. He then attempted to get loans from sympathetic European governments to circumvent the IMF (Manzetti 1991, 184). When this did not work and faced with unyielding IMF demands for a sharp reduction in the budget deficit (which stood at 15 percent of GDP in 1983; see Appendix 2, Table A.2), the Argentine government submitted a unilateral letter of intent to the then head of the IMF, Jacques de Larosière, calling for a variety of measures opposed by the IMF's local negotiators: wage increases of 6 to 8 percent, an increase in the money supply, and a budget deficit at 10 percent of GDP (Stiles 1991, 192; Tussie 1992, 158).[9] Argentina also lobbied the United States to help it obtain concessions from the IMF (Manzetti 1991, 184).

The United States wanted a more lenient treatment of Argentina, a goal distinct from its position at the time on Chile, where its hard-line position had been instrumental in increasing the leverage of the World Bank in demanding an orthodox program.[10] Not only did Washington wish to repair relations with Argentina after the Falklands Islands invasion, but it also sought to avoid harsh adjustment policies that could trigger political upheaval, endanger the fragile democracy, and raise the specter of a return to military rule (interviews with two senior Radical government officials). In addition, Argentina's ability to withstand possible retaliation from creditors, given its natural resource endowment and lower degree of vulnerability to interruptions in capital and trade flows, enhanced its negotiating position (Aggarwal 1996, 410). Hence Washington pressured American banks to be flexible and supported Argentina's 1984 agreement with the IMF with a $500 million bridge loan (Aggarwal 1996, 417; Oliveri 1989, 172). In addition, the United States gave strong support to the heterodox Austral Plan about which the IMF had grave reservations (interviews with senior-level Radical government officials and senior IMF official).

The formulation of the Austral Plan involved intense discussions with World Bank and IMF officials.[11] The IMF was strongly resistant to the plan's heterodox elements (particularly price controls), and Paul Volcker, chairman of the Federal Reserve Board, played a key role in inducing the IMF to accept the plan (Dornbusch and de Pablo 1990, 147; Peralta Ramos 1992a, 97). The country's bargaining edge at the time combined with its debt strategy made it possible to delay but not avoid radical reform. Already in these meetings, World Bank officials were making a strong pitch for trade liberalization, insisting on the reduction of import restrictions and restructuring of public enterprise in exchange for loans (interviews with senior LAC official and senior Radical government official). It is likely that these discussions, although at times conflictive, formed an important part of the social learning process. The experience certainly strengthened the resolve of Argentine officials inclined toward policy reform. One leading member of the Argentine economic team interviewed in the course of this research remarked when asked about his receptivity to the bank's trade liberalization recommendation: "My personal opinion at the time was that this was certainly needed, but I would not likely have pursued it on my own; it was too politically difficult to carry out." The discussions with multilaterals also facilitated reform by giving Argentine policy makers someone to blame when faced with the opposition of the private sector to trade liberalization.[12] Moreover, because the World Bank was of crucial importance at this time in mobilizing funds for a cash-strapped Argentina, a fairly cooperative working relationship began to develop with the Sourrouille economic team, a relationship that would become even closer and more important in carrying the reform process forward once it was under way.

THE WORLD BANK AND ARGENTINA: THE GROWTH OF INTERNATIONAL POLICY NETWORKS

Further economic deterioration in 1988 giving rise to the World Bank's leading role in the Primavera Plan was the first step in the evolution of a closer and more intense relationship between Argentina and the bank that would continue into the 1990s. In 1988, when the IMF refused Argentina's request for a standby loan, the bank stepped in with a loan of $1.25 billion (U.S.),[13] thus initiating the bank's heavy involvement in Argentina's market reform (see Table 5.1). Although some World Bank officials opposed the IMF's rigid targets and did not want to tie bank programs to them, pressure from the United States was the determining factor in the bank's offer to lend even though Argentina had failed to meet IMF performance criteria (interviews with LAC official and two senior Radical government officials). Facing an election year, senior U.S. officials were anxious to mollify Argentina so as to avoid a confrontation with a major debtor. The result was an unparalleled involvement of the bank in a client country's economic policy development. In the words of a senior World Bank official interviewed, "The World Bank was never as involved so closely in policy as it was in the Argentine case; particularly in trade policy, public sector reform, and privatization."

The development of the Primavera Plan was the work of the first high-level international policy network, which was considerably more conflictive and lacked the high degree of trust of later ones. Discussions over several months occurred between the top level of the Argentine Economy Ministry and a total of about twenty-five World Bank officials. The plan was, for the most part, a bank initiative, and bank officials used the opportunity to push a full reform program (interviews with senior LAC and Radical government officials). During these talks a wide-ranging dialogue occurred on the basic features of a policy reform program: privatization, state reform, labor flexibilization, and tariff policy (interviews with senior LAC and Radical government officials).[14] Given the country's deteriorated economic situation, the Sourrouille team was now more than ever open to suggestions of the need for reform while the country's desperation for funds gave bank officials the opportunity to press their agenda. With renewed economic crisis in the form of hyperinflation, the reform agenda would move rapidly forward.

But even before 1988, the lower echelons of the bank had been cultivating a wide variety of Argentine policy actors in their attempts to press for policy change. Indeed, the number and value of World Bank loans made to Argentina do not reflect the extent of the policy discussions. In fact, the bank and Argentine officials held discussions in a variety of policy areas in which loans were not ultimately forthcoming.[15] The result was the emergence of a large number of international policy networks. Table 5.2 outlines all of the areas in which international policy networks operated between approximately 1987 and 1998. The two right-hand columns illustrate the full range of bank involvement with Argentine policy reform: from top-level macropolicy formulation and the generation of broad economic plans (such as the Primavera Plan) to involvement in sectoral policies and the restructuring and, later, privatization of public firms. Some of the key features of this process cannot be fully captured in a table, particularly the fluidity and the informality with which individuals in the World Bank and the Argentine state maintained ongoing contacts, generally without a great deal of regard to formal rank. Middle-ranking officers of the bank, for example, appear to have had easy access to the Argentine economy minister and even to the president under the administration of Alfonsín's successor, Carlos Menem. Another distinguishing feature of these networks is that they were not, initially at least, purely technocratic. Indeed, it was precisely the relative absence of highly trained technocrats in the Argentine state that made the bank's role in providing technical support so important. Relationships of trust between LAC officials at all levels and Argentine officials developed in the context of ongoing policy dialogue, often in the form of informal discussions on a broad range of reform issues.

The development of policy networks involving public enterprise managers and World Bank officials illustrates how extensive such networks were. By 1987, discussions on public enterprise reform were under way. Bank offi-

TABLE 5.2. ARGENTINE POLICY NETWORKS (STATE AND EXTRASTATE PARTICIPATION IN NETWORKS BY POLICY AREA)

WORLD BANK	STATE	SOCIETY
MAJOR POLICY REFORMS: PRIVATIZATION, TRADE LIBERALIZATION (POLICY INITIATION)		
LAC*: Senior to midlevel officials	President, minister of the economy, key cabinet members (see text), and their respective teams	Private sector excluded
TRADE POLICY		
Trade Liberalization LAC officials, director level and below	Minister of the economy and team	Private sector excluded
MERCOSUR *agreement* LAC, from director level down	Ministers of the economy, foreign relations, and teams	Export conglomerates consulted (periphery)
LABOR AND SOCIAL SECURITY REFORM		
LAC officials, director level down	Ministers of the economy, labor, and teams	Conglomerates consulted (periphery)
		Trade union leaders** (collaborationist on periphery)
PUBLIC ENTERPRISE RESTRUCTURING AND PRIVATIZATION (TELECOMMUNICATIONS, RAILWAYS, GAS, WATERWORKS, ELECTRICITY, SHIPYARDS, PETROLEUM, STEEL)		
LAC: country and sectoral specialists, outside consultants	Minister of the economy, public works minister (until 1991), public enterprise managers, military commanders (for companies under military control)	Private contractors linked to conglomerates (support base), trade union leaders** (collaborationist on periphery)

*Latin American and Caribbean Section of the World Bank.
**The role of trade union leaders in labor policy is dealt with in Chapter 7.

cials took an activist approach in pushing for reform, sometimes, though not always, encouraged to do so by Argentine officials. Bank officials moved freely within the labyrinth of the Argentine state, speaking to public enterprise managers and trade union leaders.[16] In these activities, they played an important role in spreading the new market policy culture. The bank funded studies on public enterprise price policies, on restructuring, and on privatization.[17] Bank officials organized conferences to bring both state enterprise managers and trade union leaders in contact with outside experts on public enterprise reform. Finally, the bank brought in outside consultants to help carry out restructuring in specific public firms. These consultants, along with bank officials, concentrated on persuading public enterprise managers of the need for substantial change. Once state managers had been won over, bank officials worked with the new reform converts, developing the close personal relationships characteristic of policy networks (interviews with three middle-ranking LAC officials).[18] And though many of the senior managers of public firms willing to entertain reform were forced out in the face of bureaucratic and trade union resistance, the legacy of a positive attitude toward public enterprise reform among the senior executive levels of many public enterprises often survived (interviews with three middle-ranking LAC officials).

Initially, and in line with the bank's position at the time, bank officials pushed for restructuring rather than privatization of public enterprises. Over time, however, with the repeated failure to reform public enterprises sufficiently, both bank and Argentine officials came to the conclusion that only drastic action—in the form of privatization—would solve the problem of the inefficiency of public enterprise. There occurred, in this sense, a process of mutual social learning among Argentine public enterprise officials and World Bank middle-ranking officers. Even when bank officers were committed to privatization as the optimal policy solution, they tended to operate pragmatically, accepting the less optimal policy of restructuring if resistance to privatization was too great and focused instead on building up a constituency for later change.[19] The restructuring of public enterprise was not only a learning experience for both bank and Argentine officials and an essential part of the policy dialogue, it also played an important role in breaking down resistance. Bank actors sometimes played a crucial role in this process. In one case, a bank official's promise to a trade union leader that the bank would provide funding for severance pay was important in inducing trade union support for restructuring and eventually for privatization.[20]

By 1988, attitudes within the Argentine state toward far-reaching reform were already changing in substantial ways. But it was hyperinflation that was key to bringing around the reticent and in solidifying commitment to deep market reform. Moreover, by early 1989, U.S. support for Argentina had cooled. The new American administration no longer felt any need to support Argentina in its conflicts with the multilaterals. By early 1989, the World Bank too had suspended disbursements on its loans and the IMF warned that it would consider a new standby loan only after the Argentine national election scheduled for May 1989. As dollars were massively withdrawn from the banking system, the country's reserves plummeted and the inflation rate exceeded 4,000 percent by June 1989. Public order disintegrated as mobs rioted and the government declared a state of emergency (Smith 1992, 39). Newly elected Peronist president Carlos Menem, whose public statements had suggested a populist bent, now moved rapidly toward market reform. As this process got under way, the bank's role increased while new actors, domestic technocrats, became an increasingly important part of the process.

MENEMISMO, THE TECHNOCRATS, AND THE BANK: PULLING IT ALL OFF IN RECORD TIME

Probably no other country carried out a market reform program as rapidly and as thoroughly as did Argentina under Carlos Menem. Tariff rates were consistently reduced, quantitative controls on imports were removed, drastic cutbacks occurred in state expenditure, and privatization of the country's largest and most important companies (telecommunications, airline, railways, petroleum, steel, and companies in the military defense) was virtually complete by 1994 (see Table 5.3). By 1993, the market value of privatized assets was estimated at $18 billion (U.S.) (OED 1996, 66). The strategy of privatization differed markedly from the cases of Chile and Mexico, where "strategic" sectors of petroleum and minerals were kept in state hands. Another feature of the Argentine process was the importance of debt equity swaps in privatization. By 1995, the reform process struggled with the "tequila effect," the negative effect of the Mexican crisis on the Argentine economy. The lack of business confidence and the economic slowdown gave rise to a tough adjustment program involving a sharp reduction in government expenditure and tax increases. Another adjustment occurred in 1998 with the Asian crisis, followed by yet another in 1999 with the Brazilian crisis. After 1995 policy reform moved into the restructuring of provincial governments

TABLE 5.3. ECONOMIC REFORM UNDER CARLOS MENEM

ECONOMY MINISTER	POLICIES
Miguel Roig and Nestor Rapanelli (July 1989–December 1989)	Law for the Reform of the State gives executive power to privatize Economic Emergency Law (see Table 5.4 for details of these laws) Price agreement between government and private sector Import duties reduced 15 percent
Erman González (January 1990–January 1991)	Privatization moves forward Average tariff rate from 26 to 17 percent Plan Bonex converts short-term domestic debt to medium-term external debt Drastic cut in state expenditure, layoffs Increase in public utility rates Omnibus decree increases power of economy minister to carry out reform
Domingo Cavallo (January 1991–July 1996) *Convertibility Plan*	Monetary base fully backed by Central Bank reserves Tax increase; public sector budget cuts By 1994 most important public enterprises privatized, including telephone, airlines, petroleum, railways, electricity, gas, military hardware companies Social security privatization Drastic reduction in tariffs: average level lower than 10 percent; end to most nontariff barriers; complete deregulation of prices Two labor laws providing some flexibility 1995 adjustment (second reform of the state)
Roque Fernández (July 1996–October 1999)	Continues Convertibility Plan Congress changes tax bill/resists privatization (airports, banks, hydro) 1998 labor flexibilization law Provincial state reform and privatizations Creation of regulatory agencies for privatized companies

RELATIONSHIP WITH INTERNATIONAL FINANCIAL INSTITUTIONS

Negotiations with IMF resume in August

IMF approves tough standby ($1.4 billion)

World Bank resumes disbursements of trade policy loan, opens office in Buenos Aires, and carries out intensive dialogue with Argentine officials although no new loans are approved

Fails to meet standby criteria for fiscal deficit; IMF stops disbursement of funds

Proposed plan of ruthless adjustment unlocks IMF funds

Loans from World Bank for public sector reform (restructuring, privatization of public enterprises, administrative reform, provincial financial reform)

Intensive dialogue with World Bank

Continued difficulty with IMF targets

Negotiations for standby and EFF and with private creditors successful providing for debt relief under Brady

Debt relief of $2.55 billion and $21 billion refinanced

World Bank returns to high lending policy in 1992, contributing $750 million for Brady

World Bank disbursement of $5 billion between 1992 and 1996

Last structural adjustment loan in 1995

Argentina gets waivers on targets in standby agreement with IMF

IMF pushes labor flexibilization

Agreement for three-year EFF; granted waivers on fiscal targets

World Bank loans for health services, for provincial decentralization

1999: requests another extension on fiscal target from IMF

and the privatization of provincial banks and services. And after 1995, policy reform met increasing resistance from Congress.

The rapidity and depth of policy reform are even more striking because it was carried out by a Peronist regime. As we saw in Chapter 2, the Peronist Party had been closely associated with the historical expansion of the state. Menem, with the support of the traditional wing of the labor movement,[21] had run a traditionally populist, albeit vague, election campaign promising wage increases, more jobs, and a unilateral moratorium on foreign debt payments (Waisman 1992, 230; Erro 1993, 196). But important changes were under way in the Peronist Party, which saw the growing influence of party activists who had returned to Argentina following the proceso with graduate degrees and new market reform ideas. These new technocratic activists backed the party's "renewalist" movement (Teichman 1997a, 45), the faction that would gain predominance over the older, traditional trade union wing by 1987 (Erro 1993, 165; Fraga 1991, 165), and campaigned to win converts to market reform within the party. The renewalists had supported Antonio Cafiero rather than Menem for the Peronist presidential candidacy. But when Menem won the candidacy, he quickly moved to recruit market reform renewalists as his advisers.[22]

The domestic policy core that initiated and drove policy reform consisted of President Carlos Menem and two of his closest collaborators, who, at different times, became his minister of the economy — Erman González and Domingo Cavallo. Menem's personal commitment to market reform, a subject of considerable speculation, was absolutely essential to the process.[23] The hyperinflationary context of the election campaign period and its aftermath cannot be overstated as a reason for inducing Menem's new policy direction.[24] Just as important as commitment to reform in ensuring the depth and rapidity of the reform process was Menem's leadership style.[25] The predominant feature of that leadership style and the authority it established was patrimonial. As such, Menem's appointments to state and party positions were based on personal loyalty to himself. These appointments produced a downgrading of the importance of Peronist militancy and the appointment of many outsiders to government and party positions (Canitrot and Sigal 1994, 136; McGuire 1997, 243–52). The predominantly patrimonial authority established by Menem has been linked to his political origins as governor of one of the country's poorest provinces, La Rioja. An economic backwater, La Rioja lacks both industry and a modern trade union movement; in such a context, politics is much more personalistic, even more heavily based on clans, caudillismo, and clientelism than is Argentine national politics generally (Sidicaro 1995, 140).

It is for this reason that Menem and his closest collaborators have been termed an "antielite"—a group that, because it lacked acceptance by the established elite groups, recognition, and prestige, was able to act much more autonomously and flexibly than would otherwise be the case.[26] In Menem's first cabinet, for example, six of the eight members were originally from the provinces of the interior and only two were originally from Buenos Aires, the reverse of the situation under Alfonsín. Of the total cabinet of forty-seven ministers and secretaries (the rank below the ministerial level), only three belonged to the Peronist union sector (Sidicaro 1995, 125). Erman González, an accountant who had worked closely with Menem in La Rioja, was the most important market reform proponent among Menem's antielite cabinet appointees. Menem and most of his entourage were not committed to Argentina's corporatist politics, which involved "pacts" between powerful competing social forces; nor were they particularly wedded to the institutionalized party politics of liberal democracy. Menem would use these processes or override them as the policy necessity dictated. Both Menem and González moved freely and fluidly among the officials of multilaterals, powerful members of the private sector, the military, and collaborative trade union leaders, establishing personal links that would concentrate power, break down resistance, and propel the reform process forward.

Hence while the Argentine market reform process in its heyday (1991–94) would acquire a technocratic character, not unlike the Chilean and Mexican cases, the turning point in the process (when the decision to carry forward a deep and fast program was taken) was dominated by this antielite. In the absence, at this point, of a sufficient domestic technocratic capability within the state, international policy networks with World Bank officials became a necessary and critical part of the process. Throughout 1989, the bank continued its activist role. During the 1989 election campaign, a bank official explored with Menem and his brother Eduardo their positions on market reform and was satisfied that Menem would be willing and able to push such a program, including privatizations, forward. The bank then offered to make arrangements to brief the Menem team, should they win the election, on the discussions and economic reform plans that had been developed with the Alfonsín administration (interviews with two senior and middle-rank LAC officials).

At the same time, Argentina had compelling practical reasons to accelerate reforms, which without doubt encouraged a pragmatically minded leadership to privatize large and important public companies. One of the most decisive elements was the depth of the economic crisis, including the fiscal crisis faced by the state and the pressing necessity to convince external creditors of Argentina's firm commitment to structural reform, especially important given Argentina's less than glowing track record in this area. All government officials interviewed stressed that the first set of privatizations (of the state-owned telephone company, ENTEL, and Aerolíneas Argentinas, the airline) was carried out explicitly for this purpose. Bank officials pressed Argentina to make such a gesture, and the IMF made the conclusion of the 1989 standby agreement conditional on a public deficit target of 1 percent of GDP, a monumental task given the state of the public deficit at the time. Privatization was perceived by all government officials interviewed as essential to confronting the public deficit problem, the issue that had been the key bone of contention with the IMF and would continue to be so through the early 1990s. Indeed, privatization was linked to debt reduction in a very explicit way through allowing debt for equity conversions.

As Menem assumed the reins of political power, even World Bank officials were caught off guard by the extent of the new administration's commitment to policy reform.[27] At the end of 1989, the new Argentine administration invited the bank to become involved in a thorough reform program. A discussion involving senior LAC officials, President Carlos Menem, soon-to-be-appointed economy minister Erman González, and the then foreign minister Domingo Cavallo took place and a reform program involving trade liberalization, the privatization of all public companies, and the establishment of a currency board, an idea that came from Domingo Cavallo, was worked out (interviews with senior and middle-rank LAC officials). Thereafter, dialogue accelerated and intensified on an ever-expanding array of policy issues, and World Bank lending to Argentina picked up. International policy networks involving bank and Argentine officials now worked intensively on privatization, social security reform, labor flexibilization, and policy reform at the provincial level.

Menem's personalist leadership style and his predisposition to patrimonialism and discretionary decision making marked the privatization drive, particularly in its early years. Hence while bank actors in international policy networks played an important role in getting public enterprise reform on the agenda and in helping to push privatization forward, they often could not, much to their distress, influence the way reform was carried out.[28] Menem appointed committed privatizers who were personally loyal and accountable only to him as intervenors in public firms to be privatized and gave them and Minister of Public Works Roberto Dromi broad discretionary powers. Because there were no mechanisms of accountability, the process became one in which kickbacks and commissions were given in return for rigging bids and selling privileged information to entrepreneurs (Saba and Manzetti 1997, 355). Two of Menem's closest public enterprise intervenors (Jorge Triaca, who became the intervenor for the steel company SOMISA, and Maria Julia Alsogaray, who took over the telephone company ENTEL and SOMISA) were charged with corruption as a consequence of their actions in privatization processes. Menem himself intervened directly, modifying the original terms of tenders after bids had been asked for in two of the most controversial cases widely believed to have involved irregularities, ENTEL and Aerolíneas Argentinas (*Latin American Weekly Report*, March 1, 1990, 11). The discretionary actions that characterized privatization were not simply a feature of patrimonial rule, however. Wide discretionary powers and attendant irregularities were integral to the rapidity of the process because officials had no need to spend time securing approval for their decisions or justifying them before higher authorities (Saba and Manzetti 1997, 353; interviews with government official).[29]

As a close adviser of the president and as minister of the economy, Erman González was a key actor in getting reform off the ground, and he continued to play an important role in policy reform as minister of defense (1991–93) and as labor minister after 1997. González became an ardent privatizer, and close collaborative ties of trust developed between González and bank officials at various levels in LAC as international policy networks worked on a widening array of reforms. By the time he was moved out of the Economy Ministry and into the Defense portfolio (replaced by Domingo Cavallo), market reforms were already well under way. As minister of defense, González headed up the very difficult negotiations with the military, necessary to secure the privatization of the various military equipment and material companies.[30] The military put up stiff resistance not only to the privatization of the various companies of Fabricaciones Militares but also to the privatization of the state petroleum company—indeed, several key informants maintained that the privatization of YPF (the State Petroleum Deposits Company) was by far the most difficult case precisely because the military opposed its privatization. Budget increases for the armed forces, granting the navy jurisdiction over the coast guard and the air force control of the airports, and the pardoning of officers accused of sedition and human rights abuses were probably all important in subduing opposition from the nationalist wing of the military (Manzetti 1993, 200). The personal trust between Menem and González, on the one hand, and top-ranking members of the military, on the other, was also widely cited as one of the most important factors in allowing these reforms to go forward.[31]

While Domingo Cavallo, seen as the country's leading technocratic market reformer, had played an important role in the development of official policy behind the scenes,[32] it was only with his appointment as economy minister that domestic technocrats began to participate substantially in the reform process. Argentina's tumultuous political history had resulted in the absence of a well-trained state bureaucracy; highly trained individuals were confined to enclaves within the state apparatus, such as the Central Bank, and were unable to have an important influence on policy (Smith 1989, 57). Market reform–oriented Argentine technocrats were much less isolated from other sectors of Argentine society than had been the Chicago boys, however, and they were more successful in building links with individual business and even trade union leaders. As a consequence of state intervention in the universities during the proceso, think tanks, private academic institutions bringing together highly trained personnel, particularly economists, to carry out studies and make policy recommendations, began to proliferate as alternative institutions of research (Thompson 1994).

One of the most important of these institutions was the Fundación Mediterránea, established in 1977 by a group of Córdoba businessmen and Domingo Cavallo, then a young Ph.D. graduate in economics from Harvard. The Fundación, through its research arm, the Institute for Economic Studies on the Argentine and Latin American Reality (IEERAL), brought together a team of trained economists, many with degrees, especially Ph.D.'s from foreign universities, and produced, from 1980, studies calling for the elimination of distortions impeding the functioning of the market, reduction of the public deficit, and privatization of public companies.[33] From 1980, the Fundación and its most important founder, Domingo Cavallo, actively sought to influence economic policy, particularly in the area of privatization, lobbying the military government and then the government of Raúl Alfonsín on policy reform (interviews with senior Radical government official).

The Fundación maintained close and friendly relations with the World Bank, which sent some of its most distinguished market reform proponents to Fundación meetings, while IEERAL presented papers to World Bank officials (N'haux 1993, 248, 267). But there was also an important educational and outreach aspect to the many activities of the Fundación and IEERAL, and they can be considered initiators of an incipient and very loose extrastate policy network. They held seminars and conferences that facilitated links to prominent members of the political right, to military leaders, to leaders of entrepreneurial organizations, to trade union leaders, to politicians, and to members of the academic community who were not economists. Among the luminaries associated at one time or another with the Fundación were Alvaro Alsogaray, right-wing politico and special adviser to Menem on the foreign debt; Pablo Llach, former official of the 1973–76 Peronist government and secretary of planning under Menem; Peronist economists Roberto Lavagna and J. Luis Machinea; and Jorge Triaca, a strong Menem loyalist and Menem's first labor minister (N'haux 1993, 236, 248, 285). In short, the Fundación appears to have been a key link in the development of both domestic and international policy networks and in spreading the social learning that was important to the cohesion on goals needed to carry reform forward rapidly.

The speed with which Argentina's leadership was able to implement the country's economic reform program did not signify the absence of intense opposition — indeed, fierce opposition came from many quarters: from public servants, especially those in public enterprises, from the military, from Congress, from within the cabinet, from the private sector, and from trade unions. From the outset, the architects of reform recognized the necessity of obtaining policy isolation and in concentrating economic decision-making power in the hands of the president and minister of the economy. The most important measures in achieving this end are outlined in Table 5.4. The greatest success in achieving policy isolation occurred at the beginning of the market reform process, a consequence of the traumatic impact of hyperinflation, which contributed to public support for emergency measures to deal with the economic crisis. Two 1989 laws enabled the president to bypass Congress and proceed with policy reform through presidential decree. Indeed, the use of presidential decrees became the standard means by which the executive achieved the reform of the state. From 1989 to the end of 1994, the number of emergency presidential decrees used by Menem exceeded the total number issued by all the constitutional presidents in more than 130 years (Blutman 1994, 61). In 1996, additional emergency powers were obtained for the second reform of the state, which called for the elimi-

TABLE 5.4. MEASURES CONCENTRATING ECONOMIC DECISION MAKING

YEAR	MEASURE	POWERS CONFERRED
1989	Law for the Reform of the State	Executive decree powers to carry out privatization in telephone, highways, railway, and maritime sectors Reduction of state enterprise personnel through voluntary retirement
1989	Economic Emergency Law	Executive decree power to modify a wide variety of legislation such as suspension of subsidies, establishment of tax rates, and elimination of legal requirement for state to purchase domestically and of laws distinguishing between foreign and domestic capital
1989	Judicial reform	Judiciary is enlarged and stacked by Menem to ensure that his reforms are not overturned by the courts
1989–94	Public enterprise restructuring	Uncooperative managers of public enterprises are removed and intervenors committed to reform and personally loyal to Menem are appointed
1990	Administrative reform	Energy Secretariat in the Ministry of Public Works is moved to the Ministry of the Economy
1991	Administrative reform	Ministry of Public Works, responsible for most public enterprises, is absorbed by Ministry of the Economy
1996	Emergency powers for the second reform of the state	Executive decree power to set tax rates and to eliminate or merge government agencies

nation and merging of government departments and agencies, a speedup of privatization, and an increase in taxes to solve the fiscal deficit. In cases in which presidential decree powers were not used, the president often threatened their use (such as in the case of social security and labor reform) in an attempt to bully reluctant congressmen into submission. Increasing the membership of the Supreme Court from five to nine allowed Menem to reduce the likelihood of successful judicial challenges to his economic reform measures.[34] Administrative reforms, most notably the transfer of the responsibilities of the Public Works Ministry (responsible hitherto for public enterprises) to the Ministry of the Economy, concentrated the power for economic policy making.

Hence by the time Domingo Cavallo assumed the position of economy minister, he had full powers to complete and consolidate reform. Under his tutelage, the economic policy network based in his ministry was fiercely resistant to outside interference.[35] When Cavallo took over the Ministry of the Economy, he brought with him a highly qualified economic team, many from the Fundación Mediterránea, virtually all of the top echelons of which had graduate degrees from U.S. universities.[36] His successor Roque Fernández, who held a Ph.D. in economics from the University of Chicago, drew his team of advisers, many with graduate degrees from the University of Chicago, from another of Argentina's think tanks, the Center for Macroeconomic Studies (CEMA) (*Latin American Weekly Report*, August 8, 1996, 350). From 1991 on, economic policy development came under the tight control of the minister of the economy, his policy clique, and his growing base of technocratic supporters, largely within the Ministry of the Economy. This technical capacity, now added to the support provided by the World Bank, combined with the various pieces of enabling legislation, drove the reform process forward. Domingo Cavallo's highly concentrated policy-making style tended to exaggerate the concentration of economic policy-making power even further. Cavallo dominated the process, calling together two or three of his top-level officials (not necessarily the same ones) on a weekly basis or more often to develop policy initiatives. He surrounded himself with like-minded, intensely loyal technocrats—so loyal and so like-minded that three of them suggested that consultation and discussion were not important because Cavallo's team knew him and therefore knew what he wanted done (interviews).

Cavallo was an extremely powerful economy minister, so powerful that his relations with President Menem became strained and those with other members of the cabinet increasingly conflictive.[37] This tension, according to informed observers, stemmed from Cavallo's increasing power, rooted in the apparent success of his economic program (the Convertibility Plan),[38] at least compared with his predecessors, and his grip on the Ministry of the Economy (interviews with two senior Economy Ministry officials). Most important in accounting for Cavallo's power, however, were his preeminent role in debt negotiations and his international ties. With Cavallo as economy minister, Argentina's relations with the IMF became cordial while the close working relationship with the World Bank was reinforced by Cavallo's

long history with the bank and his many personal friendships there.[39] Under
Roque Fernández, a former official in the IMF, Argentina developed even
more cordial relations with its officials.[40]

But there were limits to Domingo Cavallo's ability to isolate economic
policy making from other members of the cabinet; indeed, Cavallo depended heavily on Menem to prevent other cabinet members from inter-
fering with his economic policy initiatives. Persistent conflicts occurred between Cavallo and the "political side" of the cabinet: the minister of social
action, the defense minister, and the secretary general of the presidency resisted accelerated reform of the state and continued cutbacks in government
expenditures (*Latin American Weekly Report*, November 19, 1991, 2).[41] Their
opposition, they claimed, was not to the principle of economic reform but
to its pace and timing and to the failure to give sufficient consideration to
social issues such as unemployment (interviews with two senior government officials). Various cabinet members expressed the belief that Cavallo's
power should be reined in (*Latin American Weekly Report*, April 11, 1996, 8).
While Menem steadfastly defended Cavallo's economic policies and under-
lined that his new appointee, Roque Fernández, would continue with the
same policies, Cavallo's departure was likely linked in some way to this ongoing struggle.[42]

Once Cavallo had taken over the Economy Ministry and the economic
reform program was well under way, some of the reform legislation was
put before Congress, which held rancorous debates and had the opportunity to delay, if not to revise, executive policy initiatives.[43] This occurred,
for example, in the case of the 1993 social security reform, forcing Cavallo
to drop the provision making contribution to the private system obligatory
(*Latin American Weekly Report*, May 20, 1993, 228), and in the case of Fernández's 1996 tax reform, when Congress refused to raise taxes on tobacco
and alcohol and to extend the value-added tax to cable TV and publica-
tions (*Latin American Weekly Report*, July 21, 1998, 329). Congress was able
to delay the privatization of YPF in 1992, the Yacyreta Hydroelectric Complex in 1996, and the Banco de la Nación Argentina in 1997. But the use
and threatened use of presidential decree continued until the end of the
administration in 1999. It was threatened in the cases of social security reform, labor reform, and tax reform, and it was used in 1997 to privatize
the airports when Congress balked at the executive's bill (*Latin American
Weekly Report*, September 2, 1997, 410). Probably the most important market reforms in which labor and congressional resistance was key was labor
reform, a topic of Chapter 7, where I examine the political management

of the policy reform process. For some of the most contentious measures, therefore, Congress has increasingly made alterations in policies proposed by the executive-dominated policy networks.

More than the other cases dealt with in this book, the Argentine private sector has had an enormous impact on policy reform even though the Argentine state has strengthened with the influx of technocrats. Historically, Argentina's most powerful landed and industrial interests often had direct representation in the cabinet. President Menem's initial cabinet appointments continued this tradition. Anxious to bring assurances to a private sector nervous about the intentions of a Peronist government, Menem appointed Miguel Roig, a senior executive of the economic conglomerate Bunge and Born, as economy minister. Roig was succeeded in this post by another senior executive of the same firm, Nestor Rapanelli. Although big business lost its direct control of the economy portfolio when Rapanelli resigned in 1989, it retained enormous influence over economic policy.

Members of the Argentine Business Council (CEA), the entrepreneurial organization integrating the country's top thirty to forty businessmen, claimed to have "excellent" ongoing personal contact with top officials and easy and immediate personal access to both Menem and the economy minister (interviews with two members of CEA). These business leaders appeared to be strong Menem supporters, describing him as "an excellent president" and Domingo Cavallo and his economic team as highly competent. These individuals had high praise for most aspects of economic policy.[44] Small and medium business, however, found access to the highest reaches of power blocked (interviews with two business leaders), and all members of the private sector interviewed who were not associated with the CEA saw Economy Minister Cavallo as difficult to deal with and claimed to lack easy and personalized access to authorities.[45] Indeed, institutionalized arrangements linking the state and the private sector were not important mechanisms in obtaining access to the policy core. The official consultative mechanism, the Production Council, composed of representatives of business, labor, and the government, was seen by both business leaders and government officials as "window dressing"—a forum where, in general, the government would communicate policies it had already decided upon.

The policy networks and policy areas in which big business conglomerates participated and those from which they were excluded are illustrated in Table 5.2. There was one important policy area from which even powerful members of the private sector were excluded. Industrialists, even big ones, were not happy about the reduction in industrial protection, a reform that

had been carried out without their knowledge beforehand or their participation (interviews with senior government officials and business leaders).
Industrialists did report, however, that they had been consulted during the
negotiation for MERCOSUR and had sent sectoral delegations whose members were closely consulted by government officials on specific issues.

But aside from the impact of trade liberalization, the major beneficiaries
of Argentina's market reform process have been the country's biggest companies. Big exporting firms benefited from tax breaks designed to stimulate
exports (*Latin America Weekly Report*, October 22, 1992, 3). Big private sector
firms benefited the most in the privatization program. Indeed, the inordinate benefits stemming from privatization became a key part of the process
of binding the private sector, especially the big industrialists who had been
former state contractors, to the Menemista project and in ensuring enthusiastic entrepreneurial support for Menem. Public enterprise contractors,
who had prospered under military rule, were strong opponents of privatization if it meant a reduction in business for them (interviews with business
leaders; Peralta Ramos 1992b, 103). Generosity toward the private sector,
therefore, was key to the regime's ability to move forward rapidly not only
in privatization but in other areas of reform policy (interview with senior
government official). A few domestic companies, mostly former government contractors, were part of consortia also composed of multinational
banks and foreign companies that purchased public companies (Schvarzer
1995, 142; Azpiazu and Vispo 1994, 138; Basualdo 1994, 50).[46] Indeed, one
analysis points out that the actual number of domestic firms participating
in purchasing consortia is smaller than originally thought since there are
numerous cases in which particular enterprises participated in more than
one consortium (Basualdo 1994, 45). Moreover, potential purchasers were
closely involved in the privatization process, forming a key part of the
domestic policy networks developing privatization and, later, regulatory
policy (see Table 5.2). Both technocrats and business leaders interviewed attested to the very close involvement of the private sector in the privatization process from gathering of information to the details of privatization
decrees.[47] Members of the private sector were involved in the development
of tenders assuring them not only of winning the bids but of advantageous terms (interviews with senior government officials and two business
leaders; Margheritis 1999, 142).[48] In the words of one formerly highly placed
technocrat who had been closely involved in the reform process: "The private sector has enormous influence on government policy. Although it was

the political elite who made the decision to finally make drastic changes in economic policy, once that decision had been made the private sector had enormous influence over exactly how those changes were played out." The government assumed the debts of the privatized firms, and companies were sold with less profitable activities removed and with their labor forces reduced (Felder 1994, 58).

Later on, particularly after Domingo Cavallo took over the Economy Ministry in 1991, there was increased interest in the establishment of regulatory bodies. Purchasers also became closely involved in the development of the regulatory frameworks for their recently purchased activities. Regulatory bodies have been established for telecommunications (two years after its privatization), electricity, gas, and sanitary services but have not operated transparently because appointees had links to the private sector (Azpiazu and Vispo 1994, 142). In the development of regulatory frameworks, as in privatizations, policy networks were frequently characterized by an internal tension between the private sector, at one end, and the World Bank, at the other, with the bank pushing for a transparent process. Often the bank lost out, but not always. The private petroleum companies, for example, had submitted a draft of a regulatory framework that excluded foreign companies. The report was subsequently revised by a World Bank official allowing foreign companies in. The petroleum companies protested, demanding that the bank official who had revised the document be dismissed. In this case, the bank won out when Menem supported its position (interview with middle-ranking LAC official).

Politically, the conglomerates were closely linked to Menem. They made heavy campaign contributions to the Peronist Party: officially the top six conglomerates are reported to have contributed $700,000 each to Menem's 1989 campaign, while Bunge and Born claims that its actual contribution was $3 million (U.S.) (*Latin American Weekly Report*, July 8, 1993, 308). Corrupt practices have been integral to the close integration of the private sector with policy development. Cash payments from the private sector to government officials are apparently standard practice: an estimated two hundred government officials were receiving payments of between $5,000 and $10,000 (U.S.) per month in 1992. During his tenure as economy minister, Domingo Cavallo reportedly received a monthly stipend of $8,000 (U.S.) from the Fundación Mediterránea, a think tank largely funded by the private sector (*Latin American Weekly Report*, November 26, 1992, 2). Numerous allegations and charges of corruption have been brought against top-level officials accused of taking kickbacks from the private sector.[49] In short, the domestic side of policy networks has reflected the regime's distinctly patrimonial bent.

CONCLUSIONS

The task of building up acquiescence if not outright support for market reform from within the state, from the private sector, and from the military appears to be a daunting task. Argentina was a country with a long liberal tradition, and the country's move toward market liberalization began under the period of the proceso (1976–83). Measures taken by the military contributed to the weakening of the labor movement while the regime initiated selective trade liberalization. Under Alfonsín, the expectations raised by the return to democracy combined with a flexible international environment allowed the country to delay reform. Nevertheless, changes during the period, especially the emergence of international policy networks, laid the groundwork for later reforms.

Argentina has had the weakest state among the three case studies, and social groups frequently have been able to obtain direct representation in the cabinet. But during the Alfonsín years, the first attempts were made to create policy isolation, and international policy networks composed of technocrats began to emerge. Domestic technocrats, however, were not the ones who finally got the reform process going. That achievement lay with a distinct breed of politico, for whom personalism, patrimonialism, and discretionary decision making were paramount. President Carlos Menem established close working relationships with international actors, with powerful members of the private sector, and with the military, and he maintained a close but tense relationship with his chief technocratic reformer, Domingo Cavallo. By the early 1990s, technocratic influence was evident in the Convertibility Plan to control inflation and in a strong commitment to drive further market reforms forward. Patrimonialism, probably an essential ingredient of the rapidity of the process, was manifest in the lack of transparency with which the privatization program was carried out. Argentine policy networks were a blend of technocracy, personalism, and patrimonialism, a reflection of the political environment in which they were operating. They were the least hierarchical, most numerous, and most open to penetration of the three cases.

By the late 1980s, Argentina's resistance to reform had led to almost a complete lack of confidence on the part of the international banking community in the country's commitment to policy change. This fact, along with the intense pressure exerted by the World Bank in combination with the IMF's demand for public deficit reduction, dictated the decision to begin reform with the privatization of some of the country's biggest companies. Of the three countries dealt with in this book, Argentina is the one in which the greatest role was played by international policy networks—an essential prerequisite to the process given the Argentine state's lack of technical capacity at the time market reform was initiated. The World Bank's aggressive activities in the Argentine state were important in the transmission and development of policy ideas and attitudes, in the formulation of policy reforms themselves, and, of course, in providing essential funding for many of the reforms. But bank officials often had little control over the way policy reforms, especially privatization, were carried out. Here, President Menem's highly discretionary decision-making style, combined with the personal access of powerful members of the private sector to the highest reaches of political power, defined the peculiarities of policy implementation.

Powerful members of the private sector became integral participants in policy networks—indeed, they were part of the support base in the case of privatization. This involvement appears to have been an explicit strategy designed to co-opt powerful businessmen who expected to be negatively affected by the reform process, especially by the loss of business contracts provided by the state. Especially early in the Menem years, the nature of Menem's personal leadership fit well with a process that would have to be rapid and would have to grant special privileges to break down resistance. It was a strategy that was effective in allowing reform to go forward but one that would stymie later attempts to establish impartial regulatory frameworks and encourage competition.

Over time, as the sense of urgency dissipated, policy reforms went before Congress. Often executive policy initiatives have been altered, a development indicating that market reform policy networks have become less able to prevent tampering with proposals. While agreeing to put certain reform measures before Congress, however, the executive continued to rely on the threat, if not the reality, of presidential decree. Although the initiation and final approval of market reform policies remained highly centralized in the hands of a policy core and policy development eventually came under the control of technocrats in the Economy Ministry, decisions regarding important details of policy and certainly its implementation were a wide-ranging and fluid process. Bank officials and members of the private sector were afforded ample opportunity to influence that process, and they did. Argentine policy reform networks became the vehicles through which market policy ideas (from the World Bank and from the domestic technocrats), private vested interests, and the political perceptions of a patrimonialist political leadership became translated into specific reform policies. The interplay among these components produced a policy outcome that was simultaneously pro-market and highly patrimonial.

chapter six

MEXICO
Market Reform in an
Authoritarian Liberalizing Regime

Mexico's market reform process has not involved the sharp discontinuities of those in Chile and Argentina. After getting under way in 1985, reform continued for almost a decade, accelerating and intensifying over time. A state technocratic policy elite monopolized the reform process until 1995. Mexican policy networks were second only to those of Chile under military rule in their hierarchical nature and in their ability to resist outside opposition. Following the 1995 economic crisis and especially since 1997, however, the ability of high-level policy networks to resist outside objections to their policies has altered dramatically. Congressional opposition blocked some reforms and changed others.

In the early 1980s, officials in the state financial sector were predisposed toward state streamlining, but a series of economic crises hastened and deepened the process of social learning and helped to propel the most radical market reformers to positions of predominance in the state. The country's authoritarian political arrangements facilitated the heavy concentration of executive decision-making power and also influenced the nature of international policy networks, particularly those involving the World Bank. In marked contrast with the Argentine case, international policy networks were tightly controlled by Mexico's policy elite and international policy resources used to achieve that elite's specific policy ends. Since the mid-1990s, however, Mexican policy makers have largely abandoned this tight control over discussions with international actors.

The literature on policy making in Mexico has focused primarily on the state, much of it attesting to the way in which the public, and at times even powerful organized groups, have been excluded from the policy-making process (Purcell 1975; Story 1986b; Teichman 1988). Enormous power has traditionally rested in the hands of the president, allowing the executive not only the exclusive privilege of policy initiative but also the ability to have policies approved as originally formulated. The rise of technocrats to positions of policy predominance, a gradual process beginning with the election of President Miguel Alemán in 1946, was reinforced by organizational changes in the 1970s that further centralized policy-making authority (Centeno 1997, 90–91). Whereas from the 1950s, the Mexican president and his cabinet colleagues were recruited from the federal bureaucracy rather than through the PRI (Vernon 1963), after the mid-1970s this top leadership began to come from within the finance sector of the public bureaucracy (especially the Finance Ministry [1] and the Central Bank). More and more of these recruits had specialized professional training (graduate degrees), an increasing number from Ivy League American universities, especially in the fields of economics and public administration (Camp 1985).

Investigation of the inner workings of the public bureaucracy has captured a great deal of attention, and abundant analyses have been conducted of the role of intrastate groups in policy making. One of the key concepts in the Mexican literature is the camarilla, a network of public officials bound by ties of strong personal loyalty to a camarilla leader.[2] The camarilla is the key agency of political recruitment. Members are expected to foster the career advancement and the influence of their leader, and in return they expect their leader to provide them with opportunities for their own professional advancement (Camp 1999, 118; Langston 1997, 1). Originally, these groups were characterized by their nonideological and nonprogrammatic nature and by their breadth in extending across a variety of state ministries and agencies.[3] By 1989, however, President Salinas's personal camarilla involved a narrow-based clique of graduates of American graduate schools whose career experience had been entirely within the Ministry of Finance and the Central Bank—precisely those areas of the state historically predisposed to the market and state streamlining (Camp 1990, 102). Hence the camarilla of the radical market reformers combined both personal loyalty and policy commitment. The camarilla leader and camarilla members at senior levels of government normally have *equipos*, loyal technocratic teams who work on a particular policy issue. Insofar as the market reform camarilla and its constituent equipos were agents of economic policy reform and were bound by ties of personal loyalty and trust—and this was the case for Mexico's radical market reformers—the camarilla concept coincides with the term "policy network." Like the policy networks elsewhere, the Mexican ones also extend outside of the state, into the international and domestic spheres.

While much of the literature is concerned with the state bureaucracy, Sylvia Maxfield argues that alliances between state actors and societal supporters account for swings in economic policy between episodes of expansionary interventionism and more laissez-faire restrictionist policies.[4] Most observers, however, agree that the private sector has wielded by far the greatest influence over policy than any other social group, although how great that influence has been is a topic of considerable debate.[5] As we will see, the market reform process was generated and guided by state technocrats who achieved considerable isolation from public pressure. As the reform process progressed, however, technocratic policy networks reached out to bring in powerful private sector allies who had an important impact on policy.

GETTING STARTED: RESISTANCE TO POLICY AND
RENEWED ECONOMIC CRISIS, 1982–1986

President Miguel de la Madrid (1982–88) assumed power in the wake of Mexico's devastating 1982 economic crisis, a crisis brought on by a sharp drop in petroleum prices and an increase in interest rates and made worse by reckless government spending and borrowing. Mexico secured a loan for $4 billion (U.S.) from the International Monetary Fund in return for agreeing to adopt a tough austerity program. A devastating conclusion to the hopes raised by the petroleum boom years, the economic crisis of 1982 was the first step in a major rethinking of the country's economic model. This rethinking was no doubt facilitated by the nature of the new political leadership that took over in 1983. President de la Madrid and those he brought to power with him were at the time regarded as the most technocratic and homogeneous team ever to rule Mexico. Two-thirds of this group, many of whom had specialized training in economics, held graduate degrees, and 63 percent of them had studied abroad (Camp 1985, 100, 103). Economists who had held various positions in the public finance sector (the Ministry of Finance or the Central Bank) accounted for the majority of cabinet appointments (Teichman 1995, 74). Even top-level party appointments went to technocrats who were close de la Madrid cohorts.[6] At the same time, the new team purged the public bureaucracy of the "financial populists"—those public servants regarded as responsible for Mexico's binge of public borrowing and spending in 1981–82. And the powers of the ministry that had been the bastion of these pro-state expansion bureaucrats were reduced when the Ministry of Natural Resources and Industrial Development (SEPAFIN) lost its responsibilities for industrial development and public enterprise pricing policy (Teichman 1995, 76–77).

This leadership strongly supported the recently signed IMF stabilization program insofar as it shared the fund's belief that Mexico's fiscal irresponsibility had been largely responsible for the country's economic crisis. The government's concern for austerity was reflected in its "Immediate Program of Economic Recovery," PIRE (see Table 6.1). But economic liberalization met resistance in several areas. Measures to remove import protection and subsidies were cautious, and though between 1983 and 1984 the state divested itself of more than one hundred companies, these were often paper companies or were relatively small and unimportant. Market reform was on the policy agenda, but it was blocked by resistance in the state bureaucracy, framed (as in the other two cases) as a demand for a gradually paced reform program. Resistance to trade liberalization came from SECOFI, the Ministry of Commerce and Industrial Development, and from that ministry's private sector clientele reticent about facing foreign competition (Heredia 1996, 163). The advocates of rapid trade liberalization (the radical reformers) were based in the Central Bank, in the Ministry of Budget and Planning, in the office of economic advisers to the president, and in the Ministry of Finance. Indeed, officials in the Central Bank were especially important in the drive for trade liberalization; among them, Francisco Gil Díaz played an especially important role (Heredia 1996, 168; interviews with senior government official). The push for privatization came especially strongly from Carlos Salinas and Pedro Aspe, each of whom served as minister of budget and planning under President de la Madrid. As in the case of trade liberalization, resistance to privatization came from the sectoral ministry: the Ministry of Energy, Mines, and Parastate Industry (SEMIP), the administrative unit in charge of most of the public enterprises (Teichman 1995, 108).

The core group of radical reformers included Francisco Gil Díaz, Pedro Aspe, Jaime Serra Puche, José Córdoba, Ernesto Zedillo, and Carlos Salinas. Having secured positions as ministerial advisers during the López Portillo administration (1976–82), they moved under the de la Madrid administration into a variety of top-level positions from which they vigorously pressed the case for policy reform.[7] In the Central Bank and in the Ministry of Finance, institutions already predisposed to antistatism, technocratic reformers found it relatively easy to spread their gospel of radical reform.[8] These reformers would become the key players in Mexico's market reform process during its heyday under President Carlos Salinas. All were young and highly educated with graduate degrees from American univer-

TABLE 6.1. ECONOMIC PROGRAMS IN MEXICO

ECONOMIC SHOCK	ECONOMIC POLICIES	RELATIONSHIP WITH INTERNATIONAL FINANCIAL INSTITUTIONS
PHASE 1: 1983–85 (DE LA MADRID PRESIDENCY, 1983–88)		
1982: fall in petro prices, increase in interest rates	PIRE: as in IMF agreement Reduction in public expenditures, in salaries, and in subsidies, increase in public sector prices Small public companies privatized	End 1982: agreement with IMF requires public deficit of 5 percent GDP by 1985 Mexico's attitude was conciliatory 1983: World Bank export development loan
PHASE 2: (1985–94) (SALINAS PRESIDENCY, 1989–94)		
1985: fall in petro prices 1986: further drop End 1987: petro prices fall again	1985 Emergency Program: trade liberalization and privatization pick up; replacement of licenses by tariffs for over 3,000 categories 1986: tariffs reduced, quantitative controls eliminated; Mexico joins GATT; government expenditure reduced, privatization, export promotion 1988: Anti-Inflation Pact: more trade liberalization, privatization, deregulation By 1988 mean tariff rate at 10 percent and 706 public companies privatized 1989: National Economic Plan: privatization, financial sector reform, measures easing restrictions on foreign investment 1992: ejido reform 1992: NAFTA locks in reforms but foreign investment in services and energy restricted 1993: Foreign Investment Law provides equal treatment 1994: fewer than 200 firms in state hands	1985: dialogue with World Bank opens, leading to two trade policy loans; World Bank support in debt negotiations IMF suspends loan disbursements when Mexico fails to meet performance criteria 1986: Mexico takes stronger stand versus IMF Agreement under Baker Plan provides contingency funding Conflict with IMF over public deficit reduction Negotiations for agreement under Brady: three-year EFF with IMF; three policy loans with World Bank worth $500 million (U.S.) each 1990–94: World Bank sectoral loans in agriculture, water, housing, environment, decentralization 1992: EFF with IMF 1993: credit line with IMF allowed to lapse

sities.[9] These young technocrats were linked personally; many had shared a common mentor and had attended the same universities.[10] Very much like Chile's Chicago boys, they formed a tight, ideologically homogeneous group, bound by personal friendship and with a sense of their own mission.[11] As heads of their respective economics departments, Pedro Aspe at ITAM (Mexican Autonomous Institute of Technology) and Serra Puche at the Colegio de Mexico had been organizing seminars on economic policy reform since the late 1970s and recruiting cadres of technocratic supporters who would follow them into the Mexican government (Golob 1997, 114–21).[12] By the mid-1980s, they had become key members of the policy core that would drive market reform.

During 1983–84, however, these radical reformers were a strong yet still minority voice as the resisters to radical market reform continued to hold sway. But the country's economic recovery faltered in 1985 (see Table 6.1), giving radical reformers the opportunity they had been waiting for. Had it not been for the rapid deterioration in the country's economic situation, radical reform technocrats would no doubt have found it considerably more difficult to make a convincing case for a faster-paced change. But in the face of renewed economic crisis, they had a formula that appeared to offer Mexico a way out of its economic crisis, whereas resisters to market reform offered no viable plan. Even so, radical market reform technocrats still faced strong resistance from within the state. In the case of privatization, this resistance would continue even into the 1990s. In 1985, radical reformers gained a major victory when the government announced the acceleration of privatization and trade liberalization. Market reform continued to move rapidly through 1986 (see Table 6.1), kept on track by the continued drop in petroleum prices and difficult negotiations with the IMF.

But the decisive moment was undoubtedly the victory of radical market reformer Carlos Salinas (then minister of budget and planning) over Finance Minister Jesús Silva Herzog as the PRI candidate for the 1994 presidential election. Salinas was supported by a cohesive group of radicals whom he had recruited to work with him in the Ministry of Budget and Planning—Aspe, Zedillo, and Córdoba. Salinas was not only a strong market reformer but also an opponent of the restrictions on economic growth being advocated by the IMF. Silva Herzog, at the time the top contender for the PRI candidacy, was less enthusiastic about policy reform although he was willing to meet the IMF demands with regard to the fiscal deficit (Teichman 1995, 86).[13] Salinas triumphed in this struggle when debt negotiations bogged down in mid-1986, and Silva Herzog's public image became increasingly one of being the internal advocate of the IMF's position on the Mexican deficit. Silva Herzog's resignation in June 1986 opened the way for Salinas to become the front-runner for the PRI presidential candidacy, and the radical reform policy agenda gained increased momentum as technocrats outside of the radical core sought to become identified with the policy program of the man who would become the country's next president.[14]

Salinas's desire for economic growth drove the Mexican negotiating position and was reflected in the 1986 agreement with the IMF. Negotiated under the terms of the Baker Plan, it was hailed as a landmark agreement because it allowed for economic growth of 3.4 percent and contingency (extra) funding tied to the price of oil. But this agreement was not simply the consequence of a toughened negotiating stance on the part of the Mexicans — after all, other debtors standing up to the multilaterals did not win such concessions. Mexico's geopolitical importance ensured U.S. involvement and gave Mexican technocrats the backing to win concessions. Moreover, radical technocrats, as we shall see in the following section, also used their relationship with the World Bank to drive forward their policy goals of market reform. In doing so, they opened the Mexican state to penetration by international policy networks. The new situation gave multilaterals an opportunity to influence Mexican policy through the spread and reinforcement of social learning and to keep the reform process going through financial aid and technical support.

INTERNATIONAL POLICY NETWORKS, MEXICAN STYLE

As in the case of Argentina, international policy networks evolved out of the 1982 debt crisis. But there were some very important differences in their nature and extent arising from Mexico's historically tense relationship with the World Bank and the country's geopolitical importance to the United States. In 1958, the bank and Mexican president Adolfo López Mateos had clashed over the issue of electricity rates, and the Mexicans resented the bank's refusal to lend for petroleum development without a close look at the state petroleum company. Relations soured notably during the petroleum boom years (1976–82) when the bank criticized the country's growing dependence on petroleum exports and Mexico spurned attempts by bank officials to deal with problems of rural poverty and income distribution (OED 1994, 94). Indeed, for many years, Mexico preferred to confine bank activities to certain sectors (mainly infrastructure) and was not interested in its policy advice.

The 1982 debt crisis was of critical importance in the bank's relationship with Mexico because, in the words of one senior-level bank official, it "gave the bank a seat at the macroeconomic policy table." In 1983, Ernest Stern, at that time World Bank senior vice president for operations and a proponent of market reform, sent a letter to Mexico offering bank support for the country's economic recovery and outlining a proposed reform package that included trade liberalization, greater efficiency in public enterprises, and improved transparency in the financial sector (interview with senior World Bank official). A new technocratic administration was in office by this time, and Mexican authorities did not reject the proposal but agreed to engage in dialogue, inviting the bank to send a trade policy mission. Discussions over trade liberalization between bank and Mexican government officials during 1983–84 were acrimonious, however, because at that time those in SECOFI who resisted trade liberalization had not yet been defeated.[15] The 1983 export development loan was a disappointment to bank officials because it did not call for a generalized trade liberalization program, although in retrospect it was perceived as a first step in what would become an extensive policy dialogue between Mexico and the bank over the next decade (interview with senior LAC official).

The 1985 economic downturn provided the opportunity the bank had been waiting for. By that time the radical reformers had achieved a major victory with the announcement of a new economic program involving a variety of liberalization measures. Now discussion of trade liberalization and other reforms developed rapidly between Mexican and bank officials, as illustrated in Table 6.2. The Mexican–World Bank networks were characterized by relationships of trust and even of friendship. Several features, however, distinguish these networks from the World Bank–Argentine networks. First, Mexican authorities maintained tight control over policy dialogue until the early 1990s, determining the policy areas in which dialogue could occur.[16] Second, dialogue involved, especially in the first instance, high-level officials in the Mexican government and the World Bank. Bank officials did not have access to public enterprise officials or trade union leaders as they did in Argentina and were explicitly prohibited from initiating contacts with Mexican officials without authorization from the Finance Ministry.[17]

Unlike the other two cases, Mexico had special leverage with the bank because of its geopolitical importance to the United States that enabled it not only to resist bank policy advice it did not like but also to use its influence with Washington to suppress views of the bank that it disagreed with.[18]

TABLE 6.2. MEXICAN POLICY NETWORKS, 1985–1994
(PARTICIPANTS ACCORDING TO POLICY AREA)

WORLD BANK	STATE	SOCIETY
TRADE LIBERALIZATION		
Senior-level officials: vice president for operations, vice president of LAC, chief of mission (Mexico), leading economist	Radical technocratic reformers at senior levels of the Central Bank, Ministry of Budget and Planning, and Finance Ministry (subsecretary director level)	Business excluded, informed only
DEBT		
Senior level: president, vice president of operations and LAC, best technical advisers	Senior level (including the finance minister), Mexican external debt negotiator	
FOREIGN INVESTMENT DEREGULATION		
Leading economist and technical team	Finance Ministry, technical team	Private sector conglomerates closely consulted (periphery/support base)
PUBLIC ENTERPRISE RESTRUCTURING AND PRIVATIZATION (Telecommunications, Electricity, Transportation, Steel, Fertilizer)		
LAC sectoral specialists, outside consultants	Senior-level Finance Ministry officials and technical teams	Private sector conglomerates closely consulted (periphery/support base)
AGRICULTURE		
Sectoral specialists	Top-level Finance Ministry and Agricultural Ministry officials	

As a consequence, bank officials were unlikely to make policy demands that they felt might antagonize Mexican officials. Because of Mexico's stiff resistance to conditionality, initially conditions were often not made explicit in loan agreements but were instead "the subject of understandings and side letters" (OED 1994, xiii). The bank developed a special strategy for dealing with Mexico in which dialogue and understandings were embodied in informal agreements. As reform got under way, however, Mexican authorities often requested the inclusion of conditions in loan agreements in order to consolidate policy reforms—to ensure that groups in the state opposed to such changes could not tamper with them in the future (interviews with two senior LAC officials). The Ministry of Finance was the principal point of contact for discussions with the bank on both lending and policy. Networks also developed with officials in the Bank of Mexico, the Ministry of the Presidency, and the Ministry of Trade and, on occasion, with sectoral ministries such as the Ministry of Agriculture over agricultural policy reform (OED 1994, xxiii).

Trade liberalization was the first and one of the most important policy reforms in which a working international policy network developed. Here, the World Bank provided essential support to help win converts to the reform program and defeat resisters. In the months leading up to their victory over the resisters to rapid liberalization, radical reformers used bank studies backing trade reform to bolster their arguments and help defeat their opponents in the state. The bank financed a trade policy seminar in early 1985 to support the government's announcement of trade liberalization measures in July of that year. Soon Mexico was moving faster than bank recommendations: it announced a 60 percent reduction in tariffs as opposed to the bank's suggestion of 20 percent. From then on, discussions between the bank and radical reformers (particularly Francisco Gil Díaz, Carlos Salinas, Pedro Aspe, Jaime Serra Puche, José Córdoba, and Ernesto Zedillo, the market reform policy core) on trade liberalization intensified (Heredia 1996, 198; interviews with senior LAC officials). Meanwhile, the bank's resident mission representative in Mexico collaborated with Mexican government officials on the technical aspects of the trade liberalization policy (interviews with two senior LAC officials). A 1986 report, a collaborative effort between a bank official and Mexican officials, formed the basis of the bank's trade policy loans to Mexico and the liberalization program (interviews with two senior LAC officials; OED 1994, 70). The bank pressed for a completion of trade liberalization in 1987, as opposed to the three-year program announced in mid-1985 (OED 1994, 80). Trade liberalization was complete by 1988 (see Table 6.1).

It was the bank's role in the debt issue that was probably the most important factor in engendering trust between bank and Mexican officials. One of the key elements in that trust was the gratitude of Mexican officials for the supportive role played by the bank in debt negotiations and restructuring and in acting as a catalyst for international financial flows through co-financing and guarantees in 1986 (OED 1994, 51; interview with senior LAC official). In addition to providing advice to Mexico in its negotiations with the commercial banks, top World Bank officials intervened in Mexico's behalf at critical points during negotiations.[19] And the Mexicans found sympathetic supporters for debt reduction among LAC officials, some of whom began to articulate the need for such a policy change as early as 1984 (interview with middle-ranking LAC official). In the negotiation of Mexico's Brady (debt reduction) deal in 1989, the bank played an important advisory role in the design and formulation of options for debt and debt service reduction, and its projections of Mexico's financial needs lent decisive support for Mexico's case in negotiations with the commercial banks (OED 1994, xv). As illustrated in Table 6.2, the policy network that developed on the debt issue involved high-level officials of the bank and the Mexican government and the top technical advisers of each, with one particularly trusted bank official on call to the Mexican government for advice on the issue (OED 1994, 98). Most of the analytical work was carried out jointly by World Bank and Mexican officials (interviews with senior and middle-ranking LAC officials).

More than in the other two cases, members of Mexican–World Bank international policy networks were characterized by similarity in educational background and, sometimes, previous personal ties stemming from their days at American universities. Several LAC officials had close personal friendships with individuals among the Mexican radical reform core as a consequence of having attended graduate school together at Yale (interviews with two LAC officials). Hence once radical reformer Carlos Salinas was designated as the PRI presidential candidate in 1987, relations between Mexico and the bank became closer and policy networks proliferated. At the end of his term, President de la Madrid asked the bank to develop six policy papers assessing the government's reform program and identifying outstanding areas needing reform (OED 1994, 65). In 1988, as Salinas campaigned for the presidency, Pedro Aspe, heading up the policy clique responsible for macroeconomic policy, and top-level World Bank officials worked together on the reform program (privatization, deregulation) that would form the basis for the Brady deal and for the rapidly accelerating reform process that would characterize the Salinas years. Hence the basic direction of Mexico's economic reforms had been pretty well worked out by the time the country was ready to negotiate restructuring under Brady.

Although much of the policy dialogue between the bank and Mexico would result in loans, as was the case for Argentina, discussion occurred even in areas in which loans would not be forthcoming.[20] Joint studies were produced on public sector investment, deregulation of foreign investment, the financial sector, the industrial sector, transportation, reform and privatization of public enterprises (telecommunications, fertilizer, steel, electricity), and agriculture, including the impact of the North American Free Trade Agreement (NAFTA) on agriculture (interviews with two senior LAC officials). As they had regarding trade liberalization, Mexican officials continued to use bank studies and joint bank-Mexican studies in all of these areas to back up their arguments for extending reform. At the same time, the studies themselves formed the basis for further dialogue with the bank and propelled the process forward as reforms were evaluated and new areas for reform identified (interviews with two senior LAC officials).

Reform in the agricultural sector is probably the clearest case of the policy elite's use of the bank to push forward a reform that did not initially have widespread support in the Mexican bureaucracy. Beginning in 1985–86, the bank began the first tentative discussions with Mexican technocrats (those in the Finance Ministry) on the need for reform in agriculture. The bank had a variety of concerns, including the negative impact on incentives of extensive state intervention in agriculture through cumbersome and costly public enterprises, banks, and marketing boards; the distortion caused by food subsidies; and excessive government spending on irrigation and infrastructure. Discussions, however, did not really get under way until radical market reformer Carlos Salinas, also a strong advocate of reform in agriculture, was about to assume the presidency. Again, many of the same radical reformers who supported trade liberalization and privatization (Ernesto Zedillo, Jaime Serra Puche, and Pedro Aspe), anxious to get reform moving in agriculture, met with top bank agricultural economists to obtain bank support (interview with bank official). The Mexicans saw the ejido, a cooperative form of agricultural organization involving traditional communal practices, as the major obstacle to achieving greater agricultural productivity. The agricultural bureaucracy, however, was resisting liberalization in agriculture, and particularly any move to modify the ejido. Bank experts, however, did not see the ejido as the root of the problem and focused instead on the other agricultural policy issues mentioned above.[21]

It was in this context that discussions between the bank and Mexican Finance and Agricultural Ministry officials got under way in 1989–90. Over the next three to four years, the Mexican government sent about ten groups of officials to Washington for policy discussions (with about ten individuals per group), most from the Ministry of Agriculture and many with reservations about the social-political fallout of market reforms in the agricultural sector. The role of bank officials in this policy dialogue was not simple. They felt compelled to educate Mexican Finance Ministry officials that simply to liberalize the agricultural sector was not sufficient, while, at the same time, persuading reticent Agricultural Ministry officials of the efficacy of ejido reform—that peasants would, in fact, be more likely to stay on their land if they had personal ownership. The dialogue did produce a blueprint for reform for each subsector for agriculture, although it appears to have been less than optimal from the bank's point of view (interview with senior bank official). Mexican authorities insisted on the insertion of agricultural reforms as conditions into loan agreements, a measure that they believed would consolidate the changes.[22] But even in agriculture, an area in which the meeting of minds was considerably less than in other areas of policy dialogue, informants spoke of the development of a relationship of trust between bank and Mexican officials. The bank had played a role in the spread of social learning among Mexican bureaucrats, helping to build a consensus that was sufficient for the reform—particularly the reform of the ejido—to go forward.[23]

In addition to its role in spreading the new international policy culture, the bank provided know-how on restructuring and privatization of public enterprises (for example, information on the experience of other countries in carrying out such reforms).[24] As in the Argentine case, reform of the public enterprise sector was largely a "learning together" exercise in which strong support for privatization emerged by the late 1980s as a consequence of the ineffectiveness of various restructuring programs in improving the performance of public enterprise.[25] Even then, however, bank and Mexican officials settled for restructuring as a way to break down political resistance and pave the way for privatization. Bank officials remained more aloof from the Mexican privatization process than they had in Argentina; they pursued a soft-sell strategy, fearful of offending the Mexicans, and they remained amenable to the Mexican strategy of giving priority to privatization in those areas where there was less political resistance or where resistance could be overcome. As in the Argentine case, the bank attempted to avoid formal loans in areas in which they foresaw extensive corruption.

A close working relationship also developed between senior-level officials of the Mexican Finance Ministry and IMF officials, which also stemmed from the fact that these people often knew each other from earlier interactions, both educational and career related. But there was clearly considerably more tension in Mexican-IMF dialogue and even conflict (primarily over the issue of the public deficit) than was the case for the bank-Mexican networks (interview with senior IMF official). Still, there was a basic agreement regarding the way the economy should operate. The differences revolved around what one IMF official described as their distinct constituencies—the Mexican government having to face "political realities" and therefore demanding an alleviation of harsh austerity and economic growth and IMF officials believing that "politicians always underestimate their ability to carry out reform so we push them to do what they think they cannot do" (interview with senior IMF official). With regard to structural changes discussed in relation to EFF agreements, IMF officials stressed that policy reform was a "collaborative effort," which, in the words of one senior IMF official, was "facilitated by the fact that we saw things the same way as the Mexicans because they earned their Ph.D.'s from the same places we did." Mexican officials overwhelmingly agreed that IMF pressures for reducing the budget deficit were key in driving the privatization program because this was the only way they felt that they could meet IMF demands for deficit reduction (interviews with three senior Finance Ministry officials).

As in the Argentine case, the World Bank's influence was constrained by the domestic entrepreneurial side of policy networks. The bank could help spur policy reform forward through its expertise and financial support but could not control implementation in cases where private sector interests weighed heavily, particularly in privatizations. Bank officials were not entirely happy with reform in the agriculture sector, where they failed to see eye to eye with domestic radical reformers. More important, however, the bank had been unable to persuade Mexicans of the necessity of opening the service sector (banking and telecommunications) immediately to foreign investment. Here, as we will see, powerful private sector interests, at the other end of policy networks, played a key role in policy outcomes.

THE HEYDAY OF MARKET REFORM, 1987–1994

As international policy networks deepened and broadened, the market reform process in Mexico went rapidly forward, propelled by Carlos Salinas and his technocratic group of radical reformers (see Table 6.1). International pressures also helped push the process along: international petroleum prices fell once again in late 1987, anticipated loans failed to materialize, and inflation hit 130 percent. Now trade liberalization came to be seen by radical reformers as an effective means to combat inflation because they believed that cheaper imports would encourage greater efficiency among domestic producers and lower prices. Privatization progressed rapidly. In late 1989 the executive decided to divest the state of all public enterprises not specifically mentioned as "strategic" in the constitution, with the result that only PEMEX (Mexican Petroleum Company), the CFE (Federal Electricity Commission), FERRONALES (railways), the Central Bank, and agencies involved in mail delivery, radio, telegraph, and communications via satellite would remain in state hands once the program was complete. Moreover, de facto privatization was initiated even in those areas protected as exclusive to the state by the constitution: "basic" petrochemicals were redefined as "secondary," thereby opening them up to private, including foreign, capital, and PEMEX was reorganized, opening up the marketing of crude oil, services, and technology to private capital. In agriculture, guaranteed prices were removed from all products except corn and beans and import licenses were abolished for all agricultural products except corn, beans, wheat, and powdered milk (Martínez and Fárber 1994). By far the most important and controversial agricultural reform involved changes to Article 27 of the constitution. This reform declared the end of land redistribution and effectively put an end to the ejido. The reform gave communal farmers (*ejiditarios*) the legal right to hold title to land and therefore the right to sell or rent it or to form joint ventures with agribusiness, whether foreign or domestic. The purpose of the reform was to stimulate investment and export competitiveness in the agricultural sector. The signing of the North American Free Trade Agreement, a free trade agreement with Chile, and reciprocal trade liberalization agreements with other Latin American countries further propelled the opening of the Mexican economy. In the electricity and financial sectors, however, the opening to foreign capital was to be restricted until the year 2000.[26]

In large part, these rapid changes became possible because once Salinas took over the presidency in 1989, the economic policy core and its dominant economic policy network became more cohesive and more concentrated than ever and fiercely resistant to outside opposition. The powerful economic cabinet now completely excluded the minister responsible for public enterprises, and the minister of finance, Pedro Aspe, became dominant, while the Ministry of Budget and Planning lost power. In fact, this ministry was eliminated in 1992 and its functions handed over to the Finance Ministry. The privatization drive was directed from the presidency and the Finance Ministry, and all nonbanking sales were handled by the Finance Ministry. In addition, a new superministry, the Office of the Presidency of the Republic, was set up for the purpose of coordinating and implementing policy. It was placed in the hands of the man who was perhaps President Salinas's closest adviser, José Córdoba, who also played a central role in the debt negotiations and in the privatization drive (Teichman 1995, 77, 90–91). The most powerful actors in economic policy reform were a tightly knit group: President Salinas, Córdoba, Aspe, and Serra Puche and their respective teams.[27] This closed and concentrated decision-making style was an arrangement explicitly constructed to reduce obstacles to presidential goals presented by protracted bureaucratic conflict. The cohesiveness and policy commitment of this group and its control of the state were probably second only to those of the Chicago boys. As the market reform program went rapidly forward, Salinista market reform technocrats not only took over the key economic ministries but also wrested control of virtually all government agencies of any importance (Camp 1990, 98–99), in particular, the direction of state companies slated for privatization (Teichman 1995, 151). While Mexican intrastate policy reform networks were composed largely of technocrats, one politico, Arsenio Farell Cubillas, minister of labor from 1983 to 1994, was widely regarded as an indispensable member of the market reform team. His refusal to weaken in the face of opposition from labor was essential to the reform process.[28]

As in the other two cases, radical market reformers opened policy networks to the country's most powerful private sector interests, a development that emerged in the course of the market reform process and had an important impact on its outcome.[29] Mexico's technocrats believed in the importance of having not just the confidence but also the active support of the private sector if greater dependence on market forces was to succeed. Throughout the Salinas years, the Mexican Council of Businessmen (the CMHN), to which the country's top thirty-seven businessmen belonged, maintained the most direct and immediate access to cabinet ministers (Luna 1992, 275; Teichman 1995). The Coordinating Committee for Commercial

Export Business Organizations (COECE), established in 1988, represented the private sector in the NAFTA negotiations. Controlled by the country's most important industrial conglomerates, it allowed big business ongoing direct input into the negotiating process (Luna 1992, 16; Kleinberg 1999, 127–51).

The most important channels linking the country's most powerful businessmen and cabinet technocrats under Salinas, however, were ongoing personal contacts (Luna 1992, 5; Camp 1989, 171; Teichman 1995). Close and personal links between the heads of conglomerates and the president and radical reform technocrats in charge of the major economic ministries developed throughout the 1990s. Claudio X. Gonzalez, a shareholder and member of the boards of directors of three of the country's biggest conglomerates, was a personal friend of Salinas, arranging his meetings with other conglomerate heads, acting as his adviser on foreign investment issues, and accompanying both Commerce Minister Serra Puche and José Córdoba on official trips abroad (*Proceso*, no. 974, July 3, 1995, 39). Carlos Cabal Peniche and Carlos Slim, who purchased public companies, were both close to Salinas and accompanied him on international tours (*Proceso*, no. 1005, February 5, 1996, 8). Business deals linked the president's brother Raúl Salinas to the country's most powerful businessmen, especially those who bought public firms and who contributed very large sums of money to Salinas's election campaign (*Proceso*, no. 1005, February 5, 1996, 15–16). Big businessmen headed up Salinas's party fund-raising committee, and top businessman Miguel Alemán served as the PRI's finance secretary for the 1994 national elections. The PRI asked for enormous contributions from its powerful business supporters, and they usually complied.[30]

Indeed, these close contacts are reflected in the movement of market reform technocrats into the private sector after leaving office. Pedro Aspe left his position as finance minister to join the executive team of Pulsar International at the request of its owner and his close friend, Romo Garza, who was linked by marriage and interlocking directorships to the Garza Sada family and among the country's top ten entrepreneurs (*Proceso*, no. 1004, January 29, 1996, 29). Upon leaving his position as minister of finance, Serra Puche went into the business of consulting for the private sector. Claudio X. Gonzalez serves on the advisory board of his consulting company, which has had major companies such as TELMEX (Mexican Telephone Company) as clients. Clearly, a small group of powerful entrepreneurs enjoyed easy access to key members of the policy core, and close personal relationships developed from these interactions. The president of one large export company described government-business relations: "The process of consultation . . . is largely done on an informal basis between government ministers and individual company executives. My company has excellent relations with the current administration. I can call a minister any time to arrange a meeting. I speak personally with President Salinas every three or four days or so."

The access of the country's powerful businessmen to policy makers was paralleled, as in the other two cases, by the benefits they received. The owners of powerful conglomerates benefited the most from market reform. The firms belonging to the country's conglomerates availed themselves of President de la Madrid's export promotion program that provided preferential treatment in the areas of credit and tax relief for those enterprises already exporting an important proportion of their production. This trend continued under President Salinas. The export incentive program produced a highly concentrated export structure with a small number of internationalized firms providing the market reform technocrats with strong allies in the private sector (Heredia 1996, 249). Furthermore, the most important privatized companies fell into the hands of the most important industrial/financial conglomerates; by 1992, the country's most important financial, industrial, and service activities were in the hands of four conglomerates (Teichman 1995, 187).

While in general businessmen felt that pressure from business had been only partially responsible for the government's economic reform policies, citing the technocratic policy elite's own policy preferences, pressures from multilateral lending institutions, and the general international policy environment, powerful members of the private sector interviewed in the course of this research readily admitted that business pressure had an impact on several specific policies. The government's reclassification of basic petrochemicals so as to open them up to private, including foreign, capital investment and its privatization of the banking sector were cases in which business leaders believed change occurred more rapidly than it would have without intense business pressure.[31] Pressure from specific big business interests was key in the decision to delay the opening up of the banking sector to foreign investors, in restricting competition in telecommunications following privatization, and in keeping foreigners out of the airlines. Bankers wanting to buy state-owned banks and the conglomerate purchasers of the country's airlines and telecommunications firms demanded the restriction or exclusion of foreign competitors and were able to get the agreement of technocrats in charge of privatization because these government officials saw this concession as a means by which they could obtain higher prices for privatized companies (interviews with three senior government officials and two members of the private sector).[32]

Moreover, it is widely believed that several privatizations, such as those of the state telephone company (TELMEX), highways, and banks, were carried out in a highly discretionary fashion by the president and a few top officials in a process that privileged the close business friends of the president (interviews with a businessman and two senior officials of the Federal Competition Commission). Unlike the cases of Chile and Argentina, the decision to make public companies available to conglomerate executives does not appear to have been an explicit strategy of government officials to win support from powerful members of the private sector.[33] Nevertheless, there is little doubt that close personal links existed between privatizers and purchasers. The case of TELMEX, the sale of which provided for monopoly control of the country's telecommunications industry until 1997 to close presidential confidant Carlos Slim, is the most well known example of cronyism in the Mexican privatization process. Rumors that the country's political elite benefited personally from privatization have been numerous: businessman Cabal Peniche is accused of having been de la Madrid's front man in privatization purchases, and Carlos Slim is said to have fronted for Carlos Salinas in the sale of the public telephone company (Teichman 1995, 153). For the most part, small and medium businesses have lacked both the personal contacts and the institutional channels to the highest reaches of power and were often highly critical of Salinas's market reforms (Luna 1992, 9; Mizrahi 1992, 19; Hellman 1994, 100).

Unlike their Argentine counterparts, Mexican radical reformers during the Salinas years did not have to contend with opposition to their reforms from within Congress. The country's technocratic rulers, like those who had ruled in the past, maintained tight control of the PRI, purging from the party those critical of their economic policies and their political tactics. In 1988, the PRI held a clear majority in the House of Deputies, which it increased as a consequence of the 1991 midterm elections, and it maintained overwhelming dominance in the Senate throughout the period. With the notable exception of the bank privatization, divestitures of state companies had to receive only a simple majority in Congress.[34] But the policy elite's monopoly of decision making was soon to change, and the new situation would have far-reaching implications for the permeability of policy networks and for market reform decisions.

POLICY NETWORKS AND POLICY REFORM SINCE THE PESO CRISIS

Although the 1994 peso crisis appeared to burst forth suddenly and unex-
pectedly, its origins had become increasingly evident over the previous year
and were linked to the very exclusionary and highly personalistic form of
decision making that came to characterize the period. Mexico's current account deficit worsened steadily throughout the 1990s. But the enthusiasm of
financial institutions for the country's liberalization drive financed a healthy
inflow of short-term capital capable of financing this deficit. Mexican policy
makers remained sanguine about this development, claiming the deficit reflected the positive sign of increased investment in imported intermediate
and capital goods (*Mexico & NAFTA Report*, January 14, 1993, 3). They remained
confident, as well, that productivity gains would accrue from the country's
reform programs. While the peso, fixed in a specified band, appreciated,
the private sector foreign debt increased rapidly (*Mexico & NAFTA Report*,
July 21, 1994, 7). Newly privatized banks lent out aggressively, producing
such a rise in nonperforming loans that before the collapse of the peso, the
banking sector was already burdened with a high level of bad debts. Now
unregulated, the Mexican banks borrowed heavily in dollars to take advantage of lower interest rates, lending out in pesos at higher rates (ISLA, March
1995, 53, 79; February 1995, 39). In addition, the upcoming 1994 federal election added another ingredient when the government expanded the money
supply to stimulate the economy. But fearful of the sudden outflow of capital, it also replaced government treasury bonds with a new bond (*tesebonos*)
indexed to the U.S. dollar.

All of this rendered the Mexican economy highly vulnerable should
events trigger a sudden capital outflow—as they were soon to do. Meanwhile, Mexico had allowed its line of credit at the IMF to lapse in 1993,
thereby cutting it off from any close scrutiny by and advice from the IMF.
But Mexico's policy dialogue with the World Bank did continue (see Table
6.1), and some bank officials warned about the dangers of the current account deficit and the appreciation in the exchange rate. Mexico's ability to
ignore the bank's advice was clearly evident in the reaction of top-level officials to a 1993 World Bank report that argued that unless Mexico continued
on the road of structural reform (especially in energy, agriculture, and the
finance sector) and unless it changed its exchange rate policy, it would have
a crisis. The bank official who wrote the report was thanked for it, told
that Mexican authorities did not agree, and told to burn it (interview with
LAC official). The resistance of Mexican officials to devaluation has been ex-

plained in terms of the negative impact such a measure would have on the upcoming national election.[35] An equally if not more important factor determining Finance Minister Aspe's stiff resistance to devaluation was most probably the enormous pressure exerted by private sector interests, especially banking interests holding debt in dollars.[36]

Meanwhile, the market reform process was generating sharp divisions within the country's ruling class. Two political assassinations in 1994, those of PRI presidential candidate Luis Donaldo Colosio (in March) and of José Francisco Ruiz Massieu, secretary general of the PRI (in September), were widely believed to be related to the tension in the PRI between the political reformers and the opponents to political reform (the so-called dinosaurs) (ISLA, March 1995, 5). Both Colosio and Ruiz Massieu were known political reformers. Moreover, the technocrats themselves were by now divided on the issue of just how much political reform was necessary or feasible, and this disagreement would eventually link Salinas to the assassination of Colosio, whose last-minute commitment to a greater degree of political liberalization may have been more than his patron had bargained for.[37] These events, combined with the insurgency in Chiapas, were important triggers in the slowdown and then reversal in short-term capital inflows, precipitating growing pressure on the peso. Further, the deteriorating political situation in 1994 and the preoccupation of the president with this issue resulted in only six or seven economic cabinet meetings. As a consequence, macroeconomic policy was left in the hands of the president and his finance minister with little debate or even discussion of the choices made (interview with senior-level official).

In the final months of the Salinas administration, incoming president Ernesto Zedillo and subsecretary of finance Guillermo Ortiz pressed for devaluation, but to no avail. Hence, in the final months of the Salinas presidency, the Central Bank intervened heavily in financial markets to defend the peso while Finance Minister Aspe reassured global investors (ISLA, July 1995, 12). Finally, on December 20, newly appointed finance minister Jaime Serra Puche raised the upper limit of the exchange band by 15 percent. Two days later, he floated the currency when the Central Bank announced that it would not be able to continue supporting the currency (*Mexico & NAFTA Report*, February 23, 1995, 6–7). By March 1995, the peso had dropped 50 percent against the dollar. Recriminations flew over which administration was responsible for the currency crisis, and Carlos Salinas publicly criticized President Zedillo for his mishandling of the economy while Zedillo's officials blamed Salinas's high spending and loose credit policies and his fail-

TABLE 6.3. REFORM AND STABILIZATION AFTER THE PESO CRISIS (PHASE 3)

RELATIONSHIP WITH INTERNATIONAL FINANCIAL INSTITUTIONS AND EXTERNAL SHOCKS

January 1995: Mexico requests IMF standby loan

Talks with U.S. Treasury and IMF; $50 billion bailout from United States, IMF, and others, with oil as collateral for U.S. loan guarantees; issues discussed for loan guarantees: illegal immigration, private participation in PEMEX, reform of the political system. Late 1995: second austerity program

United States provides $20 billion aid package

IMF agreement to cut current account deficit in half, inflation at 1.5 percent, for a loan of $17.8 billion

World Bank loan of $1.5 billion (U.S.) ($1 billion for rescue of banking system)

1997: World Bank loan for reform of the pension system

1998: Asian crisis and fall in oil prices

ure to devalue (*Latin American Weekly Report,* May 11, 1995, 110; ISLA, March 1995, 62). But the dispute over the handling of the economy in 1994 was not the only issue splitting the radical reformers. The political assassinations, the lack of transparency, especially in the early privatizations, allegations of links between the political leadership, including top technocrats, and the drug cartels caused the Zedillo regime to attempt to distance itself from the previous regime.[38]

The 1994–95 financial crisis was devastating for Mexico. In 1995 the Mexican economy contracted by 6.2 percent in real terms, the biggest decline since 1932 (González Gómez 1998, 52). An enormous financial rescue operation was launched to pull Mexico out of the crisis. Meanwhile, the government announced the Economic Emergency Plan (see Table 6.3) in January

December 20, 1994: 15 percent devaluation; two days later, the peso is floated

January 1995: emergency package: spending cuts, 5.2 percent; tax and price increases; privatization of railways, power plants, ports, petrochemical plants, satellite systems, toll roads announced; limits on foreign ownership of banks loosened; program to prop up banks and help them restructure (FOBAPROA)

Alliance for Economic Recovery: wage increases, utility increases, tax cuts, deep cut in public expenditures; reform of pension system; 3 percent growth for 1996

1996: Alliance for Growth: goal of 4 percent growth in 1997, fiscal deficit of 0.5 percent of expenditures, 5 percent increase in public and private investment; fiscal and monetary policy unchanged. Last of the pacts between government, business, and labor.

Congressional investigations into privatizations

Government forced to reduce foreign stake allowed in PEMEX petrochemical plants

1997: PRONAFIDE: National Program for Financing Development

Aim to raise growth rates through boosting savings, measures to include tax reform, pension reform

Congress revises social security bill, participation of IMSS allowed

Increase in funds to state and local governments to get budget through Congress

January and March 1998: budget cuts of nearly $3 billion

1998: bill extending powers of Central Bank to supervision of exchange rate policy, bank supervision, FOBAPROA bill

Congress modifies FOBAPROA bill: audit and reduction of amount converted to public debt

July 1998: third round of budget cuts

Extension of privatization in electricity halted by trade union, party opposition

1995, calling for privatization of a variety of state enterprises remaining in state hands but denying any plans to privatize the state petroleum company (PEMEX) or the electrical utility (CFE).[39] Nevertheless, in 1999, plans were announced to further open the CFE to private capital, including foreign investment. Government officials argued that the state could not afford the investments required by the public enterprises remaining in state hands and that privatization provided a way to raise revenue for a cash-strapped state. Powerful private sector interests pushed for privatization in those areas excluded by the government's initial announcement, demanding more privatization in the electricity sector and in the petrochemical plants owned by PEMEX (interviews with senior government official and member of the private sector). Discussions for the Mexican rescue package between Mexican officials and the U.S. Treasury are reported to have involved pressure for a variety of policy reforms (see Table 6.3), but, as we will see, domestic political developments still remained key in inhibiting opening up of sensitive areas such as petrochemicals.[40] At this point, the United States was the primary external actor and American authorities remained closely involved in the monitoring of the Mexican economy (Ramírez de la O. 1996). The World Bank lent heavily to support the failed Mexican banking system by providing funding for FOBAPROA (the Bank Fund for the Protection of Savings) (Urzúa 1997, 103, 109), a private bank rescue effort in which the World Bank had little policy input and about which it maintained considerable skepticism (interview with senior LAC official).

The personal links between the private sector interests and the policy elite continued into the Zedillo administration and were reflected in the bank rescue program. The highly personalized access of bank owners to the policy elite produced a policy result that was highly discretionary in content; individual bankers made separate deals with the executive with some obtaining considerably more advantageous terms than others (interview with member of the private sector; López Obrador 1999, 60).[41] The result was a politically charged debate about the bank rescue policy. A total of fourteen banks were intervened by the Bank of Mexico (specifically by the Comisión Nacional Bancaria y de Valores, CNVB), and it supported the loan portfolios (without intervention) of seven banks (*Latin American Weekly Report*, June 2, 1998, 245).[42] FOBAPROA provided funds for banks to meet their foreign currency obligations, buying the past due portfolios of ailing banks, while the Program for Temporary Capitalization was set up to help banks meet their commitments to depositors. By 1996, $16 billion had been spent to stave off the collapse of the banks (*Mexico & NAFTA Report*, June 13, 1996, 5).

The peso crisis generated an outcry of criticism of the government's neoliberal policies not only from opposition parties, trade unions, and other organizations but also from the PRI.[43] While the owners of the biggest conglomerates remained supportive, other members of the private sector became critical (*Proceso*, no. 966, May 8, 1995, 43). A plethora of local business organizations (in Nuevo Leon, Chihuahua, and Jalisco) called on the government to revise its economic model (*Proceso*, no. 952, January 30, 1995, 14; no. 988, October 9, 1995, 26). The head of COPARMEX (Republic of Mexico Business Confederation), Carlos Abascal, even suggested that the Salinista neoliberal model had "lined the pockets of the few" (*Mexico & NAFTA Report*, February 22, 1996, 3). General public dissatisfaction with the government's performance culminated in the PRI's loss of control of Congress in the 1997 midterm elections.

Even before the 1997 elections, the executive's ability to get its own way in policy reform was being questioned (see Table 6.3). The unraveling of the economy triggered increased activism on the part of Congress, and investigations into the privatizations of the previous administration led to charges of kickbacks and cronyism (*Mexico & NAFTA Report*, October 12, 1995, 2). In its attempt to privatize PEMEX's petrochemical plants, the government faced the combined opposition of the PRD (Party of the Democratic Revolution), the petroleum trade union, and even its own rank-and-file congressmen, whose support for privatization was conditioned on a "compromise" that would limit foreign participation in the industry. In the face of this opposition, the government abandoned the plan to offer private investors an 80 percent stake in the sixty-one companies and decided to limit foreign investors to 49 percent, thereby forgoing an expected $1.5 billion in revenues (*Latin American Weekly Report*, October 24, 1996, 487).[44] In addition, the government's social security reform bill, setting up pension funds administered by private companies, was altered by PRI legislators so as to allow for the participation of the IMSS (the state-run Mexican Institute of Social Security) as a pension fund manager alongside private managers (Trejo and Jones 1998, 83).

After the 1997 elections, economic policies were tampered with in ways that were unheard of in the past, although it is certainly also true that such tampering in no way threatened the basics of the neoliberal model (Shadlen 1999, 411). The first challenge occurred over the issue of reducing the value-added tax when the opposition in the House interfered with the government's budget proposal by legislating a tax cut. The government got its budget through only by cutting a last-minute deal with the opposition National Action Party (PAN) that involved almost doubling funds for state and municipal governments, not a happy state of affairs for a policy elite whose top priority was the fiscal health of the state (*Latin American Weekly Report*, December 16, 1997, 589). In the following year, the administration ran into even more serious trouble with its bank reform proposals, which included granting increased powers to the Central Bank, and the even more controversial conversion of some $65 billion (U.S.) of bank debts taken over by FOBAPROA into public debt. The opposition demanded a complete audit of FOBAPROA, charging that it had bailed out some large business PRI supporters (*Latin American Weekly Report*, August 11, 1998, 365). Even PRI members questioned the bank rescue program, and the finance minister was not able to extract guaranteed support for his policy package from the PRI-dominated upper house (*Latin American Weekly Report*, September 15, 1998, 424). A deal was finally reached in which the government was forced to drop its original proposal, which was to convert all $65 billion (U.S.) into public debt and return some of the very large loans (although a relatively small proportion of the total) to the banks.[45] Similarly, the attempt to extend privatization in the electricity sector was halted in the face of trade union, state bureaucratic, and congressional opposition. In negotiations over the 1999 budget, the congressional opposition was able once again to get more federal money for states and municipalities although defections on the part of some PAN members thwarted the opposition PRD-PAN attempt to cut back on funds allocated to the bank rescue operation (*Latin American Weekly Report*, January 11, 2000, 6).

The economic crisis and its political aftermath, particularly the loss of control of Congress, slowed the pace of economic reform and forced the executive to take measures to limit discretionary decision making, a development that hopefully will mitigate blatant cases of cronyism and misappropriation. For instance, the process by which privatizations were decided and carried out, previously in the hands of the president and minister of finance, between 1997 and 2000 involved the participation of a broader array of ministries and officials. Decisions involving privatizations were made by an interministerial committee consisting of the ministers of finance, commerce and industrial development, and labor and the Ministry of the Comptroller. The ministry under whose auspices the enterprise to be sold falls is the administrative unit responsible for carrying out the sale (interview with senior government official).[46] Consultation with the private sector was to be carried out informally by the sectoral ministry. All documentation was reviewed rigorously by the comptroller's office before being sent to Congress. Interministerial working groups, usually just below the secretarial level, were used to provide the analytical work and initial recommendations for regulatory reform and privatizations, again a departure from the heyday of market reform, when ministries other than finance and commerce and officials below the top levels were largely excluded.

At the same time, however, in some respects, aspects of the old, tight personalistic policy network dominated by the Finance Ministry remained. President Zedillo, an economist by profession, was reportedly intimately involved in all economic policy reforms.[47] In a departure from normal practice, the minister of finance, Angel Gurría, was not allowed to bring in his own team (interview with official in the Office of the Presidency). Rather, President Zedillo had his own group of personally loyal technocrats in the Ministry of Finance with whom he had ongoing personal interaction. Moreover, several officials involved in policy working groups in the Zedillo administration reported that the recommendations of their groups had been ignored by ministers and by the president. Resistance to the further opening to foreign capital in electricity and in petrochemicals was fairly widespread in the Mexican state, among highly placed officials outside the Finance Ministry, in the Ministry of Energy, and in the state enterprises themselves (interview with middle-level Finance Ministry official; *Proceso*, no. 961, April 3, 1995, 31). Nevertheless, the president and top officials in the Finance Ministry attempted (and failed) to push ahead with these policies. In contrast, the Finance Ministry, or at least one highly placed individual in it, has been considerably more successful in defining social policy. PROGRESA (Education, Health, and Food Program), a policy developed to combat extreme poverty, emanated from the work of the subsecretary of expenditure, Santiago Levy, who is known to be personally close to President Zedillo. The policy was implemented despite stiff resistance from the Ministry of Social Development (SEDESOL).[48]

Moreover, the country's most powerful businessmen continued to have personal channels to the highest reaches of power and to influence policy, indicating the continuation of personal networks involving the private sector. The FOBAPROA issue is by far the most notorious example. Government officials and powerful business leaders admit to the ongoing involvement of business in most aspects of economic policy; in fact, two businessmen interviewed claimed that the involvement of the private sector in economic policy was now even greater than it had been under the previous administration. Direct and immediate access to the most powerful ministers continued, and the most important means by which this consultation occurred was informal (interviews with three business leaders). President Zedillo has integrated top businessmen into his policy team. The son of powerful businessman Claudio X. Gonzalez, for example, became head of special projects in the president's office (*Proceso*, no. 1972, May 18, 1997, 9). As in the previous administration, the country's most powerful businessmen contributed heavily to Zedillo's election campaign (*Proceso*, no. 1005, February 5, 1996, 6). Government decisions regarding monopolistic practices are a further reflection of this privileged access to executive decision making. The ability of conglomerate magnate Carlos Slim to influence executive decision making with regard to antimonopolistic measures pertaining to his telecommunications empire was attested to by three highly placed officials close to the issue. Indeed, in 1995, the Federal Competition Commission admitted that the will of the president was involved in its decision to allow TELMEX to acquire controlling interest in one of the television companies owned by media conglomerate Televisa—a decision that was protested in the Chamber of Deputies and by other business interests (*Proceso*, no. 973, February 26, 1995, 36, 38). Although long distance telephone service has been opened to foreign competition, Carlos Slim remains fiercely resistant to attempts to encourage competition in the local telephone industry and uses local telephone prices to subsidize international ones. And he has been remarkably successful in fending off attempts to make the local telephone industry more competitive.[49] The peso crisis, however, forced the bankers to allow their sector to be opened up to foreign involvement (interview with senior Finance Ministry official). The private sector has remained opposed to the breakup of the airline monopoly and its opening to foreign competition, now 50 percent government owned (interview with business leader).[50] One private sector informant believed that the private sector's position on this issue was decisive in the government's decision not to break up the airline holding company.

The international side of policy networks continued to operate during the Zedillo administration in the key areas of pension reform, decentralization, and poverty alleviation. Policy dialogue with the Mexicans in the area of poverty alleviation had traditionally been closed to the World Bank but began to open up in the 1990s. The architect of the country's most important antipoverty program, Santiago Levy, had worked on a contract basis for the World Bank before joining the Ministry of Finance, where he produced a report for the bank entitled *Poverty Alleviation in Mexico* (World Bank 1991).[51] President Zedillo was reportedly impressed by the report, eventually directing that the program be considered for adoption (interview with senior Finance Ministry official). The dialogue on decentralization occurred more slowly, in part because domestic pressure for decentralization came from opposition state governments which the PRI regime did not wish to see strengthened. By the end of 1999, however, there appeared to be some movement on the issue. Increased funding was allocated to state governments for distribution to municipalities, although funds were earmarked for specific purposes, giving municipalities little latitude to establish their own priorities or programs. Meanwhile, the bank's policy lobbying activities are fairly extensive on this issue so that when the government decides to move forward with this policy change, the bank will likely have key interlocutors in place. In recent years, the bank provided contracts to disaffected government technocrats, some of whom were involved in decentralization projects such as the improvement of state-level administrative capacity.[52]

CONCLUSIONS

Mexico's market reform process was the most technocratically driven of the cases dealt with here. A cohesive and homogeneous technocratic policy elite, originating among young academics newly returned from graduate work at U.S. universities, came to dominate and guide the process. Like the Chicago boys, they were bound by common experiences and often friendships. Unlike the Chicago boys, they made few initial attempts to convert members of the private sector although economic policy was a topic of seminars and discussion among themselves before any of them acquired important formal positions in the state. Entering the state via the finance sector, they found fertile ground from which to propound their market philosophy. Indeed, some bureaucrats in the Central Bank were already predisposed to trade liberalization, and the Finance Ministry had a long history of opposition to state enterprise and expansionary state spending. Some of the strongest resistance to market reform came from state bureaucrats with a more statist predisposition who blocked trade liberalization until 1985 and privatization into the 1990s. It was only when market reform technocrats succeeded in isolating the policy-making process from intrastate resistance and, initially, from the private sector that they were able to move it forward. Trade liberalization and the more rapid progress in privatization after 1989 reflected the policy idea commitment of these technocrats and their international allies. In the area of privatization, however, radical reformers had always to be content with less than they considered optimal. As we shall see in the following chapter, what is possible in market reform is also a feature of the strength of the opposition—and important sectors of Mexican state and society remained unalterably opposed to privatization in such sacrosanct areas as petroleum.

After trade liberalization, however, market reform policy networks began to bring in powerful private sector interests, and these vested interests would temper the free market ideas of those technocrats with whom they had the most contact. Like the process in Argentina and Chile, the height of the reform process saw the development of personalistic channels of policy influence between the leaders of big conglomerates and the most powerful members of the executive. Although powerful business leaders did not participate directly in the writing of legislation and regulations, they were heavily consulted and have had a determining influence on policy reform. They played an important role in privatizations, encouraging the sale of public enterprises in specific areas and benefiting from an often nontransparent process that included, among other things, the granting of monopoly control in certain cases. Pressure from powerful private sector interests was instrumental in persuading key policy core technocrats to delay the opening of the financial and telecommunications sectors. Similar personal links likely played a role in the delay to devalue, in the special rescue deals that bankers were able to work out with the government, and in the failure to break up monopolies.

The ability of Mexican technocrats to use the resources of multilaterals, particularly the World Bank, for their reform goals sets the Mexican case apart from those in Chile and Argentina. While international policy networks played a role in the spread of social learning in the Mexican state bureaucracy and in technical and financial support for reforms, they did so, until the early 1990s, only in those areas and to the extent allowed by the country's technocratic reformers. Furthermore, Mexico's geopolitical importance has given that country clout over the bank not available to the other two countries. As a consequence, bank officials learned not to push too hard, which may have contributed to the more leisurely pace of Mexico's reform program and to the ability of reformers to resist privatization and foreign investment deregulation in areas such as petroleum where such a move would have been politically difficult. As in the Argentine case, the international side of policy networks often had little or no influence over the way reforms, particularly privatizations, were implemented. Although personalized policy networks at the highest reaches of power continued under the presidency of Ernesto Zedillo, growing public criticism of government policy and the loss of executive control of Congress represented an important challenge to the permeability of market reform policy networks. Indeed, the extent of public disillusionment with Mexico's technocratic reformers was further reflected in their loss of control over the selection of the PRI presidential candidate and the PRI's loss of the 2000 presidential election. Following the 1995 economic crisis, several proposed policy reforms were stopped, at least for the time being, while others were altered. While on the one hand, the executive took measures to reduce discretionary decision making, on the other hand, economic policy making remained a fairly concentrated process and the dominance of the

Finance Ministry in setting policy within the state bureaucracy remains largely intact.

Mexico's policy networks have in large part reflected the country's history and its authoritarian clientelistic corporatist political arrangements. These arrangements provided the political stability necessary to build a stable (at least by Latin American standards) state bureaucracy, providing an institutional basis for the rise and expansion of radical market reformers. At the same time, within the state, as elsewhere in the Mexican political system, political groupings were hierarchical and cemented by highly personal relationships that demanded unquestioned loyalty. Radical market reformers combined their institutional basis inside the state with tight personalistic policy networks and strong policy commitment—and they became a force to be reckoned with once the opportunity for change arose. The predisposition for hierarchy was reflected also in international policy networks, where Mexican officials controlled the issues and the participants. As the Mexican political system has undergone changes, however, so have the opportunities and challenges represented by international policy networks. The increased plurality of the Mexican political system has apparently given freer reign to international policy pressures, with the World Bank, for example, now operating in Mexico in the more freewheeling manner characteristic of the Argentine case. The bank has been busy building interlocutors for its policy preferences in poverty and decentralization—but the bank's activities are not subject to public scrutiny and the issues raised by its policy priorities have not been debated publicly. So, while the opportunity for policy debate has increased in the Mexican political system, those debates have not, as yet, included an examination of the priorities of the international side of policy networks, which now reach more deeply than ever into Mexico.

chapter seven

MANAGING THE POLITICS
OF MARKET REFORM

Market reform generates strong opposition, which is not surprising given the many interests it challenges. As the preceding chapters have suggested, intrastate opposition and opposition from the private sector presented a problem especially at the beginning of the process, but the private sector, particularly the most powerful conglomerates, invariably secured a privileged position in the policy process, gaining direct access to the policy elite or core. No other extrastate social group gained comparable access to the policy process. This chapter deals with how policy elites managed those they wished to leave outside of policy networks. This management involved actions that affected the sequencing and nature of reforms and, in addition, had important longer-term political implications. Historical legacies determined the relative strength of opposition groups and the instruments available for their management. Management of opposition from labor, the organized group most threatened by market reform, was an integral part of market reform programs. In general, a relatively minor component of the process involved discussion, persuasion, negotiation, and consensus building. Corporatism, clientelism, legal manipulations, appeals to traditional identities and loyalties, threats, and punitive actions were more common. But while radical reform networks resisted penetration by critical and opposition groups, over time their ability to do so declined and they were increasingly forced to accept policy outcomes they regarded as less than optimal. In Argentina and Mexico the very methods of political management used to propel market reform forward have been discredited and weakened, at least for the moment. In these cases, when market reform was perceived as failing to provide sustained prosperity, employment, poverty reduction, and greater economic equality, the control of radical market reformers over policy came under threat from critics demanding greater emphasis on social policy, accountability, and less executive discretionary decision making. In Chile, where neoliberalism and concern for poverty alleviation have existed in an uneasy marriage for a decade, political tensions pressuring for change have arisen within the state and within the ruling coalition of parties.

MENEMISMO: THE PATRIMONIAL MANAGEMENT OF MARKET REFORM AND ITS AFTERMATH

President Carlos Menem faced fierce resistance to market reform, particularly from the labor movement and from members of his own political party. Within a relatively short period of time, however, Menem was able either to overcome or to contain this resistance. The hyperinflationary episodes of 1989 and 1990 are often seen as essential events in producing public support for far-reaching changes. As we saw in Chapter 5, the failure of the previous regime's heterodox policies also increased the opportunity for change, as did a prolonged social learning process. Undoubtedly, the success of the Menem administration in controlling inflation after 1991 was important in incurring public support for a radical market reform agenda. But Menem's political survival and radical market reform were far from inevitable.[1] The ability of the Menem administration to carry forward market reform stemmed not just from an advantageous context but also from reliance on a pragmatic management of the institutions of liberal democracy, the manipulation of corporatist arrangements, and the particular combination of patrimonial features (charisma, personalism, loyalty, and clientelism) that has become known as *menemismo*. Chapter 5 dealt with the various institutional changes related to the concentration of decision-making power, a common and probably necessary feature of market reform. The personalization of that concentrated power was equally important in making those institutional changes politically palatable, especially among trade union leaders and rank-and-file workers.

As the previous administration of Raúl Alfonsín demonstrated, neither liberal democratic institutions nor negotiation with major corporate groups alone could provide the political authority that Argentina needed to achieve market reform. Menem, unlike Alfonsín, tapped into an important reality of Argentine politics—its tradition of patrimonialism and personalism—while abandoning neither liberal democracy nor corporatism, which he used or overrode according to their usefulness in achieving his purposes. Patrimonialism, on the other hand, would remain the central axle of his regime and was key to his success in dealing with labor and his own party.

Without links to established corporate interests or any special attachment to the institutions of liberal democracy, Menem's position as an antielite figure allowed him to shift methods easily and fluidly. His use of patrimonial authority, however, entailing the appointment of personal loyalists and discretionary and concentrated decision making, was ultimately his political undoing because these methods, combined with the failure of sustained economic prosperity to materialize, reinforced the role of electoral politics as a means to register public disenchantment with both Menem's political leadership and his market reform program.

Between 1989 and 1995, Menem's reform program focused on the national level in urban developed regions, while he used government spending to maintain clienteles in the poorer regions of the country. This reform strategy ensured control of Congress because poorer regions were overrepresented, particularly in the Senate. The strategy also ensured control over the majority of provincial governorships (Gibson 1997b, 3–5). Hence the major source of opposition before 1995 came from organized labor and from traditional Peronists.

Table 7.1 illustrates the wide array of instruments used to manage opposition, particularly the larger dose of positive incentives than in the other two cases. It is in the area of privatizations that Menem's combination of methods was particularly important because presidential decree powers could not stem the prospect of rebellion in the Peronist Party or massive labor unrest, which had the potential of derailing privatizations, especially in such politically sensitive areas as petroleum, steel, and the defense industries. Working in his favor was the fact that Menem, like Alfonsín, confronted a divided labor movement.[2] The collaborationist trade union organization known as the Group of 15 (named for its fifteen founding unions) became Menem's closest ally, thereby giving Menem the support of some of the most important public sector unions faced with privatization: light and power, telephone, and petroleum. By the time of the presidential election, some of these unions were already disposed to accept market reforms and some were even willing to negotiate on labor flexibilization (Kelsey and Levitsky 1994, 11). The leaders of the telephone workers' and petroleum workers' unions supported privatization (Bunel 1992, 127; Murillo 1994, 10–13; interviews with two labor leaders), and the railway leaders gave enthusiastic support to the restructuring of the railway enterprise (Felder 1994, 58). Eventually a majority of Peronist labor union leaders supported Menem's reform program (McGuire 1997, 216).

Menem held many meetings with trade unionists to explain his eco-

TABLE 7.1. THE POLITICAL MANAGEMENT OF LABOR OPPOSITION

ARGENTINA (1989–1998)	MEXICO (1983–1994)	CHILE (1974–1989)
Patrimonialism (loyalty and rewards)		
Government and party appointments, candidacies	Payoffs for cooperation reduced or eliminated	
Personal material payoffs		
Discussion	Discussion minimal	
	Frequent use of threats	
Universalistic rewards	Severance packages follow	
Severance packages	threats and hard line	
Shares of privatized companies		
Clientelistic rewards	Clientelistic rewards re-	
Targeted wage increases	duced and targeted	
Manipulation of *obras*		
Corporatist rewards	Corporatist rewards decline	Almost no corporatist
Legal recognition	Opportunity to influence	rewards
Representation on tripartite councils	policy declines	Corporatist proposal defeated, 1975
Policy input		Labor excluded from policy input
Concertación/negotiation	Pacts but little or no input	
Corporatist sanctions	from labor	
Withdrawal of legal recognition	Delay in granting or threats to withdraw legal recognition	Withdrawal of legal recognition
	Use of labor code to end strikes	Parallel unions
	Imposition of pliable labor leaders	
Aggressive interference in unions	Questionable legal actions: Bankruptcy of public enterprises Manipulation of labor code	Closed door policy toward all worker organizations
Occasional repression	Repression Arrests of labor leaders Police/military occupation	Repression Disappearances Removal of leaders Closure of unions, confiscation of union property

nomic reform as the hyperinflationary crisis reached its crescendo in 1989. His arguments were practical and especially compelling to trade union bureaucrats accustomed to pragmatic compromises: the country was broke, and privatization was the only way to obtain the desperately needed funds (interviews with two trade union leaders and senior government officials). But President Menem's effectiveness in securing labor quiescence for his new policy agenda had as much to do with his personal style, his charisma, and his appeal to personal loyalty as it did with the logic of his arguments. The comment of one labor leader very close to Menem regarding the president's ability to garner worker support for unpopular reforms was typical of explanations given for worker acquiescence in market reform: "Menem has excellent relations with labor leaders because of the way he speaks to and relates to both labor leaders and the rank-and-file trade unionists. He has a way of speaking to them that is extremely effective and as a consequence they have great loyalty to him. Even when they did not agree with what he wanted to do, they went along—due to their loyalty to the party and to its leader."

In addition, Menem provided selective material incentives that were effective in keeping his labor allies on his side—rewards that helped him maintain just enough support to prevent a united labor from calling general strikes (as occurred under Alfonsín) and disrupting the progress of his reform program. Loyal union leaders were given government appointments: Jorge Triaca of the Plastics Workers Union, who was head of the Group of 15, was appointed first labor minister and in 1991 intervenor in SOMISA (the state steel company). Two other labor leaders were given under secretary positions in the Labor Ministry (Kelsey and Levitsky 1994, 7). But the loyalty of these labor leaders was first and foremost to Menem and to his market reform project. They fully understood that their responsibility was to explain policy to the labor movement, not to represent the views of labor before the cabinet (interviews with three senior officials). At the same time, strategic unions were targeted for material benefits, especially through the manipulation of the social welfare funds (obras sociales). Once Menem loyalists were placed in charge of these funds, they were distributed in a highly discriminatory fashion favoring those unions such as the railway workers and the civil employees whose support Menem needed for privatization (Grassi, Hintze, and Neufeld 1994, 153–54).[3] Targeted wage increases providing privileges to some unions and private deals giving union leaders access to additional funds were other tactics (Kelsey and Levitsky 1994, 8). Finally, financial incentives and offers of houses and cars were made to labor leaders to ensure their quiescence in market reform measures, if not their active support (interview with labor leader).

Under Menem's leadership, the brief trend toward greater institutionalization of the Peronist Party initiated by the renewalist faction was reversed (McGuire 1997, 22), a process that was key in quelling opposition within the party. In late 1990, Menem consolidated his control over the party when he took over its presidency and appointed loyalists to its top positions, including the appointment of his brother Eduardo as vice president. With tight control of the party's primary patronage resource, the list of candidates for electoral office, Menem was able to marginalize those opposed to his policies, including labor leaders. Dissidents within the party were expelled and replaced by staunch loyalists (McGuire 1994, 22; Acuña 1993, 53). By the mid-1990s, there was no room in the Peronist Party for opponents to market reform. In the words of one disgruntled Peronist trade unionist: "It is not possible to change the policies supported by the Peronist Party because it is not at all democratic. It is controlled from the top down. There is no longer any discussion within the Peronist Party on economic policy. So it is impossible to change it."

At the same time, Menem made full use of the control afforded by the corporatist arrangements governing state–trade union relations. The government officially recognized the Adreoni Group of the CGT (the General Confederation of Labor), the nationwide labor confederation of unions, which supported Menem's market reforms, thereby marginalizing the combative Ubaldini CGT group, which was opposed to his reforms (Epstein 1991, 143). The officially recognized CGT thereupon got seats on various government committees and backed the government's request for a moratorium on strikes and for reform of the constitution that would allow Menem's reelection. It also refused to join labor protests against the government's economic policies (Kelsey and Levitsky 1994, 11). But in addition, the regime used strong-arm tactics. The 1990 law prohibiting strikes in essential services, legislation imposed by presidential decree when it was blocked by former labor leaders in the House, became instrumental in handling the sectors subject to restructuring and privatization such as electricity, gas, water, and health. A faction of anti-Menemista striking telephone workers saw their leaders fired, their organization forcefully dissolved, and their facilities taken over by police (Erro 1993, 212). Government manipulation of union voting regulations secured a change in leadership in the trade union of the state gas company, putting in power union leaders supportive of government policy (Dinerstein 1993, 22).

Menem also made use of compensatory rewards made available to workers and unions more generally. Agreements on severance pay were often key in getting trade unions to agree to restructurings that involved thousands of layoffs (interviews with World Bank officials, two senior-level government officials, and two labor leaders). Labor unions were also given the opportunity to own the shares of privatized companies. Ten percent of the shares of ENTEL, Aerolíneas Argentinas, and YPF (the petroleum company) were ceded to the workers for free (Editors 1993b, 118; Editors 1993c, 106). Wealthier unions such as the Petroleum Workers' Union and Federation of Electrical Workers not only managed their unions' shares but bought into other privatized companies, using such business opportunities to generate union resources (Murillo 1994, 10–13).

Menem's authoritarian patrimonial bent, however, did not preclude attempts at *concertación*—agreements on policy negotiated between collaborative labor, business, and government leaders. Indeed, labor participated in policy discussions in tripartite commissions for three labor bills (1991, 1995, and 1998) and for the social security reform. Collaborative labor leaders also claim to have had ongoing contact with the ministers of both labor and the economy over these issues.[4] Although the positions labor put forward met with enormous resistance and negotiations were described as "very tough," labor participants believed that the results were considerably better than would have been the case had labor not had this opportunity for policy input.[5]

As a consequence of labor's involvement in policy, labor flexibilization, including reform of the labor code, was the area in which the government's reform program lagged well behind other market reforms. As in Mexico, there was de facto flexibilization as a consequence of fear of job loss on the part of Argentine workers, but overall there was considerably less labor flexibilization than in the Mexican case.[6] In Argentina, a timid labor reform program went through Congress in 1991, and a more extensive proposal providing much greater flexibility in hiring and firing was withdrawn from Congress in the face of stiff union and congressional resistance (*Latin American Weekly Report*, August 11, 1994, 351). It was only in 1995 that Congress passed the Labor Law for Small and Medium Enterprises (PYMES), providing greater flexibility in layoffs for small and medium firms (*Clarín*, January 19, 1995, 5)—legislation that excluded large firms at labor's insistence (interviews with business and labor leaders). A more extensive reform in 1996 faced congressional resistance and intense opposition from the labor movement.[7] Menem responded by threatening implementation through presidential decree. After first backing off, Menem then attempted to impose both the labor reform and deregulation of the social welfare funds by presidential decree in 1997. This move resulted in a court ruling declaring the labor legislation unconstitutional and was followed by an appeal by the executive. In the midst of this wrangle, the new labor minister, Erman González, and the peak labor confederation, the CGT, reached agreement on a watered-down labor reform bill that gave labor several of its key demands. The 1998 law protected collective negotiations by industrywide unions and ended temporary employment contracts (*Latin American Weekly Report*, September 8, 1998, 410). It was only in 2000, after Menem's electoral defeat, that notable progress was made in labor reform, although the reform was less radical than the 1996 proposals.[8]

Reform of social security in 1993 occurred only after some concessions were granted to the strong opponents in Congress and the trade unions. To get its bill through Congress, the government agreed that there would be no obligation to participate in the private system and it agreed to administer a parallel distributive pension system. Further, the unions secured an amendment to the government's original pension bill allowing unions to set up their own pension funds (*Latin American Weekly Report*, December 10, 1992, 2). While there has been some legislation reforming the health system, union opposition has blocked basic reform in that area.[9] Unions agreed to labor reforms because of state concessions providing for measures to prevent private health care providers from competing with union *obras* (the 1998 agreement) and the government's agreement that it would be more flexible in its management of the unions' social welfare funds (the 2000 agreement).

As argued in Chapter 5, Menem often circumvented the institutions of electoral democracy, putting through much of his market reform program by presidential decree. Although with Cavallo's appointment as economy minister there was an effort to accord greater legitimacy to reform measures through securing congressional approval, the policy elite (and especially Cavallo himself) fiercely resisted changes to economic policy bills in Congress.[10] The chief of Cavallo's political cabinet was responsible for ensuring that Congress made as few changes as possible in the ministry's legislative proposals and he spent most of his time in Congress for this purpose. Cavallo was widely believed to be behind the executive's request for decree powers to achieve changes in tax law (*El Clarín Internacional*, January 30–February 5, 1996, 3). And he aroused the ire of the lower chamber when he preempted a tax bill under consideration by imposing his own version.[11] He then threatened to resign if his adjustment measures were tampered with by Congress (*Latin American Weekly Review*, July 18, 1996, 316).

Indeed, Cavallo was well known to have had little tolerance for criticism of his policies; those interviewed agreed that he favored the imposition of policies by presidential decree if deliberative mechanisms were too slow or threatened what he viewed to be the integrity of his policies.[12] The president of the Peronist bloc in the Chamber of Deputies, Jorge Matkin, who had ongoing dealings with Cavallo, publicly complained of Cavallo's pressure for the rapid expedition of the pension reform legislation through Congress, declaring Cavallo to be "philosophically authoritarian because he does not understand the democratic mechanisms of Congress" (*Clarín*, February 15, 1995, 1). And it is alleged that Cavallo used his ministry's revenue collection responsibilities to discourage media criticism of his policies (interviews with senior government officials). Disgruntled critics also charge that Cavallo used his influence in international circles to silence criticism from other economists, including those in the Peronist Party whose consulting companies ceased to receive funding from such sources as the World Bank (interviews with economist and former Peronist activist).

By 1995, there was increasing resistance to the executive's decision-making style and to its policy agenda (see Table 7.2). Congress and the Peronist Party balked at granting further emergency powers, and the president, sensing unrest in the ranks, become more reluctant to use the emergency powers he had (interviews with senior government official and party activist).[13] As market reforms and budget cutbacks affected the provinces after 1995, protest marches, strikes, and riots spread throughout the interior. Violent clashes between government and protesters became common.[14] As unemployment reached a high of 18.4 percent in 1995 (Appendix 2, Table A.3), labor unrest increased. A general strike, a consequence of grassroots labor pressure and supported by thirteen Peronist deputies and senators, occurred in 1996 to protest the new adjustment measures and the economic model in general (*Latin American Weekly Report*, October 10, 1996, 458). Two more general strikes occurred in 1997. Peronist congressmen demanded that the government respond (*Latin American Weekly Report*, June 17, 1997, 278). Indeed, by the mid-1990s, Menem faced increasing pressure from the Peronist Party to make revisions in economic policy. By 1996 supporters of Menem's intra–Peronist Party opponent, Buenos Aires governor Eduardo Duhalde, were demanding greater emphasis on unemployment, wages, health care, and education (*Latin American Weekly Report*, September 26, 1996, 439). And Duhalde himself had come out against Menem's

TABLE 7.2. SECOND-STAGE MARKET REFORM POLITICS

ARGENTINA (POST-1995)	MEXICO (POST-1995)	CHILE (POST-1991)
Regional protests, strikes, marches, 1995–98	South and southeast: rural guerrilla insurgency	Antiprivatization demonstrations
		Demonstrations over Pinochet's arrest
General strikes, 1996, 1997	Independent labor organs set up; unions abandon official labor organizations	Strikes from 1991
Opposition in Peronist Party	Opposition in the PRI	Opposition in Concertación
Elections	*Elections*	*Elections*
1997: Peronists lose majority in House	1997: PRI loses majority in House	1996: socialist gains in municipal elections
1999: Alianza defeats Peronists, but protests over unemployment spread in the provinces; general strike of combative trade unions	2000: PRI loses the presidency to the right-wing PAN	1997: socialist and communist gains in congressional elections
		Communist gains in union and occupational elections
		1999: Concertación narrowly wins presidential election against strengthened right-wing alliance

labor reform proposals, calling for a more interventionist state and for the replacement of Menem's economic model with one based on "social justice" (*Latin American Weekly Report*, October 17, 1996, 490, November 21, 1996, 530, August 4, 1998, 350).[15]

In the 1997 midterm elections, the Peronist Party lost its majority in the House of Deputies, although it retained its ability to legislate with the support of third parties. Despite opposition calls from his own party for increased attention to social issues, particularly unemployment, and for the suspension of government austerity measures, Menem proposed further budget cuts in 1999, including cuts in housing and education. The opposition united in a five-party coalition known as the Alianza[16] and promised greater attention to social development (health, education) and to the unemployment problem, an end to corruption, and a commitment to fiscal discipline (*Latin American Weekly Report*, June 1, 1999, 246–47). In 1999, Alianza presidential candidate Fernando de la Rúa was elected president with a working majority in Congress.

The management of political opposition to market reform in Argentina involved the widest array of political methods of the three cases, ranging from universal compensatory practices to corporatist and patrimonialist ones. These features aided in the rapidity and depth of the original reformist thrust, particularly in securing labor acquiescence and even support for privatizations. Between 1989 and 1995, the radical reformist core and its economic policy reform network were fairly successful at containing and resisting the growing opposition from labor, from within its own party, from organized publics, from within the state, from opposition political parties, and from regional protest movements. But by 1995, as reform moved into the provinces and unemployment skyrocketed, the efficacy of the regime's methods began to wear thin. At the same time, the regime's strategy of labor containment had afforded collaborationist labor leaders sufficient input into the policy process that they were able to stall labor flexibilization and alter other reforms such as social security. Had Argentina not had to face the economic difficulties created by the Mexican crisis, the Asian crisis, and the Brazilian crisis, the political fortunes of the Peronist government might not have declined so precipitously. It is also true, however, that the very process of market reform, in particular its authoritarian, discretionary, and personalistic form of decision making, became an integral component of subsequent economic and political problems. As argued in Chapter 5, market reform policies developed by personalistic networks corrupted the process of market reform, particularly privatization. Although a substantial proportion of the public supported privatization, the majority of these supporters did not like the way it had been carried out (Mora y Araujo 1993, 316). Further, the market reform process had excluded almost all critical voices, including those advocating a greater focus on social issues. The policy core had lost touch with public sentiment and by the late 1990s was confronted with widespread political unrest. By 1998, only a minority of the Argentine public gave priority to economic stability, while over half wanted social problems, especially employment, addressed, even if there was a cost to economic stability. They also wanted an end to corruption.[17] These were precisely the concerns reflected in the platforms of opposition parties. Electoral democracy provided the avenue through which to push for policy change, sweeping away the policy elite that had proved so resistant to alterations in its objectives. But the new regime, faced with an ongoing economic slump following the Brazilian devaluation, has been mightily constrained in its ability to address some of the social issues, particularly unemployment, that are at the root of much of the disillusionment with the previous regime.[18] In 2000, it signed a tough EFF agreement with the IMF, and its budget for 2000 was an austere one, slashing the public deficit and increasing taxes (*Latin American Weekly Report*, January 4, 2000, 12). As illustrated in Table 7.2, political protest has continued.

MEXICO: FROM THE AUTHORITARIAN MANAGEMENT OF POLITICS TO THE POLITICS OF TRANSITION

Mexico's pre-1982 corporatist political arrangements figured heavily in the control of opponents to market reform. But in performing this role, these mechanisms were severely weakened and became less and less capable of containing opposition. Until 1994, Mexico's rulers lacked the legitimacy accorded by a just electoral process, and their leadership contained no charismatic figure capable of attracting strong personal loyalty among rank-and-file workers. And while *menemismo* used a combination of rewards and punishments to contain opponents of reform, Mexico's market reformers used a considerably larger dose of the latter (see Table 7.1). As the old corporatist arrangements unraveled under the pressure of economic crisis and the economic reform process, Mexico's technocratic rulers sought new allies, particularly among the owners of the country's conglomerates, along with alternative ways to shore up public support. A targeted form of clientelism proved effective for a time. By 1995, faced with yet another economic crisis and growing criticism, the country's policy elite moved more decisively than ever toward political reform. The ultimate consequence was two electoral upsets that ended the policy elite's monopolization of the policy reform process. But a growing portion of the country's politics is expressed outside of the electoral/party framework in the form of growing political violence.

The stiffest resistance to restructuring and privatization came from the powerful public enterprise trade unions, which opposed government efforts to change collective agreements (a prelude to privatization) and privatization. Unlike Argentina, none of the big public enterprise unions, with the exception of the Telephone Workers Union, supported the restructuring and privatization of their companies. Although persuasion was certainly not absent from among the various methods used to deal with opponents in the labor movement, unlike the Argentine case, lengthy discussions and negotiations with labor leaders to build interlocutors for economic reforms were not a principal feature of the process. Nor did collaborative trade union leaders receive government appointments that would allow them access to policy networks. Especially initially, attractive severance packages were not offered to encourage workers to agree to company restructuring and privatization and such incentives never became an important part of the process (interviews with two senior Finance Ministry officials). Declaration of bankruptcy, which was threatened in almost all cases and carried out in three of them, meant that management did not have to provide the severance compensation stipulated in collective agreement and could (and did) delay or avoid paying.[19] In only a few cases (for example, TELMEX) a very small percentage of shares of public firms were offered for sale to firm workers.

President de la Madrid took a hard line against labor resistance, but President Salinas's stance was even tougher. Recourse to the labor code to impose contract changes enabled the government to end strike activity quickly. By declaring strikes illegal, management was able to dismiss workers or call for police or military intervention, and by declaring strikes "nonexistent," it could force workers back to work within forty-eight hours (Teichman 1995, 118–19). As in Argentina, divide-and-rule tactics were employed. When the official CTM showed signs of resisting government policy, the government threatened to bestow official status on more cooperative labor organizations such as the Revolutionary Confederation of Workers and Peasants (CROC) (Middlebrook 1995, 277, 261; Murillo 1997, 55). From 1987, the authorities used anti-inflationary "solidarity pacts" (wage and price agreements) signed by government, business representatives, and labor. But by 1990, labor was participating in these agreements under duress and the government was deciding unilaterally most aspects of labor policy (Teichman 1995, 165). Government bodies such as the Minimum Salary Commission, on which labor had official representation, had virtually ceased to function.[20]

Repressive methods of dealing with labor opposition were increasingly common from 1986 onward. De la Madrid made repeated use of the *requisa*, a constitutional provision intended for truly exceptional circumstances, which allowed the government to intervene in labor disputes, terminate labor rights and the collective agreement, and force workers back to work.[21] Workers were told to accept government demands for restructuring and changes in collective agreements or public companies would be declared bankrupt—a status that would result in the dissolution of the trade union and its collective agreement. Faced with labor resistance, government troops were ordered to occupy company property in the cases of SICARTSA (the state steel company) and PEMEX (the state petroleum company). In the latter, President Salinas had the union's leadership jailed, and in the fashion of old-style charrismo, a new leader was imposed. This new leader readily agreed to the dismantling of the union's collective agreement in exchange for the opportunity to enrich himself through securing the allocation of PEMEX contracts to his privately owned petroleum contracting company (Teichman 1995, 125). The imposition of compliant leadership in the Federation of Unions of State Workers (FSTE) ensured that streamlining of the state remained relatively unfettered by union opposition. When discontent grew within the organization and a democratic movement threatened to take over its direction, the state imposed the pliant leadership of Jesús Lozano Contreras (Aguila Garcia 1990, 68–69).

While in the short term such tactics allowed the government's reform program to go forward, over the longer term, rank-and-file unrest set in motion a weakening of the old corporatist arrangements. Labor leaders lost their access to personal wealth and union resources as revised agreements removed or drastically reduced their access to union funds and government contracts (Barboso Cano 1992, 20–23). In addition, however, as the economic situation of workers deteriorated, leaders came under growing pressure from the rank and file to press for improvements. Rank-and-file unrest and union disillusionment weakened trade union support for the PRI. The most well known case was that of the Petroleum Workers' Union. Government imposition of contract changes damaging the welfare of workers and its removal of the union's source of wealth were instrumental in the Petroleum Workers' Union's abandonment of the PRI in the 1988 federal election and its support for the opposition National Democratic Front (FDN) led by Cuauhtémoc Cárdenas (Loyola Díaz 1990, 290).

An alternative labor federation, representing unions from the public enterprise sector, the Federation of Unions of Goods and Service Workers (FESEBES), was formed in 1989 as a consequence of the failure of the official CTM and the CT (Labor Congress) to stand up against privatization. Nevertheless, FESEBES is sometimes viewed as a government collaborator (La Botz 1992, 101–2; Murillo 1997, 64) given its support for Salinas's objectives of transforming the state and increasing productivity through modernization. FESEBES's first leader and head of the telephone workers union Hector Hernández Juárez had supported privatization of the state telephone company and personally endorsed Salinas for the presidency in 1988 (Teichman 1995, 168). But the regime showed little interest in collaboration even with a cooperative and supportive worker organization. The Salinas administration withheld legal recognition of FESEBES in response to that organization's persistent pressure to become involved in public policy and its desire for a restructuring of the labor movement ("Conflictos obreros-patronales" 1990, 53–54) and refused the telephone workers' requests to be allowed to participate in discussions for the modernization of the company (*Proceso*, no. 652, May 2, 1989, 11).

Through all of the means described in the preceding paragraphs, Mexico's technocratic policy core was able to achieve de facto labor flexibilization in Mexico. The government secured labor's agreement to changes in collective contracts involving alterations in working conditions, reduced benefits, and removed union prerogatives—all changes contrary to the labor code. In addition, under President Salinas, the government chose to avoid the rancor that would have occurred with an attempt to change the Labor Law and opted instead to negotiate productivity agreements with the officially recognized CTM (Murillo 1997, 57). With a weakened labor movement subject to instruments of corporatist control and with little hesitation about the use of strong-arm tactics, the government was able to alter labor relations and restructure and privatize public companies. In short, mechanisms of corporatist/clientelist control were invoked by Salinas and became important ingredients in enabling market reformers to reject labor demands and exclude them from the policy process.

Despite the efficacy of the regime's corporatist/clientelist mechanisms of political control, they had their limits, even under Salinas. This was especially evident in the area of privatization. Although the Salinas regime used legal manipulations to initiate privatization in sacrosanct sectors such as petroleum, it did not dare alter the constitution so as to move more decisively in this direction. Although trade union opposition was certainly important in inhibiting the privatization of strategic public companies, opposition from within the PRI was even more decisive (interviews with two senior Finance Ministry officials). Even so, from 1986 onward, the PRI experienced a constant hemorrhage of dissidents who opposed both the government's economic policies and its political methods of imposing them (Teichman 1995, 171, 182).

Salinista agricultural policies and reforms similarly accelerated the demise of corporatist arrangements in the rural sector, and there was even less negotiation of change here than in public enterprise reform. The withdrawal of services provided by the state to the rural sector, however inefficient and controlling they may have been, further eroded the already weak position of the official CNC (National Confederation of Peasants) and strengthened independent peasant organizations. The sharp deterioration in state support sometimes resulted in local CNC leaders being repudiated by their rank and file; in other cases, local peasant leaders left the CNC with their followers and established new organizations (*La Jornada*, August 16, 1994, 1). Market reforms also disrupted the ties between various state organizations and peasant communities that had been important in the process of political co-optation. In Chiapas, the drop in international coffee prices, in combination with the termination of commercial networks and technical assistance provided by the state coffee institution, INMECAFE, factored into the rise in support for the Zapatista Army of National Liberation (EZLN) (Serrano 1997, 84; Harvey 1998, 177–83). And the 1992 reform of Article 27 providing for the privatization of ejido land had a critical psychological impact in that it ended hope for further land redistribution and destroyed the image of the state as protector of peasant rights, thereby contributing to support for the insurgent movement (Bailón 1994, 19; Serrano 1997, 80).

Mexico's market reformers were attentive to the political difficulties they faced as a consequence of economic crisis and the unpopularity of many of their policy reform measures. Indeed, the 1988 election had jolted the leadership into the recognition that measures to bolster popular support and regime legitimacy were a pressing urgency—especially in light of the widespread belief that the PRI had robbed its left-wing opponent, the National Democratic Front, of victory through large-scale electoral fraud. The National Solidarity Program (PRONASOL) aimed to increase popular support by means of a targeted form of clientelism operating under the close management of the president. Created shortly after Salinas assumed power in 1989, the program sought to alleviate poverty by providing matching funding for locally generated projects. In the agricultural sector, the program came to replace the state rural banks, and because it granted credit to individuals rather than to groups, it was able to co-opt and divide those opposed to the regime and its policies (Harvey 1993, 219). It was used in a very explicit way to promote market reforms in agriculture: the National Indigenous Institute, a major distributor of PRONASOL funds, was charged with delivering support for the reform of Article 27 (reform of the ejido) by rounding up peasant leaders for a meeting with the president in a context in which peasants' access to antipoverty programs depended on their consent to changes in the land tenure system (Fox 1994, 267).[22] More important, PRONASOL is given much of the credit for the improvement in the PRI's electoral fortunes in the 1991 midterm elections and continued to play a role in the 1994 federal election (Angel Romero 1990, 15; Dresser 1994, 155; Domínguez and McCann 1996, 135).[23]

Under pressure for democratization not only from the opposition parties but also from the PRI, the Salinas administration adopted a controlled political liberalization strategy (Centeno 1997, 64; Loaeza 1994, 197; Cavarozzi 1994, 308; Shadlen 1998, 404), ceding victories to the opposition in state elections.[24] In 1989, the government for the first time allowed an opposition party to take power at the state level; by 1995, there were four opposition PAN governorships. Several political reforms helped to push electoral democratization forward. The Federal Electoral Institute was set up to supervise elections and to hear appeals of electoral fraud, while a variety of measures (serial numbers on ballot stubs, acceptance of international electoral observers, new voting booth technologies, expanded free media access for parties, among others), designed to ensure the fairness of the electoral process, were also implemented. The 1994 federal election was widely regarded as the cleanest federal election ever.

The peso crisis of 1995 marked the beginning of a new political phase in Mexico, one characterized by more electoral reform, unprecedented gains by opposition parties, and a continued unraveling of the corporatist clientelist system of political control (see Table 7.2). To a large extent these developments were triggered by the economic crisis, which gave rise to demands from opposition parties, labor unions, members of the PRI, and even the private sector for changes in economic policy. Outside of the PRI, opposition to the government and its market reform policies quickly gathered momentum. The left PRD leader, Cárdenas, called for a referendum on current economic policy and a repudiation of the country's debt and announced a campaign to block the government's privatization plans (*Mexico & NAFTA Report*, February 23, 1995, 3; ISLA, January 1995, 94). The 1995 economic collapse brought the hostility of many PRI activists to neoliberal reforms into the open and produced a fierce challenge to the once impermeable domestic policy networks. Members of the PRI old guard were particularly vociferous in blaming the technocrats for the economic crisis and for increased unemployment and poverty (Starr 1999b, 47). The chairwoman of the PRI called for the abandonment of Zedillo's neoliberal program (ISLA, July 1995, 35).

Opposition within the PRI now took the form of a variety of measures to curtail the economic policy-making predominance of the country's technocratic rulers. In early 1996, PRI deputies sent a leader to the chairman of the PRI demanding that the government's neoliberal program be abandoned (*Mexico & NAFTA Report*, February 22, 1996, 2). At the seventeenth PRI convention, delegates approved a resolution opposing the sell-off of PEMEX petrochemical companies and committing the party to the defense of the entire oil sector (Starr 1999b, 50). Convention delegates demanded an end to the presidential selection of party candidates and to the bureau-cratic/technocratic career pattern that, in their view, had produced an ad-ministration that was out of touch with Mexican reality. At the conven-tion, the PRI adopted criteria for public office (party membership for ten years and previous electoral experience) that would have excluded Presi-dent Zedillo and most of his cabinet (Rubio 1998, 15; Samstad 1998, 18). Well-known PRI leaders jumped ship to found their own political parties: the former governor of Veracruz, Dante Delgado, founded the Conver-gencia Democrática, and former cabinet minister Manuel Camacho Solís left to found the Center Democratic Party (*Latin American Weekly Report*, February 11, 1997, 84). Demands for democratization within the PRI reached a crescendo with the emergence of no less than four critical currents (*Proceso*, no. 1081, July 20, 1997, 15).

Confronted with such widespread unrest, the political leadership allowed the electoral process to provide institutionalized channels for opposition demands even if doing so would enable the opposition to impinge on the authority of executive decision making. Following further political reforms in 1996, which, among other things, made the Federal Electoral Institute in-dependent of the government, the PRI experienced its greatest defeat ever. In 1997, the leftist PRD won the governorship of the Federal District and control of its legislature, along with control of the legislatures in the states of Mexico, Michoacán, and Morelos. Most important, the PRI lost control of the House of Deputies. This electoral change made possible revisions in economic policy legislation (in government budgets, in the bank res-cue operation) and blocked others (privatizations in electricity and PEMEX petrochemical plants).

This new situation in Congress made it necessary for the executive to develop various mechanisms for encouraging congressional support for ex-ecutive initiatives, including support among members of the PRI who had became increasingly restive. For a policy elite that was so closed to policy in-put outside of its immediate ranks, the change in circumstances was daunt-ing. Confident that their reforms have been locked in with NAFTA and that they can count on PAN support to ensure the basic features of the economic model, the Zedillo administration eventually acquiesced in Congress's more active role in policy (interviews with two senior and one middle-ranking government officials).[25] Both the Ministry of Finance and the Ministry of Commerce and Industrial Development established administrative units in charge of providing congressmen with information and of lobbying congressmen for their support of government legislation.[26] The minister of finance and his immediate subordinates had to spend long hours explaining and negotiating with parliamentarians and party leaders and appeared to have adjusted, not without considerable difficulty, to the notion that their bills would not necessarily be passed as formulated and that they would have to forgo some policy goals.[27]

Labor's tolerance for the regime's policies and political style also reached its limit, and the regime reacted with grudging acquiescence to this new state of affairs. By 1997, the Zedillo regime had abandoned the use of political pacts, largely because of the risk that noncooperation from labor would erode business confidence (interviews with two senior Finance Ministry officials). Meanwhile, the official trade union movement splintered, and former official trade unions clearly came out against the regime's economic policies and joined new union umbrella organizations claiming to be independent both of the state and of all political parties.[28] Moreover, in line with the regime's apparent greater commitment to democratic practices, labor union resistance to privatization in petrochemicals and electricity did not meet the strong-arm tactics of the previous two administrations.[29] Labor and legislators have had an impact on pension law reform (which went into effect in 1997), securing the participation of the state Mexican Institute for Social Security (IMSS) as well as private pension managers.[30]

Zedillo's strategy for dealing with the rising opposition in his own party was to allow, indeed to encourage, democratic reforms—changes that substantially diminished his own control of the party apparatus, a development that led several observers to view the power of the presidency as having been substantially weakened (Rubio 1998, 17; Cornelius 1996, 37). With the 1997 electoral defeat, pressure for democratization in the PRI became irresistible. Critics within the party charged that the PRI's poor electoral showing in 1997 had been caused by "its authoritarian leadership and antidemocracy" (*Proceso*, no. 1081, July 20, 1997, 15) and that without change more electoral defeats were in the offing. President Zedillo abandoned the *dedazo*, the traditional right of the president to choose his successor. For the first time in PRI history, in 1999 the presidential PRI candidate, Francisco Labastida Ochoa, was chosen through a primary election. Although widely recognized as the candidate supported by Zedillo, Labastida is not a typical technocrat with the same enthusiastic acceptance of the market that characterized his predecessors.[31] The defeat of Labastida in the 2000 elections marks a momentous step forward in the Mexican political transition.

Nevertheless, the Mexican regime transition of the 1990s is not easy to categorize (see Centeno 1998, 33). Alongside important progress in electoral democracy there remain vestiges of old practices, and there has been a marked increase in the level of political violence exercised both by insurgent groups and by the state. Under President Zedillo, PROGRESA, a program targeting the very poor, replaced PRONASOL. Despite its claims to political neutrality, however, the program is widely believed to have been an important clientelistic mechanism used to pressure poor voters in rural Mexico to vote for the PRI in the 2000 election (Global Exchange/Alianza Civica International Delegation 2000, 10). Certainly the efforts to combat the drug trade have contributed enormously to the level of political violence (Camp 1999, 131). But critics have argued that the use of the state's coercive apparatus to deal with drug traffickers is related to its use against insurgents and dissidents. In 1995, a civilian umbrella security agency, the National Security Council (COSENA), was established to bring together all law enforcement agencies under the control of the president. COSENA was given a full range of surveillance powers and empowered to create a special security force,[32] while the public security budget was increased by 26 percent in 1997 (*Latin American Weekly Report*, April 29, 1997, 195). At the time, the PRD and human rights groups expressed the fear that it would be used to suppress political dissent (*Latin American Weekly Report*, April 12, 1996, 152; *Mexico & NAFTA Report*, October 12, 1995, 4).

Indeed, human rights violations are especially widespread in the Mexican countryside, in poor states such as Chiapas, Guerrero, and Oaxaca, where guerrilla insurgency is present (Handleman 1997, 110). According to a 1997 report, there was, by that year, a guerrilla presence in seventeen of thirty-two states (*Latin American Weekly Report*, December 9, 1997, 582). Amnesty International's 1999 report claims that over the last five years there has been "a serious deterioration in the human rights situation in Mexico," involving the use of torture, "disappearances," and extrajudicial executions by members of the military and security forces (Amnesty International 1999, 1, 11, 17). Reports of the killing of peasants in Guerrero, Chiapas, and other states have sullied the democratic credentials of the Zedillo administration (Amnesty International 1999, 18–20), events made even worse by investigations linking such outrages to police or to paramilitaries trained by the military and to attempts by high-ranking government officials to cover up such misdeeds (ISLA, August 1995, 11, 19). Although the state military/security apparatus has been deployed largely against violent insurgents and drug dealers, opposition party members have not escaped violent repression. In the first nine months of the Zedillo administration, 68 PRD members were assassinated (*Mexico & NAFTA Report*, October 12, 1995, 4), the number reaching 150 by the end of the second year of the administration (*Latin American Weekly Report*, December 5, 1996, 564). By 1997, Mexico had achieved the number two spot after Colombia in the death toll of journalists (*Latin American Weekly Report*, September 30, 1997, 467).

The heavy arsenal of corporatist/clientelist political controls available to the technocratic policy core driving market reform, combined with the relative weakness of organized labor and societal organizations in general, ensured an accelerating market reform process in which privatization moved steadily forward and de facto labor flexibilization was accomplished. Opposition from labor, but especially from in the PRI (in addition to resistance from within the state), prevented privatization from formally moving into areas reserved to the state by the constitution. Between 1985 and 1989, the decline in resources available for co-optation, the often ruthless enforcement of contract changes and privatizations, and the use of electoral fraud when support for the PRI waned all contributed to the erosion of support for the PRI and to the increase in support for opposition parties. While a long history of economic, social, and political inequality is clearly at the basis of the country's rural guerrilla insurgency, market reforms and the way they were imposed over the last decade or more triggered the upsurge in violent political unrest. Mexico's market reform process has been key in propelling forward the unraveling of its traditional corporatist/clientelist system even as that system was used to bring about reform. By 1995, market reform, in light of its failure to generate the economic growth and improved overall living standards that were so often promised, generated irresistible pressures for democratization and strong resistance to further market reforms. The policy elite has largely responded by adapting to greater electoral pluralism and intraparty democracy, notably reducing its use of nonlegal and repressive forms of political control in urban areas. It lost its exclusive monopoly on policy and was forced to confront the policy priorities of opposition parties and of malcontents in its own party—concerns of executive discretionary decision making and corruption, social issues such as poverty, and decentralization. But though the political leadership has responded to opposition parties by negotiation and concessions, it did not do so in relation to its rural political difficulties, which, if the trend continues into the current administration, may raise some serious questions about the country's transition to democracy. The ability of the newly elected government, whose leader, Vicente Fox, is unabashedly promarket, to respond to the heterogeneous and virulent opposition criticism of the radical technocratic elite's governance of the past five years will not be easy. As in the Argentine case, the failure of radical market reformers to deliver on promises of growth and prosperity and their predisposition to corruption in the implementation of reforms were their undoing. But in Mexico, the implications in terms of regime transition were much more far-reaching and public expectations probably commensurately higher.

CHILE: MANAGING MARKET REFORM IN A DIVIDED POLITY

Chile's early market reform experience, occurring a full decade before reform got under way in the other two cases, involved by far the highest degree of repressive management. Viewed historically, this distinction may have been unavoidable. Chile lacked corporatist/clientelist forms of political control of its popular classes; indeed, as we saw in Chapter 2, the Chilean working class had a history of militant trade unionism and resistance to cooptation. Leaders were highly responsive to working-class demands. The labor movement's history of militancy meant that policy elites were unlikely to see the establishment of collaborative labor interlocutors as a viable policy choice: the cost of securing collaboration would place impossible burdens on their reform plans. The relative weakness of labor, however, made repression a viable option.

The struggle over the management of labor during the first few years of the military regime clearly illustrates the link between possibilities for reform policy and the strategy for labor management. Almost immediately upon taking power in 1973, the new military regime dismantled the political arena that had allowed the Chilean popular classes in general, and labor in particular, access to the highest reaches of political power: it closed Congress, declared the political parties of the Popular Unity illegal, and declared all other political parties in recess. It suspended the right to strike and to bargain collectively, withdrew legal recognition from the CUT and a variety of other labor organizations, confiscated the CUT's property, and prohibited union elections and meetings except for informational purposes. Nevertheless, between 1974 and 1975, a very limited political space was opened for cooperative trade unions characterized by a concerted effort to establish mechanisms of corporatist political control along with some very minimal accommodation to labor demands. The initiative failed, the victim, in large part, of the Chicago boys' perceptions of the negative impact such arrangements would have on their economic reform project.

Nicanor Díaz Estrada, minister of labor from 1974 to 1976, proposed changes in Chile's 1931 labor code that would have increased labor's opportunity to influence economic policy. His proposal involved the establishment of a centralized corporatist system somewhat reminiscent of the Mexican arrangements. Branch organizations (replacing enterprise unions) and tripartite commissions, composed of representatives of workers, employers, and the state, were to be set up for the purpose of advising the government on remuneration by branch of industrial activity in accordance with the consumer price index (Campero and Valenzuela 1984, 205).[33] Trade unions would be able to form federations and national confederations, a privilege that had been discouraged by the 1931 labor code. There would be a system of profit sharing, and unions would have the right to strike and to bargain within strict regulations (Falabella 1981, 19).[34] In addition, from January 1974 a system of automatic quarterly wage adjustments, based on the inflation of the preceding period, was implemented. The Chicago boys feared that corporatist arrangements of the sort proposed by Díaz Estrada would lead to the involvement of labor in the administration of enterprises, to serious infringements on labor flexibility, and to a negative impact on productivity (interviews with three senior officials). They were also vehemently opposed to automatic wage adjustments. But as long as the gradualist economic policy of market reform was in effect, relations between non-Marxist unions and the government were tolerable; gremialista trade unions were supportive and the Group of 10 (an umbrella labor organization including nine Christian Democratic leaders) gave the regime conditional support.

But as we saw in Chapter 4, as the country's economic difficulties increased through 1974, the Chicago boys were able to win Pinochet's support for their radical economic program. The harsh impact of the 1975 shock treatment, which alienated virtually all but a tiny fraction of trade unions, made it impossible to contain labor unrest without increasing the dosage of repression (see Table 7.1).[35] The proposed labor code, which had already been roundly criticized by conditionally supportive trade unions as too authoritarian, became even less viable in a situation in which labor's economic situation was rapidly deteriorating. In addition to rejecting the proposed labor code, unions now pressed to discuss the new 1975 economic program with government officials. Previously tolerant labor leaders characterized the 1975 plan as favoring "the most privileged sectors and the deterioration of the majority" (Campero and Valenzuela 1984, 235). Strong letters of objection were sent to Pinochet and to Finance Minister Sergio de Castro. For the Chicago boys, management of the labor issue and control of the Labor Ministry were now absolutely essential (interviews with two senior officials). By mid-1976 they were able to convince Pinochet to remove Díaz Estrada. Faithful Chicago boy adherent and loyal Pinochetista Sergio Fernández took over the Labor Ministry. His management of the labor issue ensured the defeat of Díaz Estrada's more incorporative project, a further weakening of labor, and a decisive move in the direction of market reform.

Fernández's views on the use of political repression combined the assumptions of the military-supported national security doctrine with the pragmatic concerns of the technocrats for the survival of their economic model.[36] He believed that unless the trade unions were handled very firmly, market reform would fail and that strong top-down control was ultimately the key to success (interview with senior official).[37] Fernández's first act (or lack of it) was to ensure that Díaz Estrada's proposed labor code would never become law. He sent it out for "consultations" and then made sure that it went nowhere. Although Fernández engaged in the standard practice of encouraging parallel (supportive) unionism, he was more inclined to repressive measures: he removed critical union leaders and replaced them with compliant ones and withdrew legal recognition from those who were particularly recalcitrant (Campero and Valenzuela 1984, 244). From 1976, he followed a "closed door" policy, refusing to meet with labor leaders and refusing all requests for union conventions or congresses. Labor was left with only two avenues by which to influence government: open letters and personal meetings with General Pinochet (Campero and Valenzuela 1984, 242). As labor agitation picked up during 1977 and 1978 and in the face of an impending boycott of Chilean goods precipitated by the regime's violation of labor rights, Fernández continued his hard line. In 1978, as interior minister, he passed three decrees making possible the dissolution of "illicit" union federations and empowering his ministry to declare illegal the activities of individuals and organizations that lacked legal recognition. Unions were closed and goods confiscated, affecting four hundred unions and 117,795 workers (Campero and Valenzuela 1984, 244).

For the most part, the new Labor Plan of 1979 gave the Chicago boys what they wanted: a fragmented union structure that was radically different from the Díaz Estrada proposal. While unions were now legalized and strikes could be carried out (limited to sixty days), the new plan forbade the existence of national unions and explicitly prohibited union federations and confederations from collective bargaining. Unions had to be nonpolitical, and candidates for union leadership could not have held union office before or have had any record of partisan office for the past ten years (Barrera and Valenzuela 1987, 250, 254). The new labor law permitted lockouts and eliminated labor negotiations in the rural sector. In short, labor was left with almost no mechanism through which it could protect members against arbitrary and numerous layoffs, unsafe or unhealthy working conditions, or any other arbitrary decision taken by management. There was just one aspect of the new arrangements that the Chicago boys did not like: the provision for the obligatory adjustment of salaries and the prohibition against setting salaries at a level below those of the previous year. But in 1982, this restriction was removed. Without the means to defend their interests, workers saw real wages drop and unemployment increase (Appendix 2, Tables A.3, A.4). Chile had probably the most flexible labor regime in Latin America. These arrangements would govern labor-state relations for the remainder of the military regime.

Hence, from 1975, the Chilean labor movement, militant but never organizationally strong, was weakened even further. It suffered the dual impact of political repression and economic decline. Repression caused many rank-and-file unionists, already divided by split allegiances to various political parties (by then, illegal), to prefer that their unions stick to strictly economic concerns and avoid political involvement. Moreover, following radical economic reform, the proportion of workers in the labor force declined, as did the proportion in unions.[38] With the labor movement pro-state, policy reform could quickly and decisively move into social security and health care reform. In the other two cases, in contrast, where labor movements were stronger and governments did not have such ready recourse to the repressive apparatus of the state, market reformers would see their proposals in these areas delayed or blocked or would have to be satisfied with what they viewed to be less than optimal results. In the Chilean case of social security reform the country moved to an entirely privately run system, although there was a transition period so that workers already in the state system could stay in it should they decide to so. Health care reform privatized a large part of the health field and linked health care services to workers' contributions.[39] After 1985, when privatization moved into strategic areas of the economy, there was an attempt to garner worker support by making the purchase of the shares of public companies available to workers, but the practice never extended beyond two of the privatized banks (Maloney 1992, 12).

Despite its brutality and the radical nature of the economic changes it brought about, military rule altered some, but not all, of the fundamentals of Chilean politics. During the seventeen years of military rule, the private sector had become accustomed to a quiescent and highly flexible labor force, with limited rights and even less independent political power. Military rule left a residue of fear on the part of those it had persecuted (the trade unions and the left) with the result that in the years immediately following military rule, demands were restrained for fear of awakening the specter of a return of military involvement in controlling dissent (Petras and Leiva 1994, 97; interviews with two labor leaders and three senior government officials).[40] As well, the trauma of military rule had triggered a major reassessment among the left. The CUT, along with the leaders of the socialist parties, now moderated their rhetoric, largely abandoning the notion of class struggle (Angell 1995, 199; Puryear 1994, 72–73). And there was a national consensus on the fundamentals of the market economy, at least among the political leadership. At the same time, however, links between labor and the parties had survived and party identification among trade union leadership reemerged. Although weakened and seemingly far less militant, the left and the trade union movement expected a return of some of the basic labor rights they had lost under the military and an improvement in wages and working conditions. One of Chile's political challenges would be to redress the balance between capital and labor that had become so severely skewed during the period of military rule.

While the Concertación leadership accepted the basic features of the neoliberal model, this tended to be less true among the rank and file, particularly in the case of the Socialist Party. This difference increased over time as the policy expectations of labor and the left within Concertación were not met or were not met quickly enough. Meanwhile, the private sector, with its privileged access to the highest reaches of political power, remained rigidly opposed to concessions in areas such as labor reform and pressed for more privatization, a policy strongly opposed by the left and most trade unions. These developments have, as we saw in Chapter 4, strained cohesion among the elite—there are certainly members of Concertación, even among its leaders, who recognize the importance of addressing concerns raised by labor and the left within their own alliance. In general, however, the policy elite, in which the macroeconomic policy network is dominant, resisted policy input from both the labor movement and the left in its own alliance.

Lacking effective access to the policy core, trade union opposition and other forms of political unrest gained momentum during the period of Concertación rule. Starting in 1991, strikes broke out in a wide variety of sectors: copper, coal, education, and health workers all went on strike over wages and working conditions (see Table 7.2).[41] In 1992, conflicts occurred in the textile industry, among municipal employees, against the Banco de Estado, and among port workers (Frías 1993–94, 28). The CUT was bitterly disappointed by the 1991 labor reform, which although providing some improvements, such as allowing layoffs only with cause and providing compensation for unjustified layoffs, did not fully restore collective wage bargaining. The CUT broke off relations with the Ministry of Labor in 1992 and condemned "the exclusionary elements of neoliberal policies" (Frías 1993–94, 37).

Labor unrest, much of it focusing on the government's plans for the restructuring and privatization of public companies, continued with conflicts occurring in coal, education, and hospitals in 1996. The CUT declared its opposition to the privatization of state shares in a state electricity company, ENDELNOR, and in LAN Chile (airlines) and to privatization in mining and in shipping (*Latin American Weekly Report*, August 5, 1993, 358). The teachers went on strike in 1993 and again in 1996, when they were joined by the public sector workers and the coal workers, while the port workers occupied the port authority, EMPORCHI, protesting privatization and demanding worker participation in the directorships of EMPORCHI's companies. Students mobilized against proposed restructuring of the educational system. In 1997 generalized antiprivatization demonstrations emerged. Indeed, government officials interviewed in the course of this research readily admitted that labor was not satisfied with the 1991 labor reforms, which was why additional reforms were attempted in 1995.[42] These reforms, however, languished in Congress, held up by the opposition of right-wing parties. Labor leaders interviewed clearly felt that they were pretty much excluded from policy making. In the words of one of them: "There really is no dialogue with workers. . . . There are a lot of meetings with ministers. . . . The union says what it wants. The government says it will study the matter, but there are never any results. . . . They are not willing to make any changes whatsoever." Even Christian Democratic labor leaders were dissatisfied. Manuel Bustos, the Christian Democratic head of CUT until 1996, characterized the 1992 labor reforms as "deficient for the interests of workers" (*El Mercurio Internacional*, August 24–30, 1995, 3).

The handling of labor disputes certainly involved considerably more discussions with labor leaders than was the case for Mexico under Salinas, and political leaders were not inclined to use repressive measures. But dialogue with labor leaders was not an ongoing process, as was the case with Argentina, and even Christian Democratic labor leaders did not have access to the minister of finance.[43] In some cases, the regime was notably tolerant and flexible. Teachers and public sector workers who were legally prevented from striking did strike (the teachers struck three times between 1990 and 1997), generally unhindered by military or police intervention, and were usually able to achieve pay increases and improved working conditions.[44] Port workers, however, who were resisting privatization and had occupied the port authority building, were dislodged by the Carabineros, the national police. Copper strikers in 1991 met stiff resistance to their demands until their Christian Democratic labor leader got results by threatening to leave the party. The most protracted labor dispute involved the coal workers' strike in 1996; when the government's offer meeting most of the miners' immediate demands was turned down, the government threatened to close the mines and eventually did so (*La Epoca*, June 15, 1996, 17; *Latin American Weekly Report*, April 22, 1997, 183).[45]

Concertación leaders publicly acknowledged the growing tension between themselves and their leftist ranks, particularly in the Socialist Party over adjustment measures, privatization, and labor reform.[46] Carlos Ominami, a Concertación senator and former economy minister under President Alywin, acknowledged that an important number of base Socialist Party members were unhappy with government policy and that, as a consequence, "adhesion of the socialist base to the government had weakened" (*El Mercurio Internacional*, December 14–20, 1995, 4). A document produced by the renewalist wing of the Socialist Party also admitted that renewalism (socialism supporting privatization, trade liberalization, and labor flexibilization) had in fact not penetrated the base of the party (*El Mercurio*, June 22, 1996, 1). While Socialists within Concertación opposed the government's privatization program (*El Mercurio Internacional*, December 28–January 3, 1996, 1), Socialist Party president Camilo Escalona publicly criticized the government's labor policy as inadequate (*El Mercurio Internacional*, January 4–10, 1996, 1). The 1996 coal miners' conflict created considerable tension within Concertación ranks when Escalona, leader of the party's orthodox wing, took part in a march supporting the coal workers' strike. He was reprimanded by Christian Democratic Party leader Alejandro Foxley, who declared that Escalona "could not simultaneously be with the government and take part in public acts which insult President Frei" (*La Epoca*, July 14, 1996, 15).[47] By 1996, the orthodox wing of the Socialist Party was experiencing a resurgence. At the Socialist Party Congress in 1996, it put forth proposals involving the old notions of class struggle and revolution (*El Mercurio Internacional*, February 29–March 6, 1996, 4). Indeed, the declaration coming out of the party's Twenty-fifth Congress described the party as a class party and talked about the necessity of replacing the capitalist regime with a socialist one (*El Mercurio Internacional*, February 29–March 6, 1996, 4).

In light of the opposition to its policies from members of its base, the Concertación leadership carefully managed potential congressional pressures from its own rank and file. The congressional finance commission, a joint Senate and House commission that approves all bills with financial implications, meets with the finance minister regularly to discuss bills that are to go before Congress. But such meetings are mainly for the purpose of informing parliamentarians and involved negligible policy input (interviews with senior Finance Ministry official and congressman). This is especially the case for the budget bill in view of the fact that the Senate and the House must approve the budget within sixty days of its submission to Congress. The Concertación leadership appointed only strong loyalists to the congressional finance commission, individuals who are, in the words of one parliamentarian interviewed, "opponents of populism even when it comes from within our own party."

The consequence of the labor movement's belief that its interests were not being addressed and the growing distance between the policy core and the socialist base of Concertación was reflected in the growing electoral strength of the socialists and the electoral inroads made by the Communist Party in the 1990s (see Table 7.2). In the 1996 municipal elections, Christian Democratic support declined three points while the two socialist parties, the Socialist Party and the PPD, increased their share of the popular vote by five percentage points (*Latin American Weekly Report*, March 18, 1997, 142). In the December 1997 legislative elections, the socialists (PS and PPD) overtook the Christian Democrats in their proportion of the popular vote for the Chamber of Deputies while the Communists were also able to increase their support (*Latin American Weekly Report*, December 16, 1997, 590, June 2, 1998, 264). Meanwhile, the Communist Party strengthened its position in a variety of trade and occupation unions. In 1996, Communist candidates won the presidencies of the Professors Association, the Students' Federation, and the health workers' union (*El Mercurio Internacional*, April 18–24, 1996, 1–2). And socialist trade union leaders lost their control of two of the three coal miners' unions to Communists because socialists were identified with the government's failure to meet coal miners' demands (*El Mercurio,*

July 4, 1996, 1, 9). By 1997, a "progressive block" formed by the Socialists and the PPD was discussing a possible alliance with the Communist Party, a move that, at the time, was soundly vetoed by the Christian Democrats (*Latin American Weekly Report*, July 22, 1997, 349).

The Concertación's difficulty in containing unrest within its ranks is reflective of the country's democratic pluralism, of the absence of mechanisms of corporatist/clientelist incorporation, and of the divisions that continue to exist in Chilean society. Pressure to acquiesce in the leadership's policy priorities, exerted on Christian Democratic and socialist labor leaders by the Concertación leadership, a common practice when labor unrest began to emerge in the 1990s (interviews with two labor leaders), ran into some difficulties by 1996. Disappointment among the rank and file of the labor movement over government economic and labor policy produced an alliance between socialist and communist trade union leaders that secured the election of a socialist leader of the CUT (Roberto Alarcón), defeating the Christian Democrat supported by Concertación.[48] The new Socialist CUT leader, Alarcón, spoke out publicly not only against the inadequacy of government policy in areas such as education, housing, and social security but also against government interference in what he regarded as internal CUT affairs (*El Mercurio Internacional*, May 2–8, 1996, 1).

The Concertación lacks consensus building that reaches into the rank and file of its own coalition of parties and dialogue that really includes the labor movement and the left-leaning base of its socialist allies. A Concertación (and Christian Democratic) member of Congress echoed a viewpoint repeated by others interviewed in the course of this research when he referred to the failure of the executive to hold talks with those adversely affected by the educational reform and the restructuring of the coal industry as "a deficiency in the executive's handling of the social conflicts that such changes produce." Along similar lines, Jorge Schaulsoln, coordinator of Concertación, called upon the government to gain support from its component parties before going forward with a policy (*La Epoca*, January 14, 1996, 15).

Unrest among the socialist ranks within Concertación was reflected in its demand that the next Concertación presidential candidate be a socialist, a demand that was vehemently and firmly opposed by leading Christian Democrats (*Latin American Weekly Report*, March 18, 1997, 142). By 1997, the front-running candidate supported by the two socialist parties of Concertación was former public works minister Ricardo Lagos. In the midst of growing tension within the Concertación alliance, compounded by deteriorating economic conditions and the arrest of Augusto Pinochet in London, Ricardo Lagos was elected Concertación candidate in primary elections in May 1999. This event, in turn, was followed by a narrow electoral win for Lagos and Concertación in the 1999–2000 presidential election: on the second round of voting, Lagos managed 51.3 percent of the popular vote against the right-wing alliance, Alianza por Chile, led by Joaquín Lavín. Lavín's percentage of the vote, at 48.7 percent, broke the historic ceiling for right-wing candidates (Drake and Winn 2000, 8).

While Chile's policy elite is committed to electoral democracy and has spurned the use of authoritarian mechanisms of political containment, policy networks have been resistant to penetration by trade unionists and critical groups in the Concertación alliance. Among a certain segment of socialist/left militants the separation of Concertación from its base may have spurred a strengthened resolve to force policy elites to address deeply felt concerns, but an equally common response may well have been anger, frustration, and alienation. A growing number of the poor and working class, deeply disillusioned with the failure of the Concertación, in power for a decade, to improve their social situation sufficiently, may have been attracted by the charismatic and populist appeal of Lavín, who promised them jobs, health care, education, and a reduction in crime (Winn 2000, 8, 9–10). Indeed, on these issues the electoral campaigns of Lavín and Lagos were virtually indistinguishable. At the same time, this new-right wing alliance, with a $50 million (U.S.) election war chest courtesy of the Chilean business community (Winn 2000, 7), won the votes of middle-class center/right supporters of Concertación who had benefited from Chile's economic growth and were fearful of Concertación's new socialist leadership. Hence, while a certain proportion of the electorate was growing impatient with the Concertación, other sectors of the public, particularly the private sector,[49] felt a certain degree of anxiety at the thought of a socialist taking over the reins of the presidency.

CONCLUSIONS

The relative strength of opposition groups, particularly labor, and the resources available to confront this opposition have heavily influenced market reform programs. In Chile, resistance from an organizationally weak and militant labor movement under a military regime was readily dealt with through the repressive apparatus of the state. This made possible early labor flexibilization and reforms in social security and health care which in the other cases were delayed by more powerful labor movements operating in contexts of civilian rule. Argentina, with the strongest labor movement, has had the most difficulty achieving labor flexibilization, while reforms in social security were altered by pressures from trade unionists and reforms in health care have lagged. The existence of a strong labor movement with a collaborative faction combined with a patrimonial style of political leadership afforded Argentine labor the opportunity for direct input into policy reforms. Through the manipulation of its traditional corporatist/clientelist mechanisms of political control, Mexico's policy elite was fairly successful at achieving de facto labor flexibilization. Although there is no correlation between the depth and rapidity of market reform and regime type, this analysis suggests a relationship between certain aspects of market reform and the use of repressive methods: greater labor flexibilization is associated with repressive methods and a weak labor movement; at the opposite extreme, a strong labor movement with some opportunity to collaborate directly in policy has delayed labor flexibilization.

In all of the cases, consultation and negotiation with labor leaders have not been major features of the process—Argentine radical reformers allowed only a small, select group of intensely loyal labor leaders to participate in policy networks. Nor has consultation and negotiation occurred within ruling parties or party coalitions under civilian rule. In fact, the policy elite and its various networks have been generally resistant to pressures for policy alterations from these sources. The most extreme case of authoritarian imposition of reforms (aside from Chile under military rule) is that of Mexico under the presidency of Carlos Salinas. Despite stiff opposition from both labor and the PRI, the Salinas administration even began to move into de facto privatization in such sacrosanct areas as basic petrochemicals but did not dare to pursue privatization in areas explicitly protected as strategic by the constitution. Considerably more negotiation with labor occurred under Carlos Menem but was supplemented with a wide variety of other tactics, including patrimonial and clearly punitive ones. With the return to civilian rule, the Iberian strain in Chilean politics again receded from view for a decade but may be reemerging again under the highly personalist leadership style of Joaquín Lavín. Chile, however, has not displayed the corporatist, clientelist features of the other two cases. But neither has it afforded labor and leftist party activists much opportunity to influence economic or social policy. In all three of the cases, however, as earlier chapters have demonstrated, powerful private sector interests have effective, highly personalized channels to the highest reaches of political power.

The political fallout from these highly skewed arrangements has been felt to differing degrees in each case. In Mexico, market reform has had by far the greatest political impact. It, and the manner of its imposition and implementation, has contributed to the unraveling of Mexico's authoritarian mechanisms of political control. In the rural sector, violent political insurgency has been triggered by a complex of factors that have included market reforms and their impact on mechanisms of political containment. The authoritarian and discretionary manner in which market reform measures were carried out and their apparent failure to produce sustained growth and prosperity for the majority created irresistible pressures for political opening in Mexico. The electoral defeat of the PRI in the 2000 presidential election is testimony to the depth of public disillusionment with the rule of the country's technocratic market reformers. Labor is increasingly independent, and it, and Congress, have affected policy in important ways.

Similarly, although to a lesser degree, in the case of Argentina the persistence of high unemployment, the growth of poverty, and the link between privatization and political corruption produced a political reaction in the form of the electoral defeat of the government responsible for market reform. Even in Chile, where important progress has been made in reducing poverty,[50] the frustration of those kept out of the policy loop has also had electoral ramifications, seen in the growing strength of socialist and communist parties, an invigorated socialist presence in the Concertación, and a populist right with lower-class support. In Argentina and Mexico, despite the presence of authoritarian enclaves and practices (or, perhaps, because of them), electoral politics has come to figure more importantly in public policy—within parties it ensured the candidacy of individuals who addressed concerns felt to have been ignored by the policy elite, while in electoral competitions opposition candidates critical of the policies of market reformers have been elected. These developments have added a new twist to the market reform/politics dynamic: the inadequacies of market reform appear to have contributed to greater political pluralism and an invigorated relevancy of electoral democracy to public policy. But as the case of Chile illustrates, the ability and even willingness of governments to allow a wide cross section of the public to influence policies addressing such issues as inequality, unemployment, and poverty may be mightily constrained in the era of neoliberalism. Even a Christian Democratic/socialist government can be inclined to exclude its base from policy input while affording easy access to powerful business interests. The recent Chilean election may be a positive sign, however, suggesting a decline in the polarization so damaging to the Chilean polity in the past. But the neopopulist nature of the right-wing alliance could also suggest a growing political disillusionment among some lower-class Chileans that may not augur well for the longer-term legitimacy of liberal democratic institutions. How will the Argentine electorate react when the new government, preoccupied with its public deficit and pressures for labor flexibilization, fails to address social issues, especially unemployment? What will happen when those lower-class people who voted for the new Mexican president, Vicente Fox, find that their economic situation is not appreciably improved by even further reliance on the magic of the marketplace? Will political alienation result in the reinforcement of Latin America's Iberian strain in the form of personalistic and authoritarian Fujimori-like movements? While the failures of market reforms appear to have invigorated electoral democracy and the demand for transparent and accountable government, it is now incumbent upon elected governments to make good on their most important promises—for not to do so could have negative implications for the longer-term legitimacy of these institutions.

chapter eight

FREEING MARKETS AND
FACING THE CHALLENGES
OF SECOND-STAGE REFORM

Both domestic and international factors influenced the market reform process. Table 8.1 summarizes the major features of the policy reform experience for the three cases. One aspect of the process that the table cannot capture is the interaction between the external and internal processes. Indeed, both sets of factors are so closely intertwined that it is difficult to assess their independent impacts. The most important international circumstance identified in this book as influencing policy choice was the change in the international policy culture toward greater reliance on the market. Various channels operated to convey the new ideas. Negotiation with multilateral lending institutions was one of the most important ways new ideas were conveyed and reinforced among domestic policy actors. But while international conditions and pressures defined in general terms the nature of change, countries' historical legacies and the interaction of domestic factors with international ones determined the timing, pace, and specific features of market reform programs. As this book has demonstrated, the market reform experience takes on the political attributes of the polity and society in which it is being carried out.

The relationship between market reform and politics is fairly clear in the short term but less so over the longer term. In Chile under military rule, in Argentina, and in Mexico, the market reform experience is unquestionably associated with a variety of nondemocratic political practices, spanning the gamut from brutal repression to various forms of clientelist political control. Although varying in degree and over time, market reform is associated with a closed, insulated, exclusionary, and personalistic form of decision making. It is a form of decision making that may not immediately disappear when the initial, most difficult phase of reform is complete. Although far less hierarchical than under military rule, macroeconomic policy making has been a fairly exclusive and isolated activity in Chile even under Concertación, a government that has a demonstrated concern for reducing poverty. Once the most difficult initial stage of reform is complete, electoral institutions (parties, Congress) became increasingly important as these mechanisms were the means by which dissatisfied publics attempted to redress the inadequacies of market reform: its association with cronyism (Mexico and Argentina) and its perceived failure to produced sustained growth and prosperity for all (all cases). In two of the cases (Mexico and Argentina), market reform leaderships were discredited and voted out of power. In Chile, a country that has struggled with second-stage reform for a decade, the government is facing pressures from its own leftist ranks and a growing electoral challenge from a neopopulist right-wing alliance. Below, I bring together the major findings of this study, linking domestic and international processes, and suggest some of the constraints and opportunities presented by politics in second-stage reform.

THE DOMESTIC DIMENSION: OPPORTUNITY, HISTORY, AND POLITICS

All three countries embarked on market reform in response to economic or political crises. Chile's market reform was ushered in by economic and political crises, and Argentina's adherence to neoliberal reform occurred in the wake of the chaos wrought by its hyperinflationary episode. Mexico's radical reform project got under way when international petroleum prices dropped in 1985. But though the presence of crisis was an essential condition, it was clearly not sufficient for reform. Mexico and Argentina had to face repeated crises before market reform got under way. In fact, by the mid-1970s, Argentina, unlike Chile, was plagued by violent guerrilla insurgency. Nevertheless, market reform stalled in Argentina between 1976 and 1982 and was again rejected in favor of an expansionary program when the country returned to civilian rule in 1983, following the banking collapse of the early 1980s. Nor did Argentina's financial crisis of the early 1980s—a banking collapse similar to that of Chile—open the way to reform. Rather, the country's return to civilian rule was marked by an expansionary program. Furthermore, Mexico's radical reform program was not immediately spurred by economic collapse in 1982 but awaited yet another economic crisis in 1985–86. The nature of leadership, the political resources at its disposal, and the opposition it faced were important determinants of how and when opportunity was transformed into a market reform program. These

TABLE 8.1. HISTORICAL, INTERNATIONAL, AND DOMESTIC
DIMENSIONS OF REFORM

	CHILE (MILITARY RULE)	CHILE (CONCERTACIÓN)
Preexisting conditions	Economic and political crises Political/ideological polarization Weak, militant labor movement Isolated military	Institutional legacy of military rule Elite consensus on neoliberal model
International policy networks	Tightly integrated, hierarchical Key in keeping reform on track, 1982–85	Not applicable
Geopolitical factors/debt strategy	Policy elite lacks leverage Model debtor strategy	Continues strategy of careful economic management to raise/maintain investor confidence
Participants in market reform core and networks	Military, Chicago technocrats, political right, conglomerates Tightly integrated, hierarchical Expands to include wider spectrum of private sector after 1985	Political technocrats Finance Ministry technocrats Finance Ministry hegemonic within the state Private sector
Opposition management (major features)	Repression of labor, parties, and other opposition	Isolation from socialist militants of Concertación and labor Pressure on CD labor leaders Negotiations and concessions
Market reform program	Major public enterprises excluded from privatization before 1982; after 1985, privatization moves into strategic sectors Extreme labor flexibilization, thorough social security, health care reform early in process Trade liberalization early in process; some reversal with economic crisis; then reestablished after 1985 Financial deregulation Delay in devaluation makes economic crisis worse	Privatization moves into strategic areas, including opening up copper Minimal change to labor law Increase in social spending Trade liberalization continues Bilateral trade agreements Financial controls on capital inflows; removed in 2000

⸱GENTINA	MEXICO
⸱83 and following transition to democracy ⸱bor, strong and collaborative ⸱ilitary with societal allies ⸱eterodoxy fails, hyperinflation	Petroleum boom delays reform Economic crises, 1982, 1985 A liberalizing corporatist/clientelist regime
⸱rge number, loose structure, with World Bank penetrating state and providing essential technical and financial support	Controlled by radical technocrats Hierarchical, tightly integrated Important in spread of policy ideas and financial and technical support
⸱oderate leverage with United States, whose support for heterodoxy delays re- form but spurs relationship with World Bank, which pushes reform	Importance to United States gives special leverage with World Bank Domestic reformers determine pace; ignore advice they do not like
⸱ti–status quo politicians and technocrats (1991ff.), conglomerates; collaborative trade union leaders ⸱erarchy in technocratic network	Technocrats dominate core and networks Hierarchical, integrated Finance Ministry hegemonic Big conglomerates
⸱dest array of methods: selective and uni- versal compensatory rewards; corporatist ⸱control; negotiation with collaborative faction, concessions	Corporatist mechanisms Targeted clientelism Political liberalization Post-1995 ceases labor repression Militarization of countryside
⸱st important and largest public enter- ⸱prises privatized quickly and immediately ⸱gh degree of corruption ⸱or flexibilization stalled ⸱mpromises on social security and reform ⸱of social funds ⸱de liberalization completed quickly ⸱o tied to dollar (Convertibility Plan)	Privatization starts with small, unimportant firms; moves into strategic firms after 1989 De facto labor flexibilization Compromise on social security reform Delay in devaluation worsens 1994–95 peso crisis Post-1995 attempt at further privatization in key sectors blocked Trade liberalization completed quickly, NAFTA

factors were also important determinants of what parts of a reform agenda went forward, how quickly, and what parts become stalled or blocked.

In Chile, the combination of a weak but militant labor movement and a military regime without ties to societal groups created a situation in which the political obstacles to reform were considerably less than was the case for Argentina. In the latter case, labor, which had a long tradition of collaboration with a variety of different regimes, including military ones, represented an insurmountable obstacle to market reform for many years. The Argentine military, with its vested interests in state industry, also blocked reform. In Chile, in contrast, the personalist control that Pinochet was able to establish, particularly over the army, kept the military from blocking the process in the way the Argentine military did. In Mexico, the bonanza of the petroleum boom years, in combination with a long-standing statist tradition, delayed consideration of reform until the mid-1980s.

In all cases, the market reform policy process was a highly concentrated activity, invariably resting in the hands of a small policy elite (core) from whom policy networks spanned outward, incorporating domestic actors who closely collaborated in the market reform project—usually powerful members of the private sector. The exception was Argentina, where policy networks also included a group of collaborative trade unionists. The arena in which market reform ideas and interests interacted in the formulation of policy was the highly personalistic policy network. As in no other period in Latin American history, policy ideas advocated by radical technocratic reformers came to play a central role in economic policy making, but the impact of powerful societal and intrastate interests continued to be felt and in tempering market reform ideas often determined the extent of market reform accomplishments. Bound by personal relationships of loyalty, trust, and often personal friendships, policy networks are where policy ideas, vested interests, and political calculations interact and are translated into policy outcome.

Often, policy actors advocating market reform ideas took the risk of pursing policies contrary to the wishes of their extrastate allies and broader electoral constituencies. In Chile, for example, privatization of strategic public companies went forward after 1985 despite stiff resistance from the military because Pinochet had been personally won over in a tightly knit, highly integrated policy network, involving himself and the Chicago technocrats. Rapid trade liberalization is probably the best example in which policy elites, convinced of a policy idea, isolated themselves momentarily from their broader support base in the private sector and pushed reform forward. The PRI had private sector backing in 1985 and yet moved decisively to implement trade liberalization even though the private sector was either opposed or reticent. The same was true for Argentina under Menem in 1989. Clearly, ideas, specifically market reform ideas held by key actors in the policy elite and in policy networks, played a powerful role in policy reform and, at times, were able to override the wishes of societal groups who were part of ruling or broader support coalitions. At other times, market ideas coincided with the wishes of vested interests incorporated into policy networks. This was the case for all privatization programs in which the technocrats' wish to privatize coincided with the desire of private sector interests to acquire public companies. In this way, individuals incorporated into policy networks succeeded in blocking or altering reform policies in ways beneficial to their personal interests or to the interests of their group. The Chilean military's resistance to the privatization of major public companies blocked progress in this area until after 1985. The incorporation of a collaborative group of labor leaders into policy networks in Argentina stalled labor flexibilization and affected social security reform.

Probably the most striking similarity among the three cases is the access of the owners/executives of very powerful conglomerates to the economic policy process—an access and an influence unmatched by any other social group. The attitude and behavior of the private sector at the early stages of market reform were ambivalent and even outright hostile. While virtually all factions of the private sector, even the owners and executives of the big conglomerates, opposed rapid and radical trade liberalization, most members of the private sector were nevertheless antistatist and thus strongly supportive of the state's withdrawal from the economy in other respects. Hence once the initial and difficult phase of trade liberalization was complete, many of those businessmen who survived the experience became increasingly amenable to subsequent market reforms.[1] This was especially true for the owners and executives of the biggest conglomerates, who were in the best position to take advantage of the opportunities afforded by the new economic model, particularly in the areas of export promotion and the opportunity to purchase state companies. Moreover, as policy makers opened up channels of communication to the private sector, powerful private sector actors seized the opportunity to influence policy. This meant pushing for a market reform agenda in tune with their particular economic interests. The result was privatization programs that, whether originally intended or not, secured powerful private allies for the policy core.[2]

Although institutionalized channels to policy makers were certainly present, personal access and personal institutional relationships between businessmen and policy makers were a predominant feature of the process in all cases. This situation usually emerged fairly soon after the launching of radical reforms (1975 in Chile, around 1988–89 in Mexico, and the early 1990s in Argentina). In Chile, particularly between 1975 and 1982, and in Argentina and Mexico by the early 1990s, big conglomerates, with the greatest influence on policy, were also the major beneficiaries of the new economic programs, buying up public companies, taking advantage of new export promotion programs, and often extracting monopoly profits. Even where institutionalized channels were present, the relationships between private sector leaders and state managers remained highly personal. The impact of the participation of big business in market reform and in economic policy making more generally has been substantial. Political pressure from powerful conglomerates was probably important in delaying devaluation in Chile and Mexico, thereby making their economic crises worse than they otherwise would have been. In Mexico and Argentina private sector involvement in privatization produced nontransparent privatization programs and blocked effective regulatory measures thereafter. In Mexico, in addition to delaying the opening of the financial and service sectors to foreign investment, the privileged access of the private sector to policy produced a costly bank rescue program with unequal benefits. In Argentina, the private sector has been the most intimately involved in policy making, even participating in the drafting of privatization bills and regulatory frameworks. After the return to civilian rule in Chile, with a coalition alliance of Christian Democrats and socialists in power, the private sector has privileged and personalized access to the highest reaches of political power and has been successful in influencing market reform policy in important ways, particularly in pushing for privatization and in slowing down reforms that would restore some of the lost labor rights. As we saw, this skewed access to policy and its consequences triggered rank-and-file socialist and trade union unrest in the 1990s and may undermine the legitimacy of formal democratic institutions.

Latin American policy networks have distinguishing features that reflect their historical context, particularly the Iberian strain of the heritage. Market reform policy networks echo the predisposition to centralize and personalize political authority and to accord wide discretion in decision making. Policy networks usually involve strong personal loyalty to policy leadership figures. Although policy networks have or acquire an institutional basis, they are nevertheless informal groupings that tend to have their origins, at least in part, outside of the state in individuals with long histories of personal interaction in shared educational and other experiences. Personalism became important as an organizing principle because of its effectiveness in winning and keeping converts to reform, in organizing power, and in concentrating it. Concentration of power, as indicated in Chapter 1, is widely recognized as a key element of the process. In the market reform era, personal trust and loyalty are reinforced by strong policy goal commitment, a combination that helps to ensure commitment to policy goals and keep reform on track. Indeed, certain aspects of the Latin American political tradition have been highly miscible with a technocratic modus operandi that required the opportunity to educate and persuade through ongoing personal interaction and demanded unwavering policy commitment.

Nevertheless, the specific features of these policy networks depended heavily on the political conditions in which they arose and operated. The more authoritarian the regime, the more hierarchical, closed, and fewer were the policy networks. Chile under military rule, especially during its earliest years, was characterized by the most tightly intertwined, hierarchical, and closed networks—networks that bore the imprint of the resurgence of the country's Iberian strain during this period and the repressive nature of military rule. As the system liberalized and finally returned to civilian rule, policy networks were opened to a wider array of private sector and state bureaucratic participants, although labor continued to be pretty much excluded. At the other extreme, Argentina, under an electoral democracy and despite the heavy concentration of power in the executive and the use of presidential decree powers, was characterized by a myriad of policy networks extending from state into society, involving intrastate supporters of reform, powerful private sector participants, and collaborationist trade unionists. Mexican policy networks, during the heyday of market reform, reflected the country's authoritarian political arrangements. Mexican networks were closer to the Chilean case (under military rule) in terms of the concentration of power in the policy core and the tightness, number, and hierarchical nature of policy networks. They were highly selective, incorporating only powerful conglomerate owners within their ranks. Although the basic character of Mexican policy networks has not yet altered in the face of greater democratization, their ability to resist changes to policy has declined.

Technocrats had important roles in all cases, but the nature and extent of that role differed from country to country. While technocrats dominated the process from the beginning in Mexico, in Chile, technocratic power was tempered by the military, in the person of General Pinochet, and by its dependence on important allies in the political right. In Argentina, technocrats entered the picture in an important way only after significant reforms had already been initiated, and they remained heavily dependent on the caudillo political leadership of President Carlos Menem to prevent meddling by other cabinet members in their reforms. In all cases, technocrats were important conduits for policy reform ideas, working to convince political leaders and other technocrats and bureaucrats in the state of the new policy line. With the exception of Chilean technocrats after the return to civilian rule, technocrats were also important interlocutors between the state and multilateral lending institutions, a role that opened their states to outside policy ideas and pressures.

In all the cases, the dominant economic policy reform network was controlled by technocrats and remained lodged in the ministry responsible for macroeconomic policy, which was also the ministry with the closest and ongoing relationship with multilateral lending institutions. Finance Ministry technocrats have been dominant in Chile since 1989 under civilian rule, even though the foreign debt is no longer an issue and Chile lacks the ongoing policy networks with the multilaterals that the other two countries maintain. In the Chilean case, important institutional features inherited from the period of military rule are no doubt important in accounting for this situation, especially the 1975 military law giving the Finance Ministry power over any and all matters having financial implications. But this is not the whole story, as evidenced by the increasing influence of the Finance Ministry in recent years. Especially in Chile and in Mexico, the Finance Ministry plays a dominant role, not just defining economic policy but weighing in heavily in other areas of public policy such as social policy. In Argentina, where the weight of the Economy Ministry's technocrats (Argentina's equivalent to the Finance Ministry in the other two countries) has been relatively less, their power was more effectively challenged by other intrastate actors, particularly cabinet ministers. Nevertheless, between 1991 and 1996, market reform technocrats pretty much defined the direction of economic and public policy.

In all cases, the initial phase of reform was led by radical market reform elites who were individuals not closely integrated with mainstream societal groups or political parties — military men, technocrats, or politicos who were not tied to existing vested interests. The term "antielite" has been used with reference to Argentina's market reform political leadership but is also useful with reference to the other cases. The Chilean military lacked ties to outside groups, and the Chicago boys' attempts at forming an alliance with the private sector faltered in the face of private sector resistance to trade liberalization. The initiators of Argentina's market reform were politicos from the outlying provinces—people without strong historical ties to organized labor and the private sector—pragmatists not wedded to any particular set of political or economic ideas. Mexico's most radical market reformers were "young Turks" recently returned to the country with graduate degrees from American universities, individuals without prior political experience and therefore not answerable to important sectoral interests. This relative segregation emboldened market reformers to stand up to the private sector in the initial trade liberalization drive and override labor in restructuring and privatization of public enterprise.

The democratic propensities of technocrats varied substantially from country to country. In all cases, technocrats worked toward means to achieve policy isolation but with varying degrees of zealousness and with disparate political methods. In all cases, protection of the integrity of their reform programs took precedence over issues of substantive democracy. Consultation with a broad cross section of social groups, allowing all important societal groups access to the policy process, and consensus building were not features of market reform, even in the case of post-1989 Chile, where technocrats generally showed great respect for democratic deliberative mechanisms. Technocratic behavior in each of the countries was very much a reflection of the broader national political context, culture, and practices in which technocrats were operating. In Chile under military rule, the Chicago boys had no compunction about the use of the repressive apparatus of the state and were grateful that they had it at their disposal. In Mexico, the technocratic leaders under Carlos Salinas did not hesitate to use their country's nondemocratic corporatist/clientelist political arrangements to push market reform forward. Nor were Mexican authorities reluctant to manipulate the legal mechanisms available in the labor code to force reluctant trade unions into submission. More repressive tactics, such as the occupation of companies by the military or the police and the arrest and imprisonment of labor leaders, were employed as circumstances dictated. In Argentina, technocrats fiercely resisted congressional tampering with their policy initiatives, tried to avoid consultation with all except the most powerful business interests, and supported the use of presidential decree powers to bypass congressional participation in policy formulation.

Moreover, in Mexico and Argentina, technocrats who participated in the heyday of market reform have been tainted with the corrupt practices that have been a predominant part of the process in their countries.

At the same time, however, technocrats have shown themselves to be enormously pragmatic and imminently adaptable to new political realities. The most notable example is the case of Mexico, where the 1995–2000 technocratic leadership, under strong pressure from its own party and from the public more generally, allowed, if it did not encourage, the formal democratization process to go forward. It presided over the democratization of its own party, oversaw electoral reforms that resulted in it losing office, and acquiesced in opposition changes to its economic reform proposals in the areas of privatization and social security reform. It was not happy about the process but adapted. In Argentina, former economy minister Domingo Cavallo, after being forced out of that position, reentered the political fray as the presidential candidate in the 1999 elections and identified the country's main problems as recession and unemployment (*Latin American Weekly Report*, July 27, 1999, 338). While technocrats can be expected to do their best to prevent interference in their reforms, they will likely conform to a broader societal consensus supportive of policy change and democratic deliberative mechanisms if these are present.

The nature of opposition to market reform has also been key in determining its content. The relative weakness of Chilean labor made possible early labor flexibilization and thoroughgoing reform in areas such as social security and health that were of direct interest to workers. The one area where reform lagged in Argentina is labor flexibilization, precisely because of the continued political strength of the labor movement and a political strategy that accorded the access of a fraction of it to market reform policy networks. Mexico, with a one-party-dominant corporatist/clientelist regime until the mid-1990s, was able to achieve greater success in de facto labor flexibilization than did Argentina because of its stronger mechanisms of corporatist/clientelist control and relatively weaker labor movement.

The differences in the reform experiences of the three cases also involved important differences in style. Chile's market reform process, especially its privatization drive since 1989, stands out for its lack of corruption when compared with the Mexican and Argentine cases. It is tempting to lay the blame for corruption in the privatization process on the centralization of power in the executive, on the extent of executive discretionary decision making, and on the personalized and privileged access of big business to key policy makers. Although factors such as these are probably important ingredients in explaining the Mexican and Argentine cases and the Chilean experience under military rule, they are probably not sufficient explanations for post-1989 Chile given the continued personal access of business to the policy elite. Chile's relatively clean privatization process might be partially explained by the fact that the state's relations with the private sector are more "embedded," to use Evans's term, that is, more institutionalized than in the other two cases. The widest array of institutionalized channels would appear to exist in the Chilean case. One well-known explanation of corruption is that it is part of the leadership's strategy to thwart and contain potential political opponents—an important part of a "political survival" strategy (Migdal 1988, 171–237). This tactic emerges most clearly in the Argentine case. Chile's post-1989 civilian government was in less need of such a strategy because the most politically costly aspects of market reform, such as trade liberalization and labor flexibilization, had been completed by the military regime. Business confidence could be successfully maintained by leaving the economic model in place, particularly the very flexible labor regime, rendering it unnecessary for the Chilean policy elite to provide compensatory measures, in the form of monopoly profits from privatized companies, to ensure support from powerful members of the private sector actors for a new economic model.

But it is also useful to consider the historical context of Chilean politics. In the premilitary era (before 1973), the Iberian impulse had a considerably lower profile in Chile, where there was a greater reliance on institutionalized competitive party politics. In Chile, unlike Argentina and Mexico, there had never been widespread acceptance of clientelist mechanisms as means to contain or reduce popular demands. Nor was corruption a major feature of the relationship between the government and the private sector. Generalized use of clientelistic practices provides fertile ground for corruption because it establishes the expectation that material rewards dispensed by the state or party will be exchanged for political support. The distribution of government largesse to maintain the support of the private sector was not among the civilian Chilean political elite's arsenal of political practices. In Argentina, in contrast, privatization was carried out by a patrimonial leader and his personal loyalists, all of whom exercised wide discretion in the manipulation of tenders, producing a policy outcome in which beneficiaries were conglomerates with close political ties to the regime. The Mexican situation under President Carlos Salinas was strikingly similar.

THE INTERNATIONAL DIMENSION: THE DEBT AND THE
NEW INTERNATIONAL POLICY CULTURE

The important changes in economic organization that have occurred in Latin America since the mid-1980s cannot be separated from the phenomenon of globalization and the new international policy culture that has called for greater reliance on the market. Change in the international policy culture was the most important external factor patterning the direction of policy change. There were a variety of ways in which new policy ideas were conveyed to domestic policy makers. The training of Latin Americans abroad, especially in U.S. universities throughout the 1970s, was the earliest means by which Latin Americans were brought into contact with the new international policy culture. In Latin America's first case of market reform, Chileans began to be trained in market ideas at the University of Chicago in the 1950s, returning home eventually to lead the region's earliest market reform experiment. In other cases, many of those trained abroad became key initiators of their countries' market reform programs by the mid-1980s. Such individuals were usually deeply involved in persuading political leaders and other state bureaucrats of the efficacy of market reform measures.

Most Latin American countries had many years of experience with the World Bank and the International Monetary Fund when the debt crisis broke. Most had, at one time or another, attempted IMF stabilization policies involving many of the measures that would come to constitute structural reform programs, such as trade liberalization, improvements in the efficiency of public companies, and cutbacks in government expenditures. The 1982 debt crisis, however, triggered a process that would see the IMF and the World Bank involved in Latin American policy as never before. But it was not conditional lending that was the key external mechanism in encouraging policy reform. As elsewhere in the developing world, explicit policy conditionality attached to loans was not successful in inducing policy change on the part of Latin American governments. Rather, it was by means of the more subtle process of policy discussion, a process that involved the development of international policy networks, groupings of multilateral and domestic officials who discussed policy reform and developed reform programs. International policy networks exhibited the same basic features as domestic policy networks. Personal relationships — trust, loyalty, and even friendship — bound the client and multilateral participants together. Indeed, some participants had even developed friendships during years of training at American universities. And while many of these personal relationships were between technocrats, trained in the same discipline and at the same institutions, this was not universally the case. Close collaborative relationships also bound technocrats and nontechnocrats in international policy networks. The construction of international policy networks between the World Bank and domestic policy makers—the locus that became so important in the transmission of policy ideas and in the development of market reform programs—was not a chance development, however. An explicit change of policy in the Latin American and Caribbean Regional Division (LAC) of the World Bank encouraged LAC officials to cultivate personal relationships of trust with the officials of client countries. LAC officials pursued this new policy direction with enthusiasm and success. They spoke Spanish, personally liked the people and the countries in which they were involved, and were committed to a reform agenda.

International policy networks did not effectively come into play until the incentive structure for market reform had changed substantially. As we saw in Chapter 3, attitudes toward market reform by international actors changed over time as did the incentives for implementing market reform. Between 1982 and 1985, since priority was given to the stability of the international financial system, negative transfers from debtors occurred. This sort of harsh adjustment offered little incentive to reform, reinforcing domestic resistance. Moreover, before 1985, within the World Bank, and particularly the LAC section, there were still officials who were not averse to the old statist model. Beginning in 1985, and certainly by 1989, however, this situation had changed dramatically. Not only was the LAC section solidly behind market reform, but under Brady, debt relief provided another boost to domestic advocates of reform. Only in Chile, for the peculiar domestic and geopolitical reasons explained in Chapter 4, did harsh austerity and radical market reform go forward simultaneously in 1985. Further, as the international policy culture became increasingly radical from the late 1980s onward, later reformers, such as Argentina, came under the influence of this more radical thinking.

Although the most important ongoing policy networks developed between client countries were with the World Bank, the International Monetary Fund's role was often crucial in inducing reform insofar as domestic policy actors believed that they could meet the IMF's demand for deficit reduction only through a radical privatization program. Moreover, in two of the cases (Chile and Mexico) important macroeconomic policy networks closely involved IMF officials. But in general, discussions between domestic and IMF officials did not display the features of trust, loyalty, and friendship of those between World Bank and domestic country networks.

International policy networks played a crucial role in market reform in all three of the case studies. While training abroad provided an important avenue of entry for the new international policy culture, by itself it could not have spread these ideas as effectively and as quickly as it did when it was supported by international actors. Radical reformers used the arguments developed in discussions with their international partners and jointly written reports to win supporters and defeat resisters in their respective states. Mexico made explicit use of international policy network discussions to convince intrabureaucratic resisters of the efficacy of the market in the area of agricultural reform. In the Argentine case, international policy networks with the World Bank were the most extensive of the three cases, permeating deep into the Argentine state, where international actors and domestic supporters of privatization spread the new market reform ideas. Even in the Chilean case, the one widely regarded as a case of domestically directed reform, an international policy network was key in keeping market reforms on track when the financial collapse of the early 1980s thrust into power policy makers who wanted a return to a more statist model.

Argentina was the most obvious case of direct pressure by the World Bank and the IMF for trade liberalizations and, especially, for the privatization of major state companies, and this pressure unquestionably played a key role. By 1989, faced with an almost complete absence of international confidence in the country's commitment to policy change and in dire need of financial support, Argentine policy makers felt they had no choice but to follow World Bank and IMF urging and make a dramatic gesture in the form of the privatization of major public companies. One of the most important contributions of World Bank participation in policy development was the provision of technical support. This was especially crucial in Argentina, where state technological capacity was considerably less than in the other two countries, especially at the beginning of the process. But even in the Mexican case, World Bank technical knowledge and financial support helped privatizations to go forward. World Bank/country policy networks have continued to influence a variety of second-stage reforms, including antipoverty programs and decentralization in Mexico and Argentina.

Geopolitical factors were important determinants of the maneuverability of policy elites and therefore could influence calculations of the cost of resisting reforms. Mexico's ability to bring pressure from the U.S. administration and senior World Bank officials to bear on its discussions with LAC bank officials caused LAC officials to handle Mexico with care and not to push in policy areas in which it sensed there might be resistance, a restraint it did not practice with Argentina. Hence Mexico's reform process followed a pace pretty much dictated by its radical reformers, and it was able to protect key areas such as petroleum and, until recently, the financial sector from pressures to allow foreign investment. Following the return to civilian rule, the Argentine leadership balked at policy reform, and during this period Argentina benefited from the U.S. desire to ensure democratic stability in the country. As a consequence, the United States pushed the IMF to support a less severe heterodox program and later lobbied for World Bank lending to Argentina once the IMF had withdrawn in the face of Argentina's failure to meet performance criteria. This situation allowed Argentina a breathing space during which it was able to avoid structural adjustment. Unlike its handling of the Mexicans, however, the World Bank exhibited little reticence in pushing hard for reforms (trade liberalization and privatization) it thought important, a mode of operating that would bear fruit once the opportunity arose in 1989. Meanwhile, the viewpoint of Chilean radical reformers that only the position of model debtor could afford Chile the international support it required, combined with their predisposition to radical measures, was reinforced by the World Bank's use of Chile's problematic human rights situation as leverage to demand an orthodox program.

Because of geopolitical differences and also because of important differences in domestic political arrangements, the operation of international policy networks differed between countries. The more authoritarian political arrangements in Mexico, combined with the greater international clout of the Mexicans, allowed Mexican officials to use international policy networks to achieve their own policy goals and to determine in what policy areas and to what extent international policy networks would be involved. This situation lasted into the early 1990s. In Argentina, in contrast, the policy elite made no attempt to control the activities of international policy networks that rapidly spread into Argentine state and society, where they worked to build up constituencies for reform.

While the role and impact of international factors, particularly international policy networks, differed among the three cases, there is no question that this role was important. While the right combination of domestic factors was necessary before market reform could go forward, it would not have had the same momentum without this international support. International policy networks played important roles in developing support for policy change in countries, in developing reform programs, and in providing essential technical and financial support. But there was a great deal in market reform programs that international actors, particularly the World Bank, could not influence. The bank was usually not able to determine the implementation of privatization decisions, and often its views were ignored in the establishment of regulatory frameworks. Here the private sector side of policy networks often had a determining impact and would sometimes conflict with the bank's recommendations.

DEMOCRACY AND THE CHALLENGES OF SECOND-STAGE REFORM

The initial period of market reform during which trade liberalization was carried out and the majority of public enterprises privatized has generally been an exclusionary experience, in which policy elites have tried to shield their reforms from opposition tampering and have ridden roughshod over opposition critics. But the extent of public exclusion from the process has varied markedly from country to country and over time. Further, it is during the initial period of reform that the harshest measures are used to manage opposition, particularly trade union opposition. While political repression was the key feature of opposition management during the initial reformist thrust in Chile, the heyday of Mexican reform was characterized by the use of the country's traditional corporatist mechanisms of political control directed against trade union opposition, the implementation of a more electorally focused form of clientelism, with state repression as a last resort. Argentina's electoral democracy featured the widespread use of presidential decree powers, patrimonial practices to maintain the loyalty of state and extrastate actors, the manipulation of corporatist arrangements, and loyalty engendered by charismatic leadership appeal. In the one case in which Congress had an important role to play in early stage reform (Argentina), the radical market reform leadership consistently attempted either to bypass it or (later on) to threaten it into submission. Concerns and criticisms within ruling parties (the Peronist and the PRI) were ignored and suppressed. In this context, opposition criticism of government policy could be and was generally ignored.

It is important to recognize that this process was more than anything else a highly political struggle, one in which there were indeed winners and losers. Market reform was never carried out fully; rather, it went forth piecemeal, often in accordance with which groups were able to protect their interests and expand their wealth and which ones were not. The evidence from this study contradicts the notion that market reform generates opposition from privileged vested interests while its beneficiaries, a diffuse cross section of the public, remain silent. In fact, the biggest winners of the initial period of reform were the powerful conglomerate owners who bought up public firms, took advantage of new export opportunities, and acquired privileged and personal access to the highest reaches of political power. They regularly joined their political leaders on jaunts to negotiate new free trade agreements and made exorbitant campaign contributions. The losers were not simply those who had benefited from the earlier import-substitution phase. Among workers, the losers in Mexico were not just corrupt charro union leaders but rather corrupt, noncooperative charros and rank-and-file workers who lost their jobs or experienced declines in real salaries (Appendix 2, Tables A.3 and A.4). Indeed, the biggest losers in Mexico were poor peasants in south and southeastern Mexico (Lustig 1998, 204), who lost their access to state technical support and subsidies, support they desperately needed, even though it had political strings attached. Violent political unrest in Mexico, particularly the rise of the Zapatistas in Chiapas, although stemming from a long history of inequality and oppression, was, in part, a consequence of these recent policy changes. In Argentina, the losers during market reform were not just corrupt trade union leaders (indeed, if they were truly corrupt, they were able to look after their own economic interests by siding with President Menem) but also workers who lost their jobs in record numbers and saw their real industrial wages stagnate (Appendix 2, Tables A.3 and A.4). In Chile's first phase of reform under military rule, the drop in employment was draconian while real industrial wages fell (Appendix 2, Tables A.3 and A.4). In this sense, the undemocratic features of the process ensured the implementation of market reform's skewed distribution of benefits and losses.

Policy networks, informal groupings based on personal ties that do not necessarily coincide with formal state policy-making bodies, are antithetical to some of the basic premises of substantive democracy: namely, accountability and universality. True, policy networks are at their most hierarchical and exclusionary in authoritarian regimes, but even in electoral democracies they operate to exclude wide public debate and input on public policy issues, and it is difficult to hold them accountable, particularly if they involve extrastate (multilateral and private sector) actors. Equally important, they are not simply artifacts of the zealous power concentration required by first-stage reform. As the case of postmilitary Chile illustrates, they also operate at the highest levels involving democratically elected authorities with a commitment to social justice.

As I have argued, international policy networks have played an important role in policy reform. There is no question that institutions such as the World Bank and the International Monetary Fund have clear policy priorities that they wish to see implemented in specific countries. The discussions that occur in international policy networks and, more important, the specific policy reforms advocated by such institutions as the World Bank for specific countries—privatizations, social security and health reform, poverty policy, labor flexibilization, decentralization—have not been presented for public or parliamentary debate in the countries for which they have been advocated. In general, the process by which international policy networks have carried out their deliberations has been a closed and secretive one. In most cases, policy elites presented projects funded by the World Bank as their own, revealing nothing about the discussion that went on in international policy networks beforehand. In short, the policy influence of multilaterals is very real, but its nature and extent are hidden from public scrutiny or debate. It may be, however, that given the high degree of integration between domestic technocratic policy elites and World Bank and IMF officials, as described in Chapter 3, it has now become difficult to distinguish between ideas generated in the domestic policy milieu and those generated in Washington.[3]

To have public knowledge and debates about the issues raised in international policy networks is important for many reasons. As I have shown, there are situations in which the position of multilateral officials would have bolstered the critics of policies favored by radical reformers. The World Bank's concern for transparency in the implementation of privatization and its concerns about the bank rescues in both Chile and Mexico are cases in which a more public airing of international network discussions might have forced domestic policy makers into different policy outcomes. As it stands, although most exaggerated in the case of Mexico, in general, reformers often ignore World Bank advice they do not like. On the other hand, the bank's favorite antipoverty strategy, involving programs targeted to extreme poverty, is one that many Mexicans, especially in the Ministry of Social Development, oppose. And yet these bureaucrats did not have an opportunity to engage World Bank officials in a "dialogue" over the issues at stake. Dialogue with a broader range of societal groups might enlighten bank officials and cause them to modify policy advice, producing ultimately different policy outcomes. The bank is understandably timid about what would be regarded as meddling in the internal domestic politics of client countries, but nevertheless it has begun to speak to organizations outside of the government about its programs (interviews with two senior LAC officials).[4] There are obvious concerns, however, about alienating domestic policy elites and breaking the trust that has become so important to policy influence. Not to hold a dialogue with a broader cross section of society, however, renders the process secretive and unaccountable and can have ultimately negative implications for policy success.[5]

Market reform has given rise to growing domestic criticism and ultimately to a growing electoral opposition for two reasons. In Mexico and Argentina, the public's perception is that market reform has not ensured sustained economic growth and reduced poverty and inequality. The disillusionment with market reform is certainly greater in Mexico, where the financial crisis of 1994–95 was followed by the continuing negative impacts of the Asian and Brazilian crises, events reflected in Mexico's markedly lower per capita growth rate (Appendix 2, Table A.1). Nevertheless, the continuation of high unemployment in Argentina became a source of growing concern among the opposition. Furthermore, in addition to the failure of market reform to deliver prosperity, there is the political fallout from the way in which reforms, especially privatizations, were carried out. In both countries, market reform in general, and privatization in particular, has become associated with a corrupt process that created costly monopolies, concentrated wealth, and lined the pockets of corrupt political leaders and their cronies. In Mexico, the traditional methods of corporatist and clientelist political control used to impose restructurings and privatizations unraveled in the face of their growing failure to deliver a minimal level of benefits to rank and file and leaderships. Indeed, Mexican labor leaders have increasingly moved to establish organizations autonomous from both the government and the party. In Argentina, opposition parties and the Peronist Party eventually began to balk at the executive's high-handed approach, discretionary decision making, and corrupt practices. Both the PRI and the Peronist Party have witnessed the rise in opposition currents within their ranks. The ultimate reflection of this growing public disillusionment occurred in 2000 with the defeat of the PRI presidential candidate, while the Peronist Party was ousted from power in 1999. Repulsed by the way market reform was carried out and disappointed at its results, the public registered its dissatisfaction at the polls.

Given that, especially in the case in Mexico, but perhaps also in the case of Argentina, old mechanisms of opposition containment such as clientelism, corporatism, and patrimonialism have been discredited because of their involvement in implementing market reform, it is important to consider the

implications of electoral politics when such means of political incorporation are absent. Indeed, Chile under Concertación (minus the authoritarian
enclaves inherited from the military regime) is the archetypical case of competitive, pluralist electoral politics. But even here, the ruling party coalition,
one clearly committed to social justice, sports policy networks that are only
selectively penetrated and that, as I have shown, have resisted input from a
broad cross section of societal groups, including militants in Concertación.
It is important to explore why this has occurred.

Chile under the Concertación was saddled with a variety of impediments
that restricted the operation of its democratic institutions (see Chapter 4).
Although these arrangements certainly imposed restrictions on policy, I
have suggested that in fact Chile is a country in which enormous power
rests in the hands of the executive. The economic policy core and the dominant economic policy network lodged in the Ministry of Finance have been
resistant to demands for policy alterations coming from rank-and-file socialists in the Concertación, from the trade union movement, and from
technocrats in other ministries, such as the Ministry of Planning, who want
a more concerted and integrated approach to poverty reduction. There is
also resistance from powerful members of the private sector to these sorts
of policy alterations.

The Concertación leadership has claimed that it is committed to both
the maintenance of the main features of the neoliberal model and to the
reduction of poverty and inequality. Indeed, with regard to the former it
has made important progress. Wage rates have increased since 1990 (Appendix 2, Table A.4), and the proportion of the population living in poverty has
dropped. But inequality has not changed and remains not much better than
Mexico's while the country's labor code remains highly flexible.[6] Furthermore, while social expenditure accounts for a substantial portion of total
government expenditure, its proportion of GDP has not been increasing
since 1993, and it remains below its 1970 level. However, the public treasury was in surplus until 1996 (Appendix 2, Table A.2).[7] As argued in Chapter 4, the leaders' failure to move more aggressively on labor reform and on
poverty reduction is reflected in the skewed nature of policy networks—
arrangements that give privileged access and consideration to the private
sector while resisting policy input from other social groups.

The policy elite has held a firm consensus that the first priority is the
state's fiscal health. Under Eduardo Frei, macroeconomic policy making became more concentrated and insulated than it was under the Concertación
during the earlier presidency of Patricio Alywin. Furthermore, the concern

of Chilean policy makers about pressures for increased spending mounted over time. The preoccupation with this issue, however, does not spring just from an ideological commitment to certain economic principles but rather (and probably more so) from pressures that the new global economic and market reform place on political leaders. In truth, these pressures are not new; they are just greater. Once having made the transformation from statism to a greater reliance on the market, the logic of the new economic arrangements mightily constrains policy choice. Power concentration in the executive and resistance to tampering with policy tend to be reinforced by an economic reality that dictates that the most important actors in the struggle for global competitiveness be accorded a privileged place in policy influence — that is, the powerful conglomerates involved in exporting. Indeed, Latin American countries must maintain both international and domestic business confidence in order to ensure a healthy rate of investment, both domestic and foreign, and to avoid the capital flight that can so quickly send their economies into an economic tailspin. The maintenance of domestic business confidence involves a careful watch over public spending (usually expressed as resistance to populist pressures for social spending that the country cannot afford), the avoidance of tax increases on the private sector, privatization of any companies remaining in state hands, and measures increasing labor flexibilization (and certainly the avoidance of measures that would reduce labor flexibility). Not surprisingly, policy elites are likely to resist pressure from societal groups demanding policies whose implementation could threaten both national and international business confidence.

This context, so very sensitive to business confidence, encourages policy elites to maintain and even expand privileged channels of policy consultation to a greater extent than in the past. Indeed, businessmen under Zedillo in Mexico and under the Concertación (Frei) in Chile reported greater access to the policy process than under previous administrations. To maintain investment, trade, and growth, policy elites are compelled to maintain what they view to be a prudent economic policy, which in practice has meant the resistance of policy networks to groups whose demands might jeopardize business confidence. In countries where personalism, wide discretionary decision making, and various forms of cronyism have been the norm, this privileged access to policy will be difficult to monitor or mitigate.

The attempt by the Concertación to balance the demands for business confidence against the demands for social justice from its own parties reflects the dilemma faced by policy elites, even ones with the best of intentions. The failure to satisfy socialist rank-and-file members and trade unionists generated sufficient pressure to secure a socialist leadership candidate. The Concertación government must not ignore the growing concerns of its socialist and trade union ranks, but neither can it ignore its powerful private sector. Chile is perhaps an exception in the longevity of its private sector's privileged policy position and in the extent and duration of labor flexibilization. Perhaps the Chilean private sector cannot be expected to make even minor concessions easily. Moreover, Chile is still in the process of overcoming political polarization between left and right. There may indeed be considerably more maneuverability in countries accustomed to a greater degree of negotiation with labor. Of the three cases, however, only Argentina, widely criticized for its slowness in adopting labor flexibility, has really negotiated with labor leaders, and even so, only a faction of them.

Electoral politics has the potential to revise reform agendas in important ways. In Mexico, Congress has already taken important steps to make the executive more accountable for reform measures, particularly privatizations. In Argentina, we do not know as yet what the impact will be for sure, but if the new government responds to the public disgust for past government practices, there may well be changes that ensure greater accountability and transparency. The difficulty, however, is that the private sector beneficiaries of market reform now have enormous economic power. In both Argentina and Mexico, powerful conglomerates have captured the regulatory boards that are supposed to ensure fair practices and competition. These arrangements are difficult to break down; even if political leaders muster the drive to reduce the market power of powerful private sector interests, they must expect stiff and even successful resistance. The demand for poverty reduction and a decrease in inequality is another area where private sector resistance, in the form of a preoccupation with populist expansionary pressures, can block governments committed to change. The private sector is overwhelmingly concerned with the fiscal health of government finances, but it is also fiercely resistant to tax increases, which are necessary if countries are to address social issues without increasing the deficit.

The difficult initial phase of market reform bequeaths a variety of problems—poverty, inequality, regulatory issues, privatization, and tax reform, among others. Publics and their political leaderships, in the three countries dealt with here, are by no means agreed about the nature of such problems, their sources, their relative priority, or their solutions. The challenges of second-stage reform are therefore overwhelmingly political. The challenge is to work out solutions to these policy problems which both the enthusiasts of market reform and its detractors can live with.[8] The differences in policy positions, however, have become glaringly apparent. In Mexico, for example, the leftist opposition parties, trade unions, and rank-and-file PRI congressmen have opposed further privatization, while the newly elected PAN president and his party, state technocrats, and the private sector wish to move more decisively in this direction. The public wants rules that ensure competition, but big business is resistant. The technocratic elite and its World Bank allies support an antipoverty program that targets extreme poverty, but the social welfare bureaucracy and the major left political party want more social welfare spending and a more broadly directed program.[9] In Chile, labor wants changes in the labor laws to allow it greater leeway to fight for improvements, while business is fiercely opposed to any such changes and in fact is pushing for even more labor flexibilization. Groups in the public bureaucracy and in the Concertación want more emphasis on measures to reduce inequality and reduce poverty; in fact, social welfare bureaucrats within the state want a qualitatively different type of antipoverty program—one that takes an integral approach rather than focusing on one issue, such as education. Many Concertación stalwarts want to increase spending on social welfare, but this is resisted by the private sector. In Argentina, labor flexibilization was seen as the most important policy priority of second-stage reform by the private sector and by the World Bank and the IMF—a policy that was fiercely resisted by labor for whom unemployment and poverty are now the important issues.[10] Reform of the social welfare funds, on the political agenda of technocrats and multilaterals as well, will also continue to be resisted by labor. Public desire for regulations ensuring competition and transparency will, as in Mexico, be resisted by private sector groups who stand to lose.

The ability of electoral politics to alter policy in the face of powerful entrenched policy networks supported by highly centralized political arrangements and the personalistic aspects of political culture is certainly fraught with obstacles. Policy networks, operating at the highest reaches of political power, have at times found critical support in multilateral lending agencies. In second-stage reform, policy networks remain the key actors in policy development, although their policies are being questioned, modified, and sometimes blocked. Because of the failure of market reform as yet to deliver sufficient prosperity to all, the discretionary and often corrupt way many of the major reforms have been carried out, and the failure of political elites to allow access to policy formulation on the part of a wider spectrum of social groups, market reform leaderships are now being challenged through electoral politics. If electoral politics is to maintain and expand its legitimacy, entrenched policy networks will have to cede their preeminence in policy formulation. Indeed, the very character of policy networks—their resistance to accountability and their exclusivity—will have to change. If democratic institutions are able to influence policy in the direction of deeply felt public preferences, mitigating some of the aspects of first-stage reform found most reprehensible by important segments of the public, then the legitimacy of these institutions will be reinforced and enhanced. If, on the other hand, electoral institutions are not perceived as capable of modifying the style and content of policies, there is the danger that such institutions will lose legitimacy as they are perceived as ineffective or as manipulated by vested interests. As pointed out in Chapter 7, some observers have suggested that the upsurge in lower-class support for a personalistic caudillo-like leader in the recent Chilean election may indicate disillusionment with the failure of electoral politics to meet public expectations. The failure of democratic institutions to meet popular aspirations, and the consequent invigoration of the Iberian strain of political culture in the form of authoritarian caudillo leadership, is an all too common theme in the history of the region. Let us hope, therefore, that electoral politics is able to meet the difficult challenges it now faces. If it does not, the sacrifices of the last decade could be placed in jeopardy.

BREAKDOWN OF INTERVIEWS

ARGENTINA

TYPE[1]	NUMBER
Ministers, Peronist government	4
Senior officials, Peronist government	6
Ministers, Radical government	1
Senior officials, Radical government	5
Middle-level official, Radical government	1
Private sector, members of boards of major entrepreneurial organizations	5
Members of Congress	2
Trade union leaders	4
Total	**28**

CHILE

TYPE[2]	NUMBER
Ministers, military rule	5
Senior officials, military rule	2
Ministers, Concertación	4
Senior officials, Concertación	4
Middle-level officials, Concertación	2
Members of Congress	2
Private sector, members of boards of major entrepreneurial organizations	3
Private sector executives	2
Trade union leaders	2
Communist and socialist militants	3
Total	**29**

MEXICO

TYPE[3]	NUMBER
Cabinet ministers, Salinas	2
Senior officials, Salinas	11
Middle-level officials, Salinas	2
Senior-level officials, Zedillo	7
Middle-level officials, Zedillo	5
Congressmen	2
Private sector, members of boards of major entrepreneurial organizations	2
Private sector executives	5
Total	**36**

MULTILATERAL LENDING INSTITUTIONS

TYPE	NUMBER
World Bank	
Senior LAC officials [4]	7
Middle-ranking LAC officials [5]	6
Other	2
International Monetary Fund	
Middle to senior level	6
Total	**21**

1. Ministries and agencies of government included the Ministry of the Economy, Central Bank, Ministry of the Interior, and Ministry of Labor.
2. Ministries and agencies of the government included the Ministry of Finance, Ministry of the Economy, Ministry of Labor, Ministry of the Interior, MIDEPLAN (Ministry of Planning), CORFO, ministry secretary general of the presidency, and the Central Bank.
3. Ministries and agencies of the government included the Ministry of Finance, Ministry of Industry, Mines, and Public Enterprises, Ministry of Commerce and Industrial Development, the Federal Competition Commission, the Ministry of Social Development, and PEMEX (the state petroleum company).
4. Includes vice presidents, division chiefs, senior and lead economists, and lead sectoral specialists.
5. Country economists (desk officers), resident representatives.

ECONOMIC INDICATORS

TABLE A.I. YEARLY AVERAGE ANNUAL GROWTH RATES
OF GDP PER CAPITA (%), MEXICO, CHILE, AND ARGENTINA

YEARS	MEXICO	CHILE	ARGENTINA
1950–71	3.1		
1950–73		1.1	1.7
1971–80	3.6	1.1	.8
1981–90	−0.3	1.3	−2.1
1991–98	1.3	5.7	4.4
1999	3.0*	−1.1*	−3.0*

Sources: 1950–73: Hansen 1980, 42; Ramos 1986, 46; 1961–89: Consejo Tecnico de Inversiones S.A. 1990, 48; 1981–99: CEPAL News 1999, 1; 1999: CEPAL; Banco Central de Chile.
*Preliminary.

TABLE A.2. STATE PARTICIPATION IN THE ECONOMY: TOTAL
EXPENDITURE AND PUBLIC DEFICIT (−)/SURPLUS (+) AS PERCENT OF GDP

	MEXICO		ARGENTINA		CHILE	
Year	Expenditure	Deficit/Surplus	Expenditure	Deficit/Surplus	Expenditure	Deficit/Surplus
1965	23.9	−0.9	31.5	−4.1	23.3	−4.1
1969	24.6	−2.2	33.7	−1.8	23.7	−0.4
1973	29.5	−5.6	34.6	−7.5	44.9	−24.7
1975	36.4	−8.0	39.6	−15.1	27.4	−2.6
1981	46.9	−13.6	49.0	−13.3	24.9	1.7
1982	55.1	−16.4	48.2	−15.1	28.5	2.3
1983	46.1	−8.6	49.9	−15.2	28.4	−3.8
1985	36.4	−9.6	47.5	−4.7	32.5	−6.3
1987	33.8	−15.0	44.8	−8.7	19.9	1.8
1989	30.8	−5.0	40.7	−16.2	16.1	2.4
1991	23.6	−.3	39.1	−1.3	17.1	1.5
1993	22.3	1.0	31.7	1.3	17.5	1.9
1994	22.9	.4	31.8	−0.1	17.5	2.0
1996	23.1	−.01	30.1	2.0	n.a.	1.0
1998	21.7	1.3	30.7	−1.2	n.a.	−1.2*
1999	n.a.	n.a.	33.2*	−3.1*	n.a.	−1.3*

Sources: Mexico: Public Expenditures: 1965–81: Ayala Espino 1988, 60; 1982–87: Aspe Armella 1993, 23; 1989–98: Poder Ejecutivo Federal 1999, 70; Deficit/Surplus: 1965: Alarcón 1989, 53; 1973–82: Brailovsky, Clarke, and Warman 1989, 421–23; 1982–87: Aspe Armella 1993, 115; 1989–93: CEPAL 1993, 26; Argentina: Expenditure and Deficit/Surplus: 1965–87: Porto 1992, 188; 1989–93: World Bank 1993, 7; Ministerio de Economía y Obras Servicios Públicos 1995, 57, 92; CEPAL 1993, 36; 1994–96: CEPAL News, February 1997, 2; 1996–99: Ministerio de Economía, Programa Economica Regional (www.mecon.gov.ar); Chile: Expenditure and Deficit/Surplus: 1965–69: Griffith-Jones 1987, 18; 1973–89: Hachette and Lüders 1994, 28–29; 1991–94: Ministerio de Hacienda, 1995, August, 40; Deficit/Surplus: 1996: CEPAL News, February 1997, 2; 1998–99: IMF Article IV Consultations (www.imf.org/external).
*Preliminary.

TABLE A.3. UNEMPLOYMENT RATES (%), MEXICO, ARGENTINA, AND CHILE

YEAR	MEXICO	CHILE	ARGENTINA
1973	3.7	4.3	5.3
1975	4.2	15.4[*]	3.1
1978	6.9	13.8[*]	2.9
1982	4.3	22.1[*]	4.8
1986	4.4	13.5	5.2
1989	3.0	9.1	7.0
1992	2.8	6.0	6.9
1994	3.6	6.0	10.7
1995	6.3	5.6	18.4
1996	5.5	6.2	17.1
1997	3.3	6.6	16.1
1998	3.2	9.1	13.1
1999	2.6	9.7	14.5
2000	n.a.	8.9[**]	15.4[**]

Sources: Chile: unemployment, 1973–92: Dornbusch and Edwards 1994, 112; 1994–95: Ministerio de Hacienda, 1995, October, 72; 1996–2000: Banco Central de Chile (www.bcentral.cl/); Argentina: unemployment, 1973–78: Ramos 1986, 60; 1986–92: de la Balze 1995, 123; 1994–2000: INDEC (www.indec.gov.ar); Mexico: unemployment, 1975–78: Gollás 1978, 4; unemployment, 1982, 1986: Murillo 1997, 58; unemployment, 1989–98: Poder Ejecutivo Federal 1999, 53; 1999: ILO, Oficina Regional para América Latina y el Caribe (www.ilolim.org.pe/).
[*] Does not include those in emergency make-work programs.
[**] Preliminary.

TABLE A.4. REAL INDUSTRIAL WAGE RATES
(1980 = 100)

YEAR	MEXICO	CHILE	ARGENTINA
1970	86.9	111.0	107.0
1973	90.4	88.9	111.7
1975	96.4	68.9	118.9
1978	106.2	84.1	77.4
1980	100.0	100.0	100.0
1981	101.2	108.2	93.5
1983	75.9	97.1	97.6
1985	73.6	93.5	104.8
1987	70.1	94.8	101.6
1989	73.1	103.0	72.3
1991	61.9	105.8	76.0
1993	69.6	122.4	75.7
1994	71.9	128.5	76.5
1995	62.1	133.1	76.5
1996	54.9	142.6	75.5
1997	54.8	146.0	75.1
1998	56.2	149.0	74.9

Sources: Mexico: 1970–87: FIEL 1990, 335; 1989–92: Dussel Peters 1995, 66–67; 1991–98: ILO, Oficina Regional para América Latina y el Caribe, Panorama Laboral '99, Anexo Estadistico (www.ilolim.pe/); Chile: 1970–81: calculated from Ramos 1986, 60; 1983–89: Banco Central de Chile; 1991–98: ILO, Oficina Regional para América Latina y el Caribe, Panorama Laboral '99, Anexo Estadistico (www.ilolim.pe/); Argentina: 1970–78: Ramos 1986, 60; 1981–89: calculated from de la Balze 1994, 172–73; 1991–98: ILO, Oficina Regional para América Latina y el Caribe, Panorama Laboral '99, Anexo Estadistico (www.ilolim.pe/).

WORLD BANK OFFICIALS
WORKING ON CHILE, ARGENTINA,
AND MEXICO, 1985–1995*

Vice President, LAC Section: S. Shahid Husain (1987–92); Shahid Javed Burki (1993–95)
Chief Economists: Marcelo Selowsky (1986–93); Sebastian Edwards (1993–95)
Principal Economist: Edgardo E. Barandiaran (1987–90)
Senior Operations Adviser: Myrna Alexander (1993–94)
Senior Adviser: Ping-cheung Loh (1994–95)

COUNTRY DEPARTMENT II: CENTRAL AMERICA, MEXICO, PANAMA

Directors: Rainer B. Steckhan (1986–92); Edilberto L. Segura (1993–95)
Senior/Lead Economists: Paul M. Meo (1985); Frederick E. Berger (1985–87); Luis
    Landau (1985–87); Sweder van Wijnbergen (1989–91); Frank Lysy (1992–95).
Country/Desk Officers: Pieter P. Bottelier (1985–87); K. Kanchuger (1993–95); K. Di
    Tulio (1993–95)
Project Adviser: Paul Knotter (1991–95)
Agriculture: Hans P. Binswanger (1987–95)
Trade and Industry: Paul Knotter (1987–91)
Infrastructure and Energy: Ricardo A. Halperin (1987–92)
Resident Mission (Mexico): Marko Voljc (1987–90); Eugene McCarthy (1991–94)

COUNTRY DEPARTMENT IV: ARGENTINA, CHILE, ECUADOR, PARAGUAY, PERU, URUGUAY

Directors: Pieter P. Bottelier (1987–90); Ping-cheung Loh (1991–94)
Lead Economist: Malcolm D. Rowat (1990–93)
Country Economists and Country Officers: Argentina: Peter R. Scherer (1985–86);
    Richard Newfarmer (1990–95); J. Morisset (1991–93); M. Hagerstrom (1992–95). Chile:
    Peter Eigen (1985–87); Paul Levy (1990–95)
Project Adviser: Malcolm D. Rowat (1987–89)
Country Operations: Donna Dowsett-Coirolo (1992–94)
Agricultural Operations: John H. Joyce (1987–90); Mark D. Wilson (1991–94)
Trade/Finance and Industrial Operations: Argentina: Peter R. Scherer (1987–90); Chile:
    Paul M. Meo (1985–88, 1993–94)
Infrastructure and Industry Operations: Alain Thys (1985–94)
Resident Mission (Argentina): Myrna Alexander (1990–92); Patricio Millan (1993–95)

Source: The World Bank Group, *Directory*, 1985–95.
*Lists those with LAC for minimum of three years, although not necessarily in the same position.

CHAPTER 1

1. There is considerable overlap between stabilization and structural adjustment programs in that both programs share a concern for state expenditure and open trade. Stabilization programs have been more firmly committed to austerity, however, while structural adjustment has been more explicitly involved with trade liberalization, deregulation, and privatization while recognizing the need for economic growth. See Chapter 3 for more detail.

2. This is also true for other indebted less developed countries.

3. Labor flexibilization refers to changes in the norms governing labor relations with the objective of increasing investment and international competitiveness. In practice, it involves reduction in the cost of labor.

4. The electoral defeat of the PRI in the 2000 presidential election was the ultimate political consequence of the peso crash.

5. The literature on this subject is vast. For a fairly extensive and up-to-date bibliography, see Agüero 1998, 14–20.

6. Other recent work has focused on the democratizing impact of the presence of active popular organizations. For example, see Smith and Korzeniewicz 1997; Alvarez, Dagnino, and Escobar 1998a; Chalmers, Vilas, Hite, Martin, Piester, and Segarra 1997.

7. Patron clientelism is, of course, present in varying forms and to varying degrees in all countries. In Latin America, unlike developed countries, it has been a central feature of the political process (Eisenstadt and Roniger 1984, 173). The key point, however, is the impingement patron clientelism can represent on the democratic ideal, including in those countries widely regarded as liberal democracies.

8. Domínguez claims that economic crises have opened "the way for democratic technopols in Argentina, Brazil, and Chile and contribute[d] to political and economic change in Mexico." He further claims that technopols in Chile, Mexico, and Brazil "take seriously the state's obligations to address the social deficit" (Domínguez 1997, 5, 35).

9. Such cases would include the governments of Carlos Menem in 1995 and Ernest Zedillo in 1994.

10. This issue will be dealt with at length in Chapter 3.

11. There is no orderly correlation between the Iberian strain and authoritarianism, on the one hand, and the liberal democratic strain and greater political participation, on the other. As we will see in the following discussion, at times elements of the Iberian tradition have been used to push open the political system while at other times, they have been used to close it to those demanding policy change. Liberal democratic institutions in Latin America have offered opportunities to participate in politics and policy, and they have been manipulated to exclude such participation.

12. *Caudillismo* has been defined as "yielding support to an individual rather than an institution and possibly also accepting that the individual in question may use powers that go beyond the limits of institutional constraints" (Calvert and Calvert 1989, 82).

13. This activism involved the opening up of new lands, measures to encourage immigration, and public works construction, particularly in areas deemed crucial for economic growth (Anderson 1967, 31).

14. Latin America's capacity to import declined 37 percent in the period 1930–34 relative to the precrisis period (Furtado 1976, 55).

15. The administrations of Getulio Vargas in Brazil, Lázaro Cárdenas in Mexico, Juan Perón in Argentina, and the Frente Popular in Chile fall into this category.

16. Chapter 2 deals with the Chilean, Argentine, and Mexican cases specifically.

17. Although in most cases the private sector prospered under this arrangement, tension between the private sector and the state nevertheless grew because of the former's unease at the extent of the state's involvement in economic and social affairs.

18. In the case of Chile, personalism was the defining feature of military rule. See Chapter 4.

19. Specialized training and the adoption of modern science do not preclude the retention of old values or old ways of doing things. Values of the preexisting culture may remain intact while the new ideas are added on. See Haas 1990, 47.

20. It should be made clear, however, that the concept as used in the British and American literature stresses the notion that access to policy is restricted to the "privileged few" in a variety of fragmented policy areas and that policy networks are believed to represent therefore a constraint on democracy. They create "privileged oligarchies" and "exclude the public" (Marsh and Rhodes 1992, 265).

21. Literature using the policy coalition approach for the three countries dealt with in this study is discussed in Chapters, 4, 5, and 6.

22. As pointed out earlier in the chapter, personalist political alliances (better know as patron-client networks) have been a standard feature of Latin American politics. In this sense, we can say that political networks operated before the market reform era, although these were not *policy* networks because policy networks as used in this book are committed to a specific set of transformative economic policy ideas.

23. The concepts of policy network *core* and *periphery* are adapted from Marsh and Rhodes 1992, 256.

24. The concept of policy network as I have developed it here is very close to the concept of *camarilla* used in the Mexican policy literature. I chose not to use this term, first, because the Mexican literature usually uses it to refer to groupings entirely within the state whereas I required a term that would allow for the inclusion of extrastate actors. Second, the Chilean use of the term has very pejorative connotations indicating substantial corruption. Corruption has frequently been a feature of the Mexican and Argentine reform processes, but it was not a feature of the post-1989 Chilean civilian regime. Also, corruption was not involved in the relationships between state and World Bank members of international policy networks.

25. Personal ties between state-based technocrats may also extend outside of the state to various "think tanks," academic research institutions.

26. International policy networks are explored in greater depth in Chapter 3.

27. The danger of a member of the elite jumping ship and mobilizing those alienated by market reform was real and certainly becomes apparent during the second phase of reform. Personal loyalty did help mitigate this threat, at least for a time.

CHAPTER 2

1. Often referred to as the "rules of the game," probably the most important components of this consensus are a willingness to accept electoral results, a respect for minority rights, and importantly, a respect for property rights that assumes that one of the key functions of the state is to protect property rights.

2. This is not to suggest the absence of clientelistic forms of attracting popular support—the Christian Democratic Party, for example, awarded peasants and shantytown dwellers with material rewards such as access to land (Angell 1988, 55; Barrera 1999, 85–86)—but, rather, its relatively less central role when compared with the other two cases.

3. Bribery for the purpose of obtaining contracts was not necessary, according to Cleaves, because government agencies were committed to expansionary programs and had ways of securing funds to spend beyond their original budget allocations (1974, 260). The state was, however, heavily permeated by societal interests, particularly private sector groups (Velasco 1994, 381).

4. Between 1940 and 1946, it created thirty-two enterprises, including ones in electricity (National Electricity Company, ENDESA), in steel (Pacific Steel Company, CAP), and in petroleum (National Petroleum Company, ENAP). Many of these companies provided cheap inputs to the private sector.

5. The "inner core" of interrelated families who controlled the major industrial, financial, and landholding assets of the country and who formed the active leadership of the right consisted of the following: the Mattes, Claros, Vials, and Edwards (Zeitlin and Ratcliff 1988, 167, 250). The latter two would play key roles in the post-1973 political scenario. See Chapter 4.

6. The prohibition against the formation of federations for the purpose of collective bargaining considerably reduced labor's leverage at the regional, national, and industrywide levels while the stipulation that plant unions could be legally set up only in enterprises with a minimum of twenty-five workers meant the absence of unions in most of Chile's industrial establishments in the 1960s. Peasant unions were outlawed on paper until 1947 and in practice until 1967 (Loveman 1988, 222–23). Because worker federations and confederations lacked legal status, they could not collect dues from member unions. In 1968, union financial contributions to the national trade union confederation, the CUT (Single Workers' Central), were explicitly prohibited (Angell 1972, 222).

7. More has been written on the years of the Popular Unity government than any other period in Chilean history. Some standard sources are Kaufman (1988), Sigmund (1977), and Stallings (1978).

8. On several occasions, economic liberals were in charge of the Ministry of the Economy, most notably in 1959–61, when well-known economic liberal Alvaro Alsogaray held the economy portfolio.

9. Between 1946 and 1951, total union membership went from 520,000 to 1,334,000, whereas from 1941 to 1945 it had increased by only 10 percent (James 1988, 9, 27).

10. The 1945 labor law provided for a legally recognized national labor confederation (CGT, General Confederation of Labor) to which all industrywide unions and federations belonged. The legislation provided for highly centralized control within the union structure: national union leaders were empowered to intervene in local union branches and overrule their decisions, and union and federation leaders were given the right to discipline recalcitrant union members (Crawley 1984, 403).

11. These were the state airline (Aerolíneas Argentinas), the state gas company (Gas del Estado), National Port Administration, State Railway Company, National Telecommunications Company (ENTEL), Mixed Argentine Steel Corporation (SOMISA), and National Administration of State Industries (DINIE), the latter involved in electrical, metallurgical, and textile production (Ugalde 1984, 19–20).

12. Credits to the private sector, mostly to manufacturing, grew by 30 percent in 1947 and 15 percent in 1948 (Gerchunoff 1989, 66).

13. The best-known explanation of these policy swings is found in O'Donnell (1977b). He

argues that stabilization is initiated with the support of the big landed interests in alliance with the most powerful industrial business sector. Once stabilization is under way and begins to have a negative effect on the interests of industrialists, however, they join the opposition labor and the weak bourgeoisie alliance to end stabilization and initiate an expansionary economic program, which is soon abandoned in the face of a balance-of-payments crisis and burgeoning public deficit.

14. Under the leadership of Augusto Vandor the Peronist trade union movement had supported the 1966 military coup, but the alliance between the military and labor was short-lived (Bunel 1992, 105).

15. The military, which later disappeared, originally formed a fifth sector in the PRI.

16. The term *charro* (literally "cowboy") originated in the nickname given to a corrupt leader of the railway workers union who had a penchant for cowboy gear.

17. Indeed, it has been argued that Mexico's co-optative control mechanisms allowed it to avoid the brutal military bureaucratic authoritarianism of the southern cone countries (Kaufman 1977).

18. In 1964, the Mexican Council of Businessmen (CMHN), composed of thirty-seven businessmen controlling around seventy economic groups, was established to oppose the "mixed economy" (Carrillo Arronte 1987, 53).

CHAPTER 3

1. With Enhanced Surveillance, the IMF closely monitors economic performance and a quantitative financial program at the request of a member country in the absence of a standby agreement. The goal is to reinforce business confidence in order to assist the country in achieving multiyear rescheduling of debt with commercial banks (Lee 1993, 38). CCFF permits borrowing for balance-of-payments problems beyond the control of developing countries (Kafka 1991, 110).

2. Banks were apparently threatened with increased regulatory attention (James 1996, 371).

3. The distinction between stabilization programs and structural adjustment programs hinges on the fact that stabilization is aimed at correcting trade imbalances and inflation in a relatively short period of time. Structural adjustment is geared to achieve fundamental changes that will liberate markets. In practice, however, there is considerable overlap in their policy prescriptions, and both prescribe trade liberalization and reduction in government expenditure.

4. In several cases negotiations of SALS with the World Bank broke down because of failure to reach agreement with the IMF (Griffith-Jones 1992, 61). In the case of SECALS, it became common for the bank to grant loans in the absence of an IMF stabilization agreement as occurred with Brazil, Argentina, and others (Mosley, Harrigan, and Toye 1995, 102).

5. On this struggle, see Chapter 5.

6. There are also a variety of institutional reasons for the failure of conditionality: internal pressure on officials to spend their budgets (and therefore loosen up on the enforcement of conditionality), the development of high and unrealistic conditionality programs to win praise from the executive board, and the inability to move funds from borrowers who do not comply to those who do (Mosley, Harrigan, and Toye 1995, 47, 113, 51, 68).

7. An early step foreshadowing the debt relief program occurred in December 1987 with the announcement of an innovative plan by which JP Morgan would retire up to $20 bil-

lion (U.S.) of Mexican debt through the exchange of loans for government bonds (Aggarwal 1996, 36).

8. The U.S. Federal Reserve Board, however, was never fully convinced about a shift to debt forgiveness and hence insisted that the plan had to include an option for new lending from the banks (Lehman 1993, 51).

9. On Stern's role in Mexican trade liberalization, see Chapter 4.

10. Indeed, this official was apparently strongly supportive of Mexico's implementation of exchange controls and bank nationalization in 1982 (interviews with two LAC senior officials). See Preface and Appendix 1 for information on officials interviewed.

11. In some cases bank officials collaborated at the request of the client country in areas where bank expertise, although not money, was deemed to be important and helpful. In other cases, after accepting technical support from the bank, the client country would decide not to take a World Bank loan for political reasons (for fear of the political fallout of having a particular reform associated with World Bank money) or because it wished to go in a direction that the bank did not approve of (interviews with senior LAC officials).

12. This situation was evident in the case of Mexico. See Chapter 6.

13. The last Argentine economy minister under President Carlos Menem, Roque Fernández, and several members of his team were formerly with the IMF, as was former Mexican finance minister, Guillermo Ortiz (interviews with senior IMF official). Another former Argentine economy minister, Domingo Cavallo, had a close relationship with the World Bank, having done a considerable amount of work for the bank on a contract basis. (See Chapter 5.)

14. As we will see in Chapter 5, however, international policy networks also included nontechnocrats from client countries.

15. Such was the case with the policy network that developed Mexico's trade liberalization program, a reform that, when it was originally suggested, triggered considerable hostility from the Mexicans. See Chapter 6.

16. Mexico's fierce condemnation of the 1995 Helms Burton law, which allowed court action against anyone benefiting from property expropriated from U.S. nationals and imposed economic and other sanctions on anyone in the country providing technical assistance to Cuba, no doubt did little to endear Mexico to those in Congress already dubious about the efficacy of U.S. foreign aid. The role of the United States in bailing Mexico out of the 1995 crisis is dealt with in Chapter 4.

17. This situation was the consequence of the failure of the bank and the Chilean government to agree to the terms for loans (Gwin 1997, 256).

18. As we shall see in Chapter 4, the harshness of the adjustment program supported by the IMF and the bank was not entirely to the liking of even Chile's most enthusiastic market reformers.

CHAPTER 4

1. The selection of key network participants shown in Table 4.1 was arrived at by first interviewing major actors identified in the literature as such and then narrowing the list to those repeatedly identified in interviews as major players in the process. Information on personal relationships between actors was obtained from the sources indicated at the bottom of the table. Because of the extreme hierarchy and tightness of relationships, I was readily able to

identify individual participants, an accomplishment that became difficult, if not impossible, in most of the other cases, including Chile after 1985 (except Mexico under Salinas).

2. There were differences in opinion on the depth and rapidity of reform; some early participants supported a more gradual approach (Silva 1996, 69). In 1974, Pablo Baraona and Sergio Undurraga were advisers to the minister of agriculture and the minister of finance, respectively.

3. The collapse of the price of copper (the country's major export) at the end of 1974 combined with the increase in petroleum prices produced an acute balance-of-payments crisis. Inflation, although not as high as in 1973, was unacceptable at 505 percent (Oppenheim 1993, 127; Aguilera Reyes 1994, 34).

4. Resistance to rapid adjustment came from General Gustavo Leigh, one of the members of the four-man military junta, from various other military officers, from Raúl Sáez, minister of economic coordination, from Fernando Léniz, minister of the economy, and from economists in the Central Bank (interviews with three senior Finance Ministry officials). The business and landowning peak organizations were also strong proponents of gradual adjustment (Silva 1996, 76).

5. Díaz Estrada's labor proposals and Fernández's management of the labor movement are dealt with in detail in Chapter 7.

6. By December 1982, banks owned by the big conglomerates had taken out more than 80 percent of the country's foreign loans (Hastings 1993, 218).

7. The network of relationships between policy makers and senior conglomerate executives was an important contributor to the borrowing binge because executives took their signals from senior policy makers who were favorably disposed to foreign indebtedness (interviews with two business leaders). Indeed, the Chicago boys believed that debt was healthy as long as it was in the private sector (Délano and Traslaviña 1989, 64; Edwards and Cox Edwards 1987, 72).

8. Established in 1979 to control inflation, the fixed exchange rate also encouraged imports and heavy borrowing. But it did not become an issue until the crisis broke.

9. My interview data support Silva on this point (1996, 151). Two sources, however, argue that the exception was Manuel Cruzat, who lobbied for devaluation because the overvalued peso was hurting the profitability of some of the group's firms, while Vial wanted a fixed exchange rate and lobbied for government-imposed adjustment in nominal wages (Edwards and Cox Edwards 1987, 90; Fontaine Aldunate 1988, 153–54).

10. Sergio Fernández, minister of the interior, and Miguel Kast, minister of labor, exited with de Castro.

11. Commissions were established and the future of each bank was assessed and negotiated separately, a process that was a requirement for World Bank support. Cruzat lost ownership of the Banco de Santiago along with most of his other enterprises but was able to keep 8.5 percent of his shares (Marín and Rozas 1988, 78). Javier Vial refused to negotiate and blamed the government for the economic collapse. In 1984, following a stint in jail, he finally signed an agreement with the government abandoning the assets of BHC to its creditors (Marín and Rozas 1988, 78).

12. The description of events and actors in this section is drawn from interviews of one multilateral and two Chilean participants in these policy discussions and from OED 1990.

13. The World Bank was very concerned about the impact of the bank rescue operation on the future financial health of the Chilean state. One bank official confided that he personally would have preferred to see most of the Chilean banks go under.

14. In addition to the loans, the World Bank also provided loan guarantees to facilitate agreement with the commercial banks. In 1986, the bank in its discussions with the steering committee insisted that commercial creditors finance Chile's remaining foreign exchange requirements for 1987 (OED 1990, 51, 9).

15. Relations with the creditor banks, the details of the Copper Stabilization Fund (a bank initiative), and the extent of financial rehabilitation for the threatened private sector banks were the major issues delaying signing of these agreements (OED 1990, 103, 128).

16. I interviewed two economists who had worked closely with Büchi during these years. Their admiration and dedication to him was obvious.

17. Another motivation was the the need to provide the pension funds with companies to invest in (OED 1990, 103, 128).

18. These included the state-owned chemical company (SOQUIMICH), the state sugar company (IANASA), the steel state company (CAP), the state electricity company (ENDESA), the state telecommunications company (ENTEL), and the state airline (LAN Chile).

19. The public enterprise sector production as a percentage of GDP was 12 percent for Mexico in 1988 and 9.5 percent for Argentina in 1990 (Teichman 1995, 139; World Bank 1993, 25). These figures are for the public enterprise sectors of Mexico and Argentina before the completion of their radical privatization drives.

20. Share packages began to be put on the market in 1982. Share packages of 49 percent for three CORFO companies, CHILECTRA (electricity), SOQUIMICH, and ENTEL, were offered for sale in 1985, and 30 percent of the shares of remaining CORFO companies were put up for sale.

21. With the 1991 reform, management was required to give a reason for dismissals, appeals could be made to a labor tribunal, and employers were required to pay compensation for wrongful dismissals. Labor policy is dealt with at greater length in Chapter 7.

22. The new appointments included two Concertación loyalists appointed by President Frei, bringing the tally for Concertación to twenty-three, but the right maintained twenty-two seats, perhaps twenty-four if two former justices (chosen by the Supreme Court) are counted, so that Concertación still lacked sufficient support for constitutional reform (*Latin American Weekly Report*, January 6, 1998, 3).

23. This legislation would have, among other things, extended collective negotiation to temporary workers and prohibited contracting replacement workers during a strike. It also would have provided for collective bargaining above the plant level.

24. In the Alywin government, in addition to trained economists in charge of the Ministries of Finance and Economics, Ricardo Lagos, who held a Ph.D. in economics, was appointed minister of education, and René Cortázar, who held a Ph.D. from MIT, became minister of labor. Under Frei, while economists remained in charge of key economic portfolios, the sociologist José Joaquin Brunner was secretary general of the government and the economist Jorge Arrate was appointed minister of labor (Puryear 1994, 2, 117).

25. Hence the new civilian government continued debt reduction through debt-for-equity swaps. Between 1985 and 1993, total debt conversion reached $11.314 billion (U.S.) (Haindl 1995, 29).

26. In interviews respondents gave two explanations for this change. The differences in the personalities of Finance Ministers Foxley and Aninat were held partially responsible insofar as Foxley was perceived as more of a consensus taker. But the conscious attempt to block pressures for increased expenditure from within the state was identified as the main reason

for restricting the discussion of macroeconomic policy because it was feared that pressure on public expenditures would become more of a problem over time (interviews with two senior officials).

27. This process was attested to by four senior-level technocrats, one in the Planning Ministry, two in the Finance Ministry, and one in the Central Bank.

28. This sense of solidarity is further reinforced by the fact that graduates of schools with a strong neoclassical economic orientation tend to gravitate toward the Finance Ministry and the Central Bank (for example, graduates of the University of Chicago), while those with training in other fields (such as sociology) and economists with more flexible training tend to find their way into other ministries such as the Planning Ministry. This situation reinforces solidarity inasmuch as friendships have often been formed during university years (interviews with two senior Finance Ministry officials).

29. Here my findings differ from those of Weyland, who claims that the Chilean state has "remained fairly free of bureaucratic infighting" (1997, 58).

30. This process was described by three senior-level officials, two from the Finance Ministry and one from the Planning Ministry.

31. The response of one senior-level technocrat was typical: "We all know each other very well because the same people from the various ministries are constantly meeting. There is a lot of shouting during budget meetings. But we have similar training and this facilitates agreement."

32. Under the first two regimes, the Finance Ministry was in the hands of Christian Democrats, as was the head of the Central Bank, while other portfolios tended to circulate among members of Concertación, with labor, health, education, public works, interior, and planning probably being the portfolios most frequently held by socialists.

33. Several senior-level MIDEPLAN interviewees suggested that the decision to increase spending in education (which finance officials saw as the panacea to inequality) had been made by the finance minister, a decision they regarded as reflecting a very superficial understanding of the roots of poverty and inequality in Chile.

34. Following considerable resistance from the Christian Democrats, Ricardo Lagos won the primary election to become presidential candidate for the Concertación for the 1999–2000 presidential election.

35. The CUT, the umbrella labor organization, was also invited to send representatives to the Foro but unlike business has not generally found it a useful opportunity to air its views. It withdrew in 1996 (*La Epoca*, June 13, 1996, E1).

36. While representatives of exporters had high praise for the government's involvement of the private sector in this area, those potentially hurt by such agreements were generally excluded. Agriculturalists, for example, were kept out of Chile's negotiations with MERCOSUR (interview with senior Finance Ministry official).

37. Business's major concern was labor policy. The private sector, which was strongly opposed to the 1995 proposed labor reform, refused to enter into the discussions of the proposed reform. But the private sector did not appear to hold the proposed reform against the government perhaps because of the belief (expressed to me by both members of the private sector and trade union leaders) that the government had allowed this proposed reform to go forward to Congress to placate labor, knowing that it would be defeated in the Senate.

38. Before taking power, Concertación announced that it would review all privatizations carried out during the last year of the military regime (*Latin American Weekly Report*, February 2, 1989, 3) and once assuming power announced that all privatizations in process would be "frozen" (Estrategia 1994, 152). Virtually all officials interviewed were reluctant to address

the privatization issue; indeed, some were outright embarrassed by it. Two denied that their policy was one of privatization, saying that it was a program of granting concessions to the private sector.

39. This topic is discussed in greater depth in Chapter 7.

CHAPTER 5

1. In the Chilean case, in contrast, military men under Pinochet did not come to occupy state positions on a massive scale, and those who did take up government posts were required to take a leave of absence from their military commissions.

2. Argentina's Ministry of the Economy is equivalent to the Ministries of Finance in Chile and Mexico. It is responsible for macroeconomic policy, for revenue collection, and for government investment and expenditure.

3. He also lacked a technocratic support base, but this was probably the least of his problems. As we will see, the Argentine program got under way before the implantation of such a technical base within the state.

4. Of course, equally important was that Argentina, unlike Chile, had developed a bureaucratized labor leadership willing to collaborate.

5. The forestry industry received a subsidy, as did the mining industry through a new fund set up in 1979, Fomento Minero, while the fishing industry was subsidized through the Fundo Nacional Pesca (Schvarzer 1981, 95).

6. As in Chile, financial liberalization had produced a rapid expansion of the banking sector and a binge of borrowing on the international market, while an overvalued exchange rate hurt exports and encouraged imports.

7. Whereas the number of workers in manufacturing was 1,165,000 in 1975, by 1982 that figure had dropped to 740,000 (Villareal 1987, 81).

8. With elections in the offing, the Radical Party's political strategists were able to convince Alfonsín of the importance of currying political favor with the Peronist trade unions.

9. This letter of intent was rejected by the managing director and executive board of the IMF (Stiles 1991, 92).

10. As we will see in the following chapter, not only was the treatment of Mexico more lenient, but it has been more consistently so. World Bank officials experienced firsthand the clout that Mexico could wield through the U.S. executive.

11. The plan was formulated in secret and involved no consultation of intra- or extrastate groups or individuals in Argentine society. The reasoning behind this process was that to have developed the plan without such secrecy would have ensured its failure as consultation would have given rise to obstructionist political resistance (interviews with two senior Radical government officials).

12. Two top-level Argentine officials of the Radical government said that they had presented trade liberalization to the private sector as a policy required by the bank and as therefore unavoidable.

13. The $1.25 billion (U.S.) lending program involved two SECALS (for banking and trade reform) and two loans (for housing and energy) (Tussie 1988, 170).

14. Specific reforms were also discussed, particularly the restructuring and privatization of public enterprises in airline, telecommunications, and railway industries.

15. There were several reasons for this. The World Bank refused official involvement if it felt that Argentine officials were unlikely to take measures to ensure a modicum of transparency in reform, refusing to lend for the Aerolíneas Argentinas privatization and privatization

of the highways for this reason. Although extensive dialogue was held over labor flexibilization and social security reform, the Argentine authorities decided against taking bank loans for these reforms because of their political sensitivity (interviews with middle-ranking and senior LAC officials).

16. In one case, World Bank officials and public enterprise managers, convinced of the need for privatization, worked together to lobby congressmen to support privatization (interview with middle-ranking LAC official).

17. According to LAC bank officials interviewed, between 1985 and 1989 the bank prepared a variety of studies that would contribute to later reforms, including a study advocating reform of the social security system, a program for the privatization of the railways, a program for the deregulation of gas, and a study dealing with historical experiences in telecommunications privatizations. The bank's internal report of its activities in Argentina says that bank officials were somewhat timid on the privatization issue, although the author of the report apparently did not interview the bank officials involved in Argentine public enterprise reform. In most other areas, however, the bank's studies coincide fairly closely with actual reform programs (OED 1996, 38–46).

18. Two bank officials expressed great admiration for public enterprise officials who supported restructuring and privatization; one characterized such individuals as the "real heroes" of Argentina's market reform.

19. With the exception of labor flexibilization, most bank officials appear to have concluded that extensive restructuring before privatization was not worth the expenditure. But this was a conclusion they reached only after attempting reform.

20. In fact, the bank official in question was not authorized to make such a specific promise. But because bank loans are fungible, he went ahead, knowing that this was necessary to bring the trade union on side and trusting that Argentine officials would honor the deal.

21. Menem, however, was supported by "the 15" and "the 62 organizations," the labor organizations that took a more moderate, conciliatory position on the debt and human rights issues. "The 15" was particularly collaborationist, having worked with both the military and the Alfonsín regimes. See McGuire 1992, 56.

22. This move on Menem's part was usually explained in terms of his pragmatism: the market reformers in the party by this time were the largest and best trained group and Menem wanted their cooperation and support (interviews with senior government officials).

23. One explanation maintains that Menem's policy conversion came as a consequence of conversations with government officials during a trip to Europe with Domingo Cavallo (his economy minister between 1991 and 1996), just a few days after he entered the race for his party's presidential candidacy. Others claim that Menem could not be described as having "converted" to market reform because he lacks political principles; rather, as a political pragmatist he simply cast his lot with the renewalist technocrats because he recognized their growing importance in the party and their usefulness as the best source of policy expertise (interviews with two senior government officials).

24. Because of the seriousness of the economic crisis, Menem agreed to take office six months early (in July). In return, the Radicals, who controlled Congress at the time, agreed to support Peronist economic measures to deal with the crisis.

25. The importance of Menem's political style has been emphasized by a variety of observers. Cavarozzi speaks of Menem's "extraordinary ability to establish direct contact with people on the basis of impression and empathy" (1997, 115). See also Gaudio and Thompson 1990, 224; Canitrot and Sigal 1994, 123).

26. Sidicaro adopts the term "antielite" from William Kornhauser (1959), cited in Sidicaro 1995, 125.

27. Menem's decision to carry out privatization rapidly and thoroughly has now become part of Argentina's political lore. The most commonly heard story has Erman González bringing a list of the country's companies to Menem in 1989 and asking him which ones should be privatized; Menem's response was "all of them" (interview with senior government official).

28. Bank officials claim to have declined to make loans where they foresaw lack of transparency (questionable legal/ethical practices) but would always keep the discussion going in the hopes of having some influence over the process (interviews with senior LAC and middle-ranking officials).

29. The rapidity of privatization and its lack of transparency were explained by Argentine officials in terms of the pressing need to provide immediate and tangible evidence to the international creditor community that Argentina was fully committed to policy reform (interviews with two senior-level officials).

30. Agreement from the military was achieved through negotiations carried out on commissions set up to oversee the privatizations, composed of government officials, representatives of the military, and private consultants.

31. Three interviewees (senior government officials) identified Menem's and González's "excellent personal relations" with members of the military as key in achieving privatizations in companies previously under the auspices of the military.

32. Cavallo had had close links with the World Bank for many years, having acted as a consultant for it. He was involved in top-level discussions of economic policy with the bank from at least 1989 and is widely believed to have had a significant impact on reform policy from the beginning of the Menem administration (interviews with senior LAC officials and senior Economy Ministry official).

33. Many of the Fundación's policy recommendations can be found in its publication, *Novedades Económicas*, from 1981 onward.

34. Hence the Supreme Court upheld the use of presidential decree powers despite serious questions as to their constitutionality (Saba and Manzetti 1997, 362). In 1990, the Supreme Court overturned a lower court decision blocking the sale of the state-owned airlines (*Latin American Weekly Report*, July 26, 1990, 12) and then went on to block all existing and potential actions against privatization (*Latin American Weekly Report*, August 2, 1990, 8). In 1998, the Supreme Court upheld Menem's airport privatization bill (*Latin American Weekly Report*, January 6, 1998, 12).

35. Its relation with Congress is dealt with in Chapter 7.

36. The total number of Cavallo's team of highly qualified personnel is estimated at around two hundred (interviews with senior Economy Ministry official).

37. Formulation of economic policy had always rested in the hands of the minister of the economy, but never had it been so insulated not only from societal forces (this trend was under way from 1983 and perhaps earlier) but also from other areas in the state.

38. The Convertibility Plan requires the Central Bank to buy the peso to keep it at par with the U.S. dollar and requires that all money issued by the Central Bank be backed fully by an equivalent amount of foreign currency.

39. Both World Bank and IMF informants stressed the trust that existed between Argentine Economy Ministry officials, particularly past minister Domingo Cavallo and current economy minister Roque Fernández, and themselves as a result of their similar educational

training and work experience with the bank and the IMF. In the words of one respondent, "Argentine Economy officials are well known to us; we speak the same language and there are not basic differences in our views—only differences in circumstances that cause us to have differences in emphases."

40. IMF officials interviewed made a point of Fernández's previous experience there and stressed the meeting of minds between themselves and the economy minister.

41. At least one of Menem's labor ministers, Enrique Rodríguez, opposed Cavallo's economic policies because they paid insufficient attention to social policies (*Latin American Weekly Report*, August 17, 1995, 364).

42. The precise reasons for Cavallo's departure still remain unclear. A variety of contentious issues created pressure for Cavallo's resignation: Cavallo's opposition to the creation of a national labor and employment council, which he said would place the economic model in jeopardy; his attempt to have a tax reform passed by presidential decree followed by his failure to make himself available for questioning; and charges and countercharges of corruption between himself and the political side of the cabinet. One explanation suggests that Cavallo's departure was the price Menem agreed to pay to get legislators to agree to pass a backlog of bills (*Latin American Weekly Report*, August 8, 1996, 350).

43. The resistance of the policy elite, especially the dominant economic policy network in the Ministry of the Economy, to changes in its legislation by Congress is dealt with in Chapter 7.

44. Business's major concern was labor policy, particularly the fear that labor resistance would slow or block changes to the labor code allowing for greater flexibility in labor relations.

45. These interviewees included two business leaders active in the Industrial Union and another in the General Confederation of Industry. Two businessmen active in the Argentine Chamber of Commerce said that although there had not been consultation up until 1992, the situation had improved markedly since then.

46. The top three are Pérez Companc Group, Compañía del Plata, and Techint (*Latin American Weekly Report*, February 13, 1993, 76).

47. This involvement was justified on the grounds that the technocratic team lacked the expertise to work out the details of a privatization program.

48. This was admitted to by a former top-level official in the Ministry of the Economy and two business leaders.

49. For example, charges were brought against then minister of public works Roberto Dromi in 1991, against then president of the state Banco de la Nación Aldo Dadone in 1996, and against Domingo Cavallo, former minister of the economy, in 1996. Rumors and allegations have circulated about Menem's involvement in corrupt practices.

CHAPTER 6

1. In Mexico, the terms *secretario* (secretary) and *secretaría* (secretariat) are used to refer to cabinet ministers and their administrative units, unlike the other two cases, where *ministro* and *ministerio* are the terms used. For the sake of clarity and comparability, the terms *minister* and *ministry* are used with reference to Mexico as well in this discussion.

2. Some camarillas have, however, included extrastate actors (Purcell and Purcell 1980, 220–21; Grindle 1977, 65; Teichman 1988, 72).

3. In this way camarillas promoted cohesion of the elite in the face of institutional or policy conflict (Rondfeldt 1989).

4. She argues that the Cárdenas alliance centered in such ministries as labor, agriculture, and industry, allied to the worker and peasant sector of the PRI, has historically supported expansionary state spending and an interventionist state, while the bankers' alliance, located in the Ministry of Finance and the Central Bank and allied with the bankers, is guided by a laissez-faire ideology (Maxfield 1990, 10–13, 35, 59).

5. Some have viewed public policy as reflecting the interests of a cohesive economic and political ruling elite, the so-called revolutionary family (Brandenburg 1964; Reyes Esparza et al. 1978; Cockcroft 1983). While some recognize the ability of the private sector to influence policy through its privileged representation on a variety of government boards and commissions (Purcell and Purcell 1977, 221), others have pointed to the 1982 bank nationalization as clear evidence that the Mexican state was powerful and autonomous enough to threaten the interests of the private sector (Camp 1989; Story 1986b).

6. For example, Adolfo Lugo Verduzco, a lawyer and public accountant who had done graduate studies in public administration, was appointed president of the PRI. Miguel Gonzalez Avelar, a lawyer employed in the Ministry of Budget and Planning, was appointed leader of the Senate by de la Madrid.

7. Carlos Salinas was minister of budget and planning (SPP) from 1985 to 1987 while Francisco Gil Díaz served as deputy director of economic research in the Central Bank. José Córdoba served as director of economic and social policy in SPP. Zedillo joined the Central Bank of Mexico, where he worked closely with Gil Díaz. Zedillo, Serra Puche, and Aspe all served as subsecretaries (one level below minister) under President de la Madrid. Aspe was replaced as subsecretary of planning and budget control in SPP by Zedillo when Aspe moved up to replace Salinas as minister of SPP in 1987. Serra Puche served as a subsecretary in finance. Guillermo Ortiz, who was close to Córdoba, was brought in as subsecretary of revenue in the Finance Ministry.

8. As an institution involved with allocating government monies, the Ministry of Budget and Planning was less predisposed to state streamlining than were the Finance Ministry and the Central Bank. But once Salinas took it over, its top levels were filled with people who supported Salinas's policy bent, and its policy predisposition began to change.

9. Among the radical market reformers holding cabinet-level positions under Salinas's presidency, Miguel Mancera (Central Bank), Jaime Serra Puche (Trade and Industry), and Ernesto Zedillo (SPP) had graduate degrees in economics from Yale. Pedro Aspe has a Ph.D. in economics from MIT. Salinas himself has a Ph.D. in public administration from Harvard and Córdoba an incomplete Ph.D. from Stanford.

10. Leopoldo Solís, head of the Office of Economic Advisers to the President under de la Madrid, was mentor to both Ernesto Zedillo and Francisco Gil Díaz. Pedro Aspe also studied under Francisco Gil Díaz (Golob 1997, 105), and José Córdoba and Guillermo Ortiz (subsecretary in the Finance Ministry under Salinas) formed a close friendship at Stanford University in the mid-1970s (*Proceso*, no. 961, April 3, 1995, 7). And it was through Ortiz that Córdoba became close to Salinas. A close friendship developed between Zedillo and Serra Puche during their graduate work at Yale University between 1974 and 1978 (*Proceso*, no. 974, July 3, 1995, 38).

11. Carlos Salinas's personal camarilla included key figures in the market reform process: Jaime Serra Puche, Ernesto Zedillo, Pedro Aspe (Camp 1990, 102), and José Córdoba (interview with senior Finance Ministry official). Jaime Serra, originally a member of former finance minister Silva Herzog's camarilla, also formed a relationship with Salinas and was able to join Salinas's camarilla once Silva Herzog had been "burned"—ousted as finance minister (Langston 1997, 1).

12. Unlike the Chilean and Argentine cases, there does not appear to have been any attempt by radical reformers to hold discussions with the private sector at this initial stage.

13. Two senior Finance Ministry officials interviewed suggested that Silva Herzog was uncomfortable with the rapid liberalization supported by Salinas.

14. For example, Gustavo Petricioli, who took over the finance portfolio following Silva Herzog's resignation in 1986, had opposed rapid trade liberalization before 1985 (interview with senior-level official).

15. The leading figure on the World Bank side pushing for trade liberalization was Fred Berger.

16. Areas traditionally kept out of the dialogue until that time included the petroleum sector, the financial sector, reform of the agricultural sector, particularly the ejido, and social issues such as health and poverty.

17. One bank official interviewed recalled an occasion in which he had met with a Finance Ministry official in the morning and had commented in passing that he was scheduled to meet with a senior-level PEMEX official that very afternoon. He was forced to cancel the appointment because he had not obtained Finance Ministry authorization.

18. The most well known case involved a junior official in the bank who wrote a minority report in 1980 critical of Mexico's rapid petroleum export strategy and predicting an economic crisis (Urzúa 1997, 74). The Mexicans used their influence with the United States and upper levels of the bank in an attempt to have the official fired (interview with senior LAC official). In another case, Mexican complaints to senior U.S. officials resulted in LAC officials being chastised for pressuring too hard for trade liberalization (Urzúa 1997, 82). In yet another case, incensed by a report calling for a review of Mexican state investment schemes, the Mexicans used the same route to have the report's author fired (interview with senior LAC official).

19. During the Brady negotiations, President Salinas complained to a senior World Bank official about the difficulties his administration was having with the commercial banks. The official in question took the problem up with the president of the bank, who went to President George Bush, who, in turn, successfully pressured the commercial banks to soften their position (interview with senior bank official).

20. An extensive dialogue along with a variety of technical studies, for example, occurred in relation to the privatization of TELMEX. But in the end no loan was made for the telephone privatization. According to the bank, the loan was rejected by Mexican officials because of the political sensitivity of the privatization; according to one Mexican official, the loan fell through because the Mexicans would not agree to the date for privatization insisted on by the bank; according to another informant, the reason was disagreement over the selling price.

21. The World Bank wanted international prices in agriculture, targeted food subsidies, and, especially, a child feeding program. Bank officials claim the Mexicans rejected the latter for fiscal reasons (interview with senior World Bank official).

22. According to one bank informant, the Mexicans wanted the reform of the ejido included as a condition of a bank sectoral loan in agriculture. The bank refused, seemingly both because of the enormous political sensitivity of the issue and because officials did not see the ejido as at the root of the country's agricultural difficulties (interview with senior bank official).

23. Agricultural Ministry officials sent for policy dialogue with the bank who were not persuaded were replaced (interview with senior bank official).

24. Even though the Mexican state had a highly trained technocracy, it lacked anyone

with experience in privatization and was unsure of how to proceed (interviews with two senior Mexican officials in the Finance Ministry).

25. A possible exception is the privatization of the banks, which one senior-level World Bank official claimed was being pressed by the World Bank from 1985 onward (interview with senior LAC official).

26. The private sector, however, was allowed to generate electricity for its own use (*La Jornada*, February 20, 1991, 30). Certain agricultural sectors also remained protected. Corn production would be protected for fifteen years and then gradually opened up to foreign competition.

27. Although Central Bank head Miguel Mancera remained an important figure in macro-economic policy, he did not play a key role in the major policy reforms during the Salinas presidency after 1992, namely privatization and further liberalization under NAFTA.

28. For a full discussion of the management of labor opposition, see Chapter 7.

29. As in the cases of Argentina and Chile, trade liberalization was carried out without prior consultation with the private sector. Consultation at the beginning of the process had blocked trade liberalization from moving forward (Heredia 1996).

30. The most notorious example occurred in 1993, when each of the country's top business leaders was invited to pledge $25 million to the PRI's 1994 election campaign; public outcry resulted in a reduction of contributions to a third of a million each (Teichman 1995, 256).

31. Four executives or owners of petrochemical companies made this point.

32. There was a strong disagreement within the policy core over this issue. President Salinas, head of the Central Bank Miguel Mancera, and Finance Minister Pedro Aspe, those reformers with the closest ongoing contacts with powerful entrepreneurs supporting the restriction of foreign investment in the banking and telecommunications sectors, championed the restriction of foreign participation. Serra Puche and Zedillo pushed for the immediate opening of these sectors to foreign competition and investment.

33. When asked, Mexican technocrats denied that this was a motivation. Nor did Mexican businessmen see privatization as an alliance-building mechanism.

34. The bank privatization required an amendment to the constitution and therefore two-thirds support from the Chamber of Deputies. The PRI was able to negotiate support from the National Action Party (PAN). In return for its support, the PAN was given assurances that no individual would be allowed to own more than 5 percent of banking stock. This stipulation was skirted, however, through the use of holding companies.

35. The argument that the Mexican government failed to adjust the exchange rate because of electoral concerns is made by Starr (1999a), who compares the Mexican decision not to adjust with the Argentine decision to adjust, the difference being accounted for by differing electoral coalitions in each case. Others have argued that policy makers simply miscalculated the weakness of the peso and the probability that confidence in the economy would return after the election (Mayer-Serra 1998, 17; Lustig 1998, 161).

36. Two top-level officials closely involved in high-level economic decisions during this period said that they believed this pressure played an important role in Aspe's resistance to devaluation. These individuals also believed, however, that Aspe had made a "technical miscalculation," which was the explanation given by three other inside observers for the decision not to devalue. The role of the private sector in this decision is borne out by private sector opposition to the float of the peso in meetings held between business leaders and Finance Minister Serra Puche (see *Proceso*, no. 959, March 20, 1995, 17, and no. 960, May 8, 1995, 43).

37. According to one source, there was a deep breach between Salinas and Colosio by the

time of the latter's murder (*Mexico & NAFTA Report*, November 2, 1995, 3). Persuaded by Camacho Solís, Colosio came around to the firm belief that deep political reforms and a real political opening were the only way to confront the political crisis facing the country (*Mexico & NAFTA Report*, November 2, 1995, 2).

38. Zedillo ordered the arrest of Raúl Salinas, who not only was linked to the assassination of Ruiz Massieu but also was believed to be implicated in state corruption and in drug trafficking. The once powerful top adviser to both de la Madrid and Carlos Salinas José Córdoba resigned his position as the Mexican representative to the Interamerican Development Bank in the midst of allegations of links to both the assassination of Donaldo Colosio and drug trafficking (*Latin American Weekly Report*, July 13, 1995, 308). Allegations of corruption against Carlos Salinas himself have been made in connection with the misappropriation of CONASUPO (the state company marketing food products) funds (*Mexico & NAFTA Report*, October 12, 1995, 2).

39. Contradictory statements were made regarding the electricity company; the energy minister said that the electricity company was not for sale, while the minister of finance declared that sale of the properties of the electrical company would raise $6 billion (U.S.) (ISLA, January 1995, 15).

40. Mexico reportedly agreed to measures to control undocumented immigration, drug trafficking, and law enforcement (ISLA, February 1995, 39).

41. Subsequent audits show a link between PRI campaign contributions and generosity of bank rescue operations (López Obrador 1999, 32–34).

42. Once the House of Deputies gained access to bank documents, several bankers with close connections to the Salinas regime were charged with fraud (*Latin American Weekly Report*, December 2, 1997, 567).

43. The political fallout of the peso crisis is discussed in depth in Chapter 7.

44. When the 49 percent shares were put up for sale in 1998, however, there was little interest (*Latin American Weekly Report*, May 12, 1998, 214).

45. Under this policy, five banks would give back $3.7 billion (U.S.) in loans (each loan over $500,000), out of a total portfolio of $16 billion that FOBAPROA had taken over from the five (*Latin American Weekly Report*, October 8, 1998, 466). The PAN supported the deal but the PRD did not.

46. The Unit for Disincorporation in the Ministry of Finance, its name changed to the Unit for Disincorporation and Investment in 1995, was no longer responsible for the sale of firms to be privatized. It became responsible for the analytical work once a privatization was decided on and for the revision of legislation to open up areas to foreign capital investment (interview with senior government official).

47. One top-level informant revealed that in his view Zedillo had tighter control of economic policy than his predecessor because he, unlike Salinas, is an economist by profession and thus absolutely nothing escaped his critical scrutiny.

48. The minister of SEDESOL, Francisco Rojas, resigned when he lost the battle over social policy. Rojas apparently supported a continuation of President Salinas's PRONASOL (National Solidarity Program), a program he saw as more politically viable because it reached more people than the more narrowly targeted PROGRESA program. The SEDESOL bureaucracy opposed PROGRESA because they did not see it as a long-term solution and favored more social spending on programs to incorporate the poor as productive members of the economy (interviews with two middle-level officials of SEDESOL).

49. The regulatory board, the Federal Commission for Telecommunications (COFETEL), submitted a proposed regulatory document aimed at curtailing TELMEX's market domi-

nance to TELMEX for its comments. TELMEX's director general declared that the company "will not accept asymmetrical regulation that regulates [the company's] growth . . . or its plans for expansion" (*El Financiera*, November 25, 1999, 31).

50. The two state-owned airlines were privatized under President Salinas but soon faltered. The government stepped in, buying shares and creating a holding company, to administer the two airlines, AEROMEXICO and Mexicana de Aviación. Foreign competitors have brought charges of monopolistic practices before the Federal Competition Commission, but to no avail (*Proceso*, no. 1103, December 21, 1997, 29).

51. The program followed the standard lines of bank policy in that it targeted extreme poverty. A pilot project for this program was carried out in the state of Mexico in 1994 (interview with middle-level government official).

52. In late 1999, senior levels of the government were taking a greater interest in decentralization. The Ministry of Finance had just brought back one individual who had ceased doing consulting work for the ministry a few years earlier and had gone to work for the World Bank because he was frustrated with the government's failure to move on the decentralization issue. Another frustrated technocrat had set up his own consulting company which was receiving World Bank funds to prepare state governments for decentralization (interviews with two Finance Ministry officials).

CHAPTER 7

1. The year 1990 saw strikes by state employees, teachers, railway workers, and telephone workers and the announcement by CGT leader Saul Ubaldini that he would seek support for the establishment of a new labor party. An estimated eight hundred thousand private sector workers were also on strike demanding wage increases (*Latin American Weekly Report*, April 19, 1990, 9; June 7, 1990, 11). Early in that year, a faction of the military known as the *carapintadas* staged a rebellion, allegedly financed by disgruntled members of the private sector (McSherry 1997, 241). In mid-1990 the government claimed to have information that this group was plotting more "direct action" against the government and seeking support from disgruntled trade union and business leaders (*Latin American Weekly Report*, August 9, 1990, 6).

2. In 1989, the labor movement split between the anti-Menemist CGT Azopardo and the pro-Menem CGT San Martín.

3. Access to the social welfare funds was absolutely critical to the ability of union leaders to maintain rank-and-file support since the funds made it possible for the union to provide such services as supply stores and medical assistance.

4. The 1991 Labor Reform Law allowed workers to be hired on a temporary basis without entitlement to severance pay, legalized the hiring of workers under twenty-four years of age as apprentices without entitlement to severance pay, and placed limitations on severance pay for unjustified dismissal and for accidents and injuries (*Latin American Weekly Report*, November 28, 1991, 3). The other bills are discussed below.

5. As one such trade union leader put it: "People think that we are in bed with the government. But that is not the case—we are struggling for political space so we can push for what we think is important." On this point, see McGuire 1992, 65–68.

6. According to McGuire (1997, 225), most collective agreements signed in 1992 and 1993 in Argentina were signed at the branch or firm level, a practice contrary to the labor code. The viewpoint that Mexico's de facto labor flexibilization was considerably greater than Argentina's was expressed to me by two senior IMF officials and all LAC officials. Moreover,

Argentine entrepreneurs saw their de facto labor flexibilization as tenuous because without changes in the labor code there was always the possibility that these practices could be successfully challenged in the courts. In contrast, labor flexibilization regarding revisions to the labor code was considerably less important for Mexican business.

7. This proposed reform would have allowed employers to alter contractual terms, change working times and holiday periods, and eliminate rules on severance pay (*Latin American Weekly Report*, October 10, 1996, 458).

8. This latest reform fosters collective agreements at the company level, eliminates the 1975 provision for the automatic renewal of collective agreements, and extends the probationary period for new workers from 30 to 180 days (*Latin American Weekly Report*, February 3, 2000, 62).

9. In 1991 the collection of workers' contributions to the social welfare funds was transferred from the unions to the state, and workers' compulsory affiliation with union *obras* (social welfare funds providing health care) was abolished.

10. Top-level officials involved in getting economic bills through Congress stated explicitly in interviews that their responsibility was to ensure that Congress did not tamper with government bills at all.

11. Cavallo pushed through a lower tax reduction on popular items than called for by the House of Deputies (*Latin American Weekly Report*, May 2, 1996, 182).

12. This image of Cavallo was held by the majority of Argentine officials, congressmen, labor leaders, and business leaders interviewed and is contrary to the viewpoint of Corrales, who assumes Cavallo's democratic proclivities because much of his legislation followed the congressional route (1997, 65).

13. For example, the 1996 tax reform bill went through Congress (and was altered) even though the Second Reform of the State emergency law had given Menem the power to implement this measure by presidential decree.

14. Labor unrest and protests occurred in Córdoba, Río Negro, Jujuy, Tucumán, Tierra del Fuego, San Juan, Mar del Plata, La Rioja, and Mendoza in 1995; in Río Negro, Corrientes, Formosa, Santa, Jujuy, La Rioja, Neuquén, and Santa Fe in 1996; in Neuquén, Mendoza, Salta, Tucumán, Santa Fe, Jujuy, and Río Negro in 1997; and in Jujuy, Salta, Río Negro, and Neuquén in 1998. The government responded with the use of security forces, producing numerous injuries in some cases (*El Clarín Internacional*, 1995–98).

15. In addition, the Menem regime became mired in a growing number of corruption scandals. For a summary of the various scandals confronting the Menem government, see *Latin American Weekly Report*, October 13, 1998, 477.

16. The two major parties in this alliance are the leftist FREPASO (Country Solidarity Front) and the Radical Party.

17. Results of a survey carried out by Sofres Ibope in all major cities (*Latin American Weekly Report*, March 10, 1998, 110).

18. Although the regime claims that the new labor reform will increase employment.

19. This occurred in all three enterprises declared bankrupt (Fundidora Monterrey, AEROMEXICO, and Cananea) and produced protracted struggles between unions and the government (*Proceso*, no. 498, May 19, 1986, 18, 20, no. 673, September 25, 1989, 8; *La Jornada* [sección laboral], April 4, 1991, 3).

20. The extent of the official labor movement's disgust with the process of labor consultation on policy is reflected by the call for the dissolution of the Minimum Salary Commission by the head of the official CTM (*La Jornada*, May 12, 1992, 5).

21. It was used five times between 1983 and 1987 (Teichman 1995, 118–19).

22. PROCAMPO (Program of Direct Support to the Countryside) also had clear clientelistic features geared to shore up the regime's support in the countryside for the 1994 national election. The program gave direct subsidies to peasant producers of corn, beans, wheat, rice, soya, sorghum, and cotton throughout a transition period during which guaranteed prices would be removed.

23. There is disagreement over whether the government sought to use PRONASOL to gain support where it was weak or to use PRONASOL to reward areas supporting the PRI in 1988. See Molinar Horcasitas and Weldon 1994, 130, 139.

24. An additional factor was the NAFTA negotiations, which prompted close scrutiny of Mexico's political practices during elections.

25. When asked if they feared any threat to market reforms as a consequence of greater democratization, all technocrats interviewed felt that there was little chance that important changes in economic policy would occur because the policy reforms had been "locked in" by the North American Free Trade Agreement—tampering with them would mean changing the agreement. There was also a consensus that since the opposition rightist PAN was solidly behind the neoliberal model, basic changes would not be made by Congress.

26. The Finance Ministry after 1997 under Zedillo's presidency had six members of its congressional liaison unit permanently in Congress lobbying for its bills, and it employed other individuals specializing in relations with the media and the public. Most other ministries either also had such units or were in the process of setting them up by 1999.

27. All who spoke about the first year of opposition control of Congress (congressmen and government officials) characterized top-level officials, especially Finance Ministry officials, as fiercely resistant to any changes in their bills. By 1999, however, this resistance appeared to have lessened although old habits die hard, as suggested by PAN allegations that the government attempted to bribe some of the opposition legislators during the 1999 budget debate (*Latin American Weekly Report*, January 4, 2000, 2).

28. FORO (Trade Unionism Facing Crisis and the Nation) was established in 1994 by FESEBES, the teachers' union, and a variety of other unions that maintained that the Labor Congress (CT) was manipulated by the government. A larger organization, established in 1997, the National Union of Workers (UNT), benefited from the desertions of a variety of trade unions that had remained compliant within the official trade union movement. The UNT claimed to be democratic and called for an end to corporatism, an increase in union autonomy, the defense of labor rights, and better salaries (*Proceso*, no. 1099, November 23, 1999, 32).

29. When asked why the government had apparently abandoned such methods, one senior-level official responded that "the public would not tolerate it." But allegations of the imposition of a charro leadership in the railway workers' union suggest that the government may not have entirely abandoned old ways. The head of the union is accused of having accepted bribes in exchange for his support for privatization (*Proceso*, no. 1086, August 24, 1997, 31).

30. Reform in the health care area has been mainly confined to changes in the Ministry of Health (Trejo and Jones 1998, 83).

31. While all of the technocrats interviewed supported Labastida over the other candidates and readily admitted he was the official favorite, they also acknowledged that Labastida did not see eye to eye with the radical market reform technocrats on economic policy and that they expected to see some changes.

32. Allegedly, some of the new security measures were designed by the old-time politicos in the PRI, the "dinosaurs" (*Mexico & NAFTA Report*, October 12, 1995, 4).

33. Worker representatives were to be chosen by the minister of labor from a list drawn up by workers and employers (Campero and Valenzuela 1984, 239).

34. In an effort to depoliticize the involvement of trade unions, parties were prohibited from any involvement in trade unions and Marxist trade unions were prohibited.

35. For the Chicago boys, the liberal use of the repressive apparatus of the state was an indispensable ingredient of their reform program. In the words of one of them: "Due to the fact that this was a military government, we could do what we wanted to do . . . we could not have done what we did otherwise because everyone was opposed."

36. Fernández justified disappearances (summary executions of political opponents) on the grounds that the country was at war (Osorio and Cabezas 1995, 238).

37. His view was premised on the belief that Chile was "the most socialist country in the world" and that only a firm hand could prevent a "political explosion" (interview with senior government official).

38. By the end of the 1980s, the number of workers in trade unions was one-half the number that had been unionized in 1970 (Drake 1996, 136).

39. Another aspect of the reform was the shift of responsibility for health care to the municipalities.

40. Healthy economic growth rates after 1985 were undoubtedly also important in accounting for the relative social peace of the period.

41. This account of labor unrest is taken from *Latin American Weekly Report* and *El Mercurio Internacional*, various issues, in addition to the citations in the text.

42. Indeed, the labor law proposal came soon on the heels of a CUT-led labor demonstration (Loveman 1995, 321).

43. Their interaction was entirely with the minister of labor (interviews with two labor leaders and a senior government official).

44. When teachers and health workers first struck in 1991, the government brought charges under the National Security Law (*Latin American Weekly Report*, October 17, 1991, 12).

45. The government's offer was put to a vote by the union leadership and turned down three times by workers. While agreeing to reinstate ninety-seven workers temporarily (the original cause of the conflict), the government stood firm on its commitment to a future reduction of the workforce in the Lota Enacar mine. This was the reason for the rejection of the government's offer by rank-and-file workers. The offer included severance packages, early retirement, and retraining for laid-off workers but would not lower the retirement age as requested by union negotiators (*La Epoca*, June 13, 1996, 16).

46. In addition to the newspaper citations, the following discussion is taken from interviews with two senior-level government officials, including one of ministerial rank, two congressmen, and one labor leader in the CUT.

47. Escalona stood his ground, responding that the Socialist Party opposed the layoffs of the ninety-seven miners that had triggered the coal strike. He insisted that the government must not deliver an ultimatum (which it ultimately did) and that the two sides must continue negotiations (*La Epoca*, June 14, 1996, 15).

48. Immediately, Alejandro Foxley, head of the Christian Democratic Party, met with his counterpart in the Socialist Party, in an attempt to work out a rotating leadership arrangement that would allow a Christian Democrat to take over the leadership of the CUT after two years of a normal four-year term (*El Mercurio Internacional*, April 25–May 1, 1996, 4)—a proposition rejected by the socialist trade unionists.

49. The polarization between business and labor over the labor reform issue is now greater

than ever. While labor wants measures to provide greater protection to labor rights, the private sector and the political right support a bill, still before Congress, that provides for further deregulation (flexibilization of labor) of the labor market (*Latin American Weekly Report,* September 8, 1998, 411).

50. Between 1990 and 1994, the proportion of poor in the Chilean population was reduced from 40 to 28 percent. The figures for Mexico (1989 and 1996) are 42 and 43 percent, respectively, and for Argentina (1990 and 1997) are 16 and 13 percent, respectively (CEPAL).

CHAPTER 8

1. This was not the case for small and medium nonexporting firms, which, if they were still around after trade liberalization, remained highly skeptical of market reform.

2. The use of privatization to bring in the private sector was widely acknowledged in the case of Argentina and was also apparent in the Chilean case, including under Concertación. Neither Mexican technocrats nor members of the private sector, however, believed that securing private sector allies was an important motivation for technocrats at any stage of the Mexican privatization drive.

3. This occurs when country officials work for multilaterals either as employees or doing contract work, a situation that exposes them to policy discussions and involves them in submitting reports and recommendations. Such officials both influence and are influenced by the environment in which they are working. When they are later employed at senior policy levels in their home governments, they are likely to lobby for policies developed while they were in Washington.

4. Officials are increasingly recognizing that good policy requires an understanding of, and support from, a broad spectrum of societal groups (interview with senior LAC official). The IMF also claims that it is increasingly attempting to speak to societal groups about its policy recommendations. The reason given is the same: if such policies do not have broad societal support, they will not be successful (interview with senior IMF official).

5. The case of reform in the Mexican agricultural sector may be instructive here. Had World Bank agricultural specialists had a more intimate knowledge of the social and political historical aspect of Mexican agriculture, a knowledge acquired through dialogue not just with agricultural bureaucrats but with the members of the social groups involved in agriculture, they might have been able to persuade the country's radical reformers to forgo ejido reform for the time being and move more decisively in support of health care, education, and other reforms for small producers—a policy toward which these bank officials were already predisposed. In any case, the dialogue that they did have could not have equipped them to imagine the political fallout of reform.

6. The Gini coefficient (family income), an inequality index that increases as the distribution of income becomes more skewed, was 56.3 for Chile (1994) (World Bank 1997, 215) and 58 for Mexico (1994) (Lustig 1998, 203). The 1975 and 1983 figures for Chile were 50 and 54, respectively (Edwards and Cox Edwards 1987, 167).

7. Social expenditure as a proportion of GDP reached 13.5 percent by 1995, while in 1970 the figure was 21.7 percent (Raczynski 1994, 65).

8. Indeed, there is also a wide variety of opinions among these critics, ranging from those who remain enthusiastic about market reform ideas but are highly critical about the way in which it has been carried out to those who question the model itself.

9. The type of poverty program supported was reflective, to a large extent, of faith in the market. Those supporting programs targeting extreme poverty maintain that the market will improve living standards for all those living in standard poverty. Those wanting a broader program are doubtful.

10. Indeed, labor has not bought into the argument often made by the technocrats that increased labor flexibilization will reduce unemployment (interviews with all labor leaders).

references

Acuña, Carlos H. 1994. "Politics and Economics in the Argentina of the Nineties." In
Carlos H. Acuña and Eduardo A. Gamarra, eds., *Democracy, Markets and Structural Re-
form in Latin America*. Coral Gables: North-South Center Press at the University of
Miami.

Aggarwal, Vinod K. 1996. *Debt Games: Strategic Interaction in International Debt Rescheduling.*
Cambridge, Eng.: Cambridge University Press.

———. 1987. *International Debt Threat: Bargaining among Creditors and Debtors in the 1980s.*
No. 29. Policy Papers in International Studies. Berkeley: Institute of International
Studies, University of California.

Agüero, Felipe. 1998. "Conflicting Assessments of Democratization: Exploring the Fault
Lines." In Felipe Agüero and Jeffrey Stark, eds., *Fault Lines of Democracy in Post Transition
Latin America*. Coral Gables: North-South Center Press at the University of Miami.

Aguilar García, Javier. 1990. "Relaciones estado-sindicatos, 1982–1990." *El Cotidiano*
7 (November–December): 68–69.

Aguilera Reyes, Maximo. 1994. "La economía chilena en el periodo 1974–1993." Docu-
mentos Docentes. Santiago: Universidad Central, Facultadad Ciencias Económicas y
Administrativas.

Alarcón, Loyola. 1989. *Desafíos de la economía mexicana*. Mexico City: ECASA.

Alonso, Antonio. 1986. *El movimiento ferrocarrilero en México, 1958–1959*. 7th ed. Mexico City:
Ediciones Era.

Alvarez, Sonia E., Evelina Dagnino, and Arturo Escobar, eds. 1998a. *Cultures of Politics and
Politics of Cultures*. Boulder, Colo.: Westview Press.

———. 1998b. "Introduction: The Cultural and the Political in Latin American Social
Movements." In Sonia E. Alvarez, Evelina Dagnino, and Arturo Escobar, eds., *Cultures
of Politics and Politics of Cultures*. Boulder, Colo.: Westview Press.

Ames, Barry. 1987. *Political Survival: Politicians and Public Policy in Latin America*. Berkeley:
University of California Press.

Amnesty International. 1999. *Mexico: Under the Shadow of Impunity*. London: International
Secretariat.

Anderson, Charles W. 1967. *Politics and Economic Change in Latin America*. London: D. Van
Nostrand.

Angel Romero M., Miguel. 1990. "Electiones: Nueva situación geopolítica." *El Cotidiano*
7 (January–February): 14–20.

Angell, Alan. 1995. "Unions and Workers in Chile during the 1980s." In Paul W. Drake
and Iván Jaksić, eds., *The Struggle for Democracy in Chile, 1982–90*. Rev. ed. Lincoln:
University of Nebraska Press.

———. 1988. *De Alessandri a Pinochet: En busca de la Utopía*. Santiago: Editorial Andrés
Bello.

———. 1972. *Politics and the Labor Movement in Chile*. London: Oxford University Press.

Aspe Armella, Pedro. 1993. *El camino mexicano de la transformación económica*. Mexico City:
Fondo de Cultura Económica.

Ayala Espino, José. 1988. *Estado y desarrollo: La formación de la economía mixta mexicana (1920–
1982)*. Mexico City: Fondo de Cultura Económica.

Azizali, F. Mohammed. 1991. "Recent Evolution of Fund Conditionality." In Jacob Frenkel
and Morris Goldstein, eds., *International Financial Policy: Essays in Honor of Jacques J.
Polak*. Washington, D.C.: International Monetary Fund.

Azpiazu, Daniel, and Adolfo Vispo. 1994. "Algunos enseñanzas de las privatizaciones en Argentina." *Revista de CEPAL* no. 54 (December): 130–46.

Babai, Don. 1988. "The World Bank and the IMF: Rolling Back the State or Backing Its Role?" In Raymond Vernon, ed., *The Promise of Privatization: A Challenge for U.S. Policy.* New York: Council on Foreign Affairs.

Bailón, Moisés J. 1994. "Semejanzas y diferencias en dos regiones indígenas del sur de México." Paper presented at the XXVIII International Congress of the Latin American Studies Association, Atlanta, March 10–13.

Banco Central de Chile. www.bcentral.cl/

Banco Central de Chile. 1996. Mimeo.

Banco de México. 1993. *The Mexican Economy, 1992.* Mexico City: Banco de México.

Barboso Cano, Fabio. 1992. "La restructuración de PEMEX." *El Cotidiano* 7 (March–April): 20–23.

Barrera, Manuel. 1999. "Political Participation and Social Exclusion of the Popular Sectors in Chile." In Philip Oxhorn and Pamela K. Starr, eds., *Markets and Democracy in Latin America.* Boulder, Colo.: Lynne Rienner.

Barrera, Manuel, and J. Samuel Valenzuela. 1987. "The Development of the Labor Movement: Opposition to the Military Regime." In J. Samuel Valenzuela and Arturo Valenzuela, eds., *Military Rule in Chile: Dictatorship and Oppositions.* Baltimore: Johns Hopkins University Press.

Basualdo, Eduardo M. 1994. "El impacto económico y social de las privatizaciones." *Realidad Económica* no. 123 (April 1–May 15): 27–51.

Bennett, Douglas, and Kenneth Sharpe. 1982. "The State as Banker and Entrepreneur." In Sylvia Ann Hewlett and Richard Weinert, eds., *Brazil and Mexico: Patterns in Late Development.* Philadelphia: Institute for the Study of Human Issues.

Berins Collier, Ruth. 1991. *The Contradictory Alliance: State-Labor Relations and Regime Change in Mexico.* Berkeley: University of California Press.

Biersteker, Thomas J. 1993. "International Financial Negotiations and Adjustment Bargaining: An Overview." In Thomas J. Biersteker, ed., *Dealing with Debt: International Financial Negotiations.* Boulder, Colo.: Westview Press.

Bird, Graham R. 1995. *IMF Lending to Developing Countries: Issues and Evidence.* London: Routledge.

Bizberg, Ilán. 1990. *Estado y sindicalismo en México.* Mexico City: El Colegio de México.

Blair, Calvin P. 1964. "Nacional Financiera: Entrepreneurship in a Mixed Economy." In Raymond Vernon, ed., *Public Policy and Private Entrepreneurship in Mexico.* Cambridge, Mass.: Harvard University Press.

Blutman, Gustavo. 1994. "Orden y desorden en la reforma del estado argentino (1989–1994)." *Ciclos* 4 (2d semester): 52–93.

Borón, Atilio. 1998. "Faulty Democracies? A Reflection of the Capitalist 'Fault Lines' in Latin America." In Felipe Agüero and Jeffrey Stark, eds., *Fault Lines of Democracy in Post Transition Latin America.* Coral Gables: North-South Center Press at the University of Miami.

Boylan, Delia M. 1996. "Taxation and Transition: The Politics of the 1990 Chilean Tax Reform." *Latin American Research Review* 31:7–36.

Brailovsky, Vladimiro, Roland Clarke, and Natán Warman. 1989. *La política económica del desperdicio: México en el periodo 1982–1988.* Mexico City: UNAM.

Brandenburg, Frank. 1964. *The Making of Modern Mexico.* Englewood Cliffs, N.J.: Prentice-Hall.

Bunel, Jean. 1992. *Pactos y agresiones: El sindicalismo argentino ante el desafío neoliberal.* Buenos Aires: Fondo de Cultura Económica S.A.

Butler, Stuart M. 1987. "Changing the Political Dynamics of Government." In Steven H. Hanke, ed., *Prospects for Privatization.* New York: Academy of Political Science.

Calvert, Susan, and Peter Calvert. 1989. *Argentina: Political Culture and Instability*. Pittsburgh: University of Pittsburgh Press.

Camp, Roderic A. 1999. *Politics in Mexico*. New York: Oxford University Press.

———. 1990. "Camarillas in Mexican Politics: The Case of the Salinas Cabinet." *Mexican Studies/Estudios Mexicanos* 6 (Winter): 85–107.

———. 1989. *Entrepreneurs and Politics in Twentieth Century Mexico*. New York: Oxford University Press.

———. 1985. "The Political Technocrat in Mexico and the Survival of the Mexican Political System." *Latin American Research Review* 20:97–118.

Campero, Guillermo, and José A. Valenzuela. 1984. *El movimiento sindical en el régimen militar chileno, 1973–1981*. Santiago: Instituto Latinoamericano de Estudios Transnacionales.

Canitrot, Aldolfo, and Silva Sigal. 1994. "Economic Reform, Democracy and the Crisis of the State in Argentina." In Joan Nelson, ed., *A Precarious Balance: Democracy and Economic Reform in Latin America*, vol. 2. San Francisco, Calif.: Institute for Contemporary Studies.

Carrillo Arronte, Ricardo. 1987. "The Role of the State and the Entrepreneurial Sector in Mexican Development." In Sylvia Maxfield and Ricardo Anzaldúa, eds., *Government and Private Sector in Contemporary Mexico*. San Diego: Center for U.S.-Mexican Studies and the University of California.

Castañeda, Jorge G. 1996. "Democracy and Inequality in Latin America: A Tension of the Times." In Jorge I. Domínguez and Abraham F. Lowenthal, eds., *Constructing Democratic Governance: Latin America and the Caribbean in the 1990s, Themes and Issues*. Baltimore: Johns Hopkins University Press.

Cavarozzi, Marcelo. 1997. *Autoritarismo y democracia, 1955–1996*. Buenos Aires: Compañía Editorial Calpe Argentina S.A.

———. 1994. "Mexico's Political Formula, Past and Present." In Maria Lorena Cook, Kevin J. Middlebrook, and Juan Molinar Horcasitas, eds., *The Politics of Economic Restructuring: State-Society Relations and Regime Change in Mexico*. San Diego: Center for U.S.-Mexican Studies and the University of California.

Centeno, Miguel Angel. 1998. "The Failure of Presidential Authoritarianism: Transition in Mexico." In Scott Mainwaring and Arturo Valenzuela, eds., *Politics, Society and Democracy: Latin America*. Boulder, Colo.: Westview Press.

———. 1997. *Democracy within Reason*. University Park: Pennsylvania State University Press.

Centeno, Miguel A., and Patricio Silva. 1998. "The Politics of Expertise in Latin America: Introduction." In Miguel A. Centeno and Patricio Silva, eds., *The Politics of Expertise in Latin America*. New York: St. Martin's Press.

CEPAL. *América Latina, magnitud de la pobreza y indigencia*, cuadro 16. www.eclac.cl/espanol/estadisticas.

———. 1999. *CEPAL News* 19 (January).

———. 1997. *CEPAL News* 17 (February).

———. 1993. *Notas sobre la economia y el desarrollo*. No. 552/553 (December).

Chalmers, Douglas A., Carlos M. Vilas, Katherine Hite, Scott B. Martin, Kerianne Piester, and Monique Segarra, eds. 1997. *The New Politics of Inequality in Latin America*. Oxford: Oxford University Press.

Ciria, Alberto. 1974. "Los partidos politicos durante la restauración conservadora." In Alberto Ciria, Nidia Areces, Norberto Galasso, Matias G. Sánchez Sorondo, Alberto J. Plá, Raúl Scalabrini Ortiz, Arturo Jaretche, and Ovidio A. Andrada, *La década infame*. Buenos Aires: Ediciones Cepe.

El Clarín. (Buenos Aires). Various dates.

El Clarín Internacional. (Buenos Aires). Various dates.

Cleaves, Peter S. 1974. *Bureaucratic Politics and Administration in Chile.* Berkeley: University of California Press.

Cline, Howard F. 1961. *The United States and Mexico.* Cambridge, Mass.: Harvard University Press.

Cline, William R. 1995. *International Debt Re-examined.* Washington, D.C.: Institute for International Economics.

Cockcroft, James D. 1983. *Class Formation, Capital Accumulation and the State.* New York: Monthly Review.

Conaghan, Catherine M., and James M. Malloy. 1994. *Unsettling Statecraft: Democracy and Neoliberalism in the Central Andes.* Pittsburgh: University of Pittsburgh Press.

Conaghan, Catherine, James M. Malloy, and Luis A. Abugattas. 1990. "Business and the Boys: The Politics of Neoliberalism in the Central Andes." *Latin American Research Review* 25:3–30.

"Conflictos obreros-patronales." 1990. *El Cotidiano* 7 (July–August): 52.

Consejo Tecnico de Inversiones S.A. 1990. *Tendencias económicas, la economia Argentina,* Edición no. 20 (Annual).

Constable, Pamela, and Arturo Valenzuela. 1991. *A Nation of Enemies: Chile under Pinochet.* New York: Norton.

Cornelius, Wayne A. 1996. *Mexican Politics in Transition.* San Diego: University of California Press.

Corrales, Javier. 1997. "Why Argentines Follow Cavallo: A Technopol between Democracy and Economic Reform." In Jorge I. Domínguez, ed., *Technopols: Freeing Politics and Markets in Latin America in the 1990s.* University Park: Pennsylvania State University Press.

Cortés, A. Guadalupe. 1984. "Golpe al movimiento Ferrocarrilero, 1948." In Victor Durante Ponte, coord., *Las derrotas obreras, 1946–1952.* Mexico City: UNAM.

Crawley, Eduardo. 1984. *A House Divided: Argentina, 1880–1980.* London: C. Hurst.

Cumberland, Charles C. 1952. *Mexican Revolution: Genesis under Madero.* Austin: University of Texas Press.

Dahse, Fernando. 1979. *Mapa de la extrema riqueza.* Santiago: Editorial Aconcagua.

Dale, William B. 1983. "Financing and Adjustment of Payments Imbalances." In John Williamson, ed., *IMF Conditionality.* Washington, D.C.: Institute for International Economics.

Damel, Mario, and Roberto Frenkel. 1996. "Democratic Restoration and Economic Policy, Argentina, 1984–1991." In Juan Antonio Morales and Gary McMahon, eds., *Economic Policy and the Transition to Democracy: The Latin American Experience.* New York: St. Martin's Press.

De la Balze, Felipe A. M. 1995. *Remaking the Argentine Economy.* New York: Council on Foreign Relations Press.

Délano, Manuel, and Hugo Traslaviña. 1989. *La herencia de los Chicago Boys.* Santiago: Las Ediciones del Ornitorrinco.

Diamond, Larry, and Juan J. Linz. 1989. "Introduction: Politics, Society and Democracy in Latin America." In Larry Diamond, Juan J. Linz, and Seymour Martin Lipset, eds., *Democracy in Developing Countries: Latin America.* Boulder, Colo.: Lynne Rienner.

Díaz, Alvaro. 1997. "New Developments in Economic and Social Restructuring in Latin America." In William C. Smith and Roberto Patricio Korzeniewicz, eds., *Politics, Social Change and Economic Restructuring in Latin America.* Coral Gables: North-South Center Press at the University of Miami.

Dinerstein, Ana Cecilia. 1993. "Privatizaciones y legitimidad: La logica de coerción." *Realidad Económica* no. 113 (January 1): 19–25.

di Tella, Guido. 1987. "Argentina's Most Recent Inflationary Cycle." In Rosemary Thorp and Laurence Whitehead, eds., *Latin American Debt and the Adjustment Crisis.* Houndmills, Basingstoke, Hampshire, and London: Macmillan.

Domínguez, Jorge I. 1997. "Technopols, Ideas and Leaders in Freeing Politics and Markets in Latin America in the 90s." In Jorge I. Domínguez, ed., *Technopols: Freeing Politics and Markets in Latin America in the 1990s.* University Park: Pennsylvania State University Press.

Domínguez, Jorge I., and James A. McCann. 1996. *Democratizing Mexico: Public Opinion and Electoral Choices.* Baltimore: Johns Hopkins University Press.

Dornbusch, Rudiger, and Juan Carlos de Pablo. 1990. "Debt and Macroeconomic Instability in Argentina." In Jeffrey D. Sachs and Susan Margaret Collins, eds., *Developing Country Debt and Economic Performance*, vol. 2, *Country Studies—Argentina, Bolivia, Brazil, Mexico.* Chicago: University of Chicago Press.

Dornbusch, Rudiger, and Sebastian Edwards. 1994. "Exchange Rate Policy and Trade Strategy." In Barry P. Bosworth, Rudiger Dornbusch, and Raúl Labán, eds., *The Chilean Economy: Policy Lessons and Challenges.* Washington, D.C.: Brookings Institution Press.

Drake, Paul W. 1996. *Labor Movements and Dictatorships.* Baltimore: Johns Hopkins University Press.

———. 1978. *Socialism and Populism in Chile, 1932–1952.* Urbana: University of Illinois Press.

Drake, Paul W., and Eduardo Silva. 1986. "Introduction: Elections and Democratization in Latin America." In Paul W. Drake and Eduardo Silva, eds., *Elections and Democratization in Latin America, 1980–1985.* San Diego: Center for Iberian and Latin American Studies/Center for U.S.-Mexican Studies, University of California.

Drake, Paul W., and Peter Winn. 2000. "The Presidential Election of 1999/2000 and Chile's Transition to Democracy." *LASA Forum* 21 (Spring): 5–9.

Dresser, Denise. 1994. "Bringing the Poor Back In: National Solidarity as a Strategy of Regime Legitimacy." In Wayne A. Cornelius, Ann L. Craig, and Jonathan Fox, eds., *Transforming State-Society Relations in Mexico.* San Diego: Center for U.S.-Mexican Studies, University of California.

Dussel Peters, Enrique. 1995. "From Export Orientated to Import Orientated Industrialization: Changes in Mexico's Manufacturing Sector, 1988–1994." In Gerardo Otero, ed., *Neoliberalism Revisited.* Boulder, Colo.: Westview Press.

Editors. 1993a. "El proceso general de la privatización." *Realidad Economica* no. 120 (November 16–December 31): 80–90.

———. 1993b. "Privatization de Aerolíneas Argentinas." *Realidad Economica* no. 120 (November 16–December 31): 114–23.

———. 1993c. "La empresa de telecommunicaciones (ENTEL)." *Realidad Economica* no. 120 (November 16–December 31): 90–112.

Edwards, Sebastian. 1995. *Crisis and Reform in Latin America.* New York: Oxford University Press.

———. 1985. "Economic Policy and the Record of Economic Growth in Chile, 1973–1982." In Gary M. Walton, ed., *The National Economic Policies of Chile.* Greenwich, Conn.: Jai Press.

Edwards, Sebastian, and Alejandra Cox Edwards. 1987. *Monetarism and Liberalization: The Chilean Experiment.* Cambridge, Mass.: Ballinger.

Eisenstadt, S. N., and L. Roniger. 1984. *Patrons, Clients and Friends.* Cambridge, Eng.: Cambridge University Press.

La Epoca. (Santiago). Various dates.

Epstein, Edward C. 1992. "Labor Conflict in the New Argentine Democracy: Parties, Union Factions and Power Maximizing." In Edward C. Epstein, ed., *The New Argentine Democracy: The Successful Formula.* Westport, Conn.: Praeger.

———. 1989. "What Difference Does Regime Type Make? Economic Austerity Programs in Argentina." In Howard Handleman and Werner Baer, eds., *Paying the Costs of Austerity in Latin America*. Boulder, Colo.: Westview Press.

Erro, David G. 1993. *Resolving the Argentine Paradox: Politics and Development, 1966–1992.* Boulder, Colo.: Lynne Rienner.

Estrategia. 1994. *El Gran Salto de Chile: La historia económica y empresarial.* Santiago: Publicaciones Editorial Gestión.

Evans, Peter. 1992. "The State as Problem and Solution: Predation, Embedded Autonomy and Structural Change." In Stephan Haggard and Robert R. Kaufman, eds., *The Politics of Economic Adjustment.* Princeton: Princeton University Press.

Falabella, Gonzalo. 1981. *Labour in Chile under the Junta, 1973–1979.* Working Paper 4. London: Institute of Latin American Studies, University of London.

Felder, Ruth. 1994. "El estado se baja del tren: La política ferrovaria del gobierno menemista. La restructuración de los ferrocarriles: Particularidades y perspectivos." *Realidad Economica* no. 123 (April 1–May 15): 53–75.

Ferrer Aldo, Mario S. Brodersohn, Eprime Eshag, and Rosemary Thorp. 1974. *Los planes de estabilizacion en la Argentina.* Buenos Aires: Editorial Paidos.

Ffrench Davis, Ricardo. 1992. "Adjustment and Conditionality: Chile (1982–88)." In Emilio Rodríguez and Stephany-Griffith Jones, eds., *Cross-Conditionality: Banking Regulation and Third World Debt.* Houndmills, Basingstoke, Hampshire, and London: Macmillan.

FIEL (Fundación de Investigaciones Económicas Latinoamericanas). 1990. *Argentina: Hacía una economía de mercado.* Buenos Aires: FIEL.

El Financiero. 1999. (Mexico City). November 25.

Finch, David C. 1983. "Adjustment Policies and Conditionality." In John Williamson, ed., *IMF Conditionality.* Washington, D.C.: Institute for International Economics.

Fontaine Aldunate, Arturo. 1988. *Los economistas y el Presidente Pinochet.* Santiago: Empresa Editora Zig-Zag S.A.

Fortín, Carlos. 1988. "Power, Bargaining and the Latin American Debt Negotiations." In Stephany Griffith-Jones, ed., *Managing World Debt.* New York: St. Martin's Press.

Fox, Jonathan. 1994. "Targeting the Poorest: The Role of the National Indigenous Institute in Mexico's Solidarity Program." In Wayne A. Cornelius, Ann L. Craig, and Jonathan Fox, eds., *Transforming State Societal Relations in Mexico.* San Diego: Center for U.S.-Mexican Studies, University of California.

Fraga, Rosendo. 1991. *La cuestión sindical.* Buenos Aires: Editorial Centro de Estudios Unión para la Nueva Majoría.

Freels, John William, Jr. 1970. *El sector industrial en la politica nacional.* Buenos Aires: Editorial Universitaria de Buenos Aires.

Frías, Patricio. 1993–94. "Sindicatos en la transición: En la búsqueda de una nueva identidad." *Economia y Trabajo en Chile.* 4th Annual Report, Programa de Economia del Trabajo, 57–69.

Frieden, Jeffry A. 1991. *Debt, Development and Democracy, 1965–1985.* Princeton: Princeton University Press.

Friedman, Irving S. 1983. "Private Bank Conditionality: Comparison with the IMF and the World Bank." In John Williamson, ed., *IMF Conditionality.* Washington, D.C.: Institute of International Economics.

Fuchs, Jaime. 1965. *Argentina: Su desarrollo capitalista.* Buenos Aires: Editorial Cartago.

Furtado, Celso. 1976. *Economic Development of Latin America.* Cambridge, Eng.: Cambridge University Press.

Galjart, Benno, and Patricio Silva. 1995. "Intellectuals, Technocrats and Development: Concluding Remarks." In Benno Galjart and Patricio Silva, eds., *Intellectuals and Technocrats in the Third World: Designers of Development.* Leiden, The Netherlands: Research School CNWS.

Gaudio, Ricardo, and Andrés Thompson. 1990. *Sindicalismo peronista/gobierno radical.* Buenos Aires: Fundación Fredrich Ebert.

Gerchunoff, Pablo. 1989. "Peronist Economic Policies, 1946–55." In Guido di Tella and Rudiger Dornbusch, eds., *The Political Economy of Argentina, 1946–1983.* Pittsburgh: University of Pittsburgh Press.

Gerchunoff, Pablo, and Guillermo Canovas. 1995. "Privatizaciones en un contexto de emergencia economica." *Desarrollo Económico* 34 (January–March): 483–511.

Gibson, Edward L. 1997a. "The Populist Road to Market Reform: Policy and Electoral Coalitions in Argentina and Mexico." *World Politics* 49 (April): 337–70.

———. 1997b. "Electoral Coalitions and Market Reforms: Evidence from Argentina." Paper presented at the XX International Congress of the Latin American Studies Association, Guadalajara, Mexico, April 17–20.

Global Exchange/Alianza Civica International Delegation. 2000. *Pre-electoral Conditions in Mexico 2000.* San Francisco: Global Exchange.

Goldwert, Marvin. 1972. *Democracy, Militarism and Nationalism in Argentina, 1930–1966.* Austin: University of Texas Press.

Gollás, Manuel. 1978. "El desempleo en México: Soluciones Possibles." *Ciencia y Desarrollo.* CONACYT no. 20 (May–June): 2–11.

Golob, Stephanie R. 1997. "Making Possible What Is Necessary: Pedro Aspe, the Salinas Team and the Next Mexican Miracle." In Jorge Domínguez, ed., *Technopols: Freeing Politics and Markets in Latin America in the 1990s.* University Park: Pennsylvania State University Press.

González Gómez, Mauricio A. 1998. "Crisis and Economic Change in Mexico." In Susan Kaufman Purcell and Luis Rubio, eds., *Mexico under Zedillo.* Boulder, Colo.: Lynne Rienner.

Grassi, Estella, Susana Hintze, and María Rosa Neufeld. 1994. *Políticas sociales, crisis y ajuste estructural.* Buenos Aires: Espacio Editorial.

Grayson, George W. 1989. *The Mexican Labor Machine: Power Politics and Patronage.* Washington, D.C.: Center for Strategic International Studies.

———. 1969. "The Frei Administration in the 1969 Parliamentary Elections." *Inter-American Economic Affairs* 23 (Autumn): 51–74.

Green, María del Rosario. 1981. "Mexico's Economic Dependence." In Susan Kaufman Purcell, ed., *Mexican-U.S. Relations.* New York: Praeger.

Greenfield, Sidney M. 1976. "The Patrimonial State and Patron Client Relations in Iberia and Latin America." Program in Latin American Studies, Occasional Papers Series no. 1, International Area Studies Program. Amherst: University of Massachusetts.

Griffith-Jones, Stephany. 1992. "Cross Conditionality or the Spread of Obligatory Adjustment: A Review of the Issues and Questions for Research." In Emilio Rodríguez and Stephany Griffith-Jones, eds., *Cross Conditionality, Banking Regulation and Third World Debt.* Houndmills, Basingstoke, Hampshire, and London: Macmillan.

———. 1987. *Chile to 1991: The End of an Era?* Special Report 1073. London: Economic Intelligence Unit.

———. 1983. "Debt Management: An Analytical Framework." In Stephany Griffith-Jones, ed., *Managing World Debt.* New York: St. Martin's Press.

Grindle, Merilee S. 1996. *Challenging the State: Crisis and Innovation in Latin America and Africa.* Cambridge, Eng.: Cambridge University Press.

———. 1977. *Bureaucrats, Politicians and Peasants in Mexico.* Berkeley: University of California Press.

Gwin, Catherine. 1997. "US Relations with the World Bank, 1945–1992." In Devesh Kapur, John P. Lewis, and Richard Webb, eds., *The World Bank: Its First Half Century,* vol. 2, *Perspectives.* Washington, D.C.: Brookings Institution Press.

Haas, Ernst B. 1990. *When Knowledge Is Power: Three Models of Change in International Organizations.* Berkeley: University of California Press.

Haber, Stephen H. 1989. *Industry and Underdevelopment: The Industrialization of Mexico.* Stanford: Stanford University Press.

Hachette, Dominique, and Rolf Lüders. 1994. *La privatización en Chile.* Santiago: Centro Internacional para el Desarrollo Económico.

Haggard, Stephan, and Robert R. Kaufman. 1995. *The Political Economy of Democratic Transitions.* Princeton: Princeton University Press.

Haggard, Stephan, and Steven B. Webb. 1994. "Introduction." In Stephan Haggard and Steven B. Webb, eds., *Voting for Reform: Democracy, Political Liberalization and Economic Adjustment.* Washington, D.C.: World Bank.

Haindl, Erik. 1995. "Chile's Resolution of the External Debt Problem." In Robert Grosse, ed., *Government Responses to the Latin American Debt Problem.* Coral Gables: North-South Center Press at the University of Miami.

Hakim, Peter, and Abraham F. Lowenthal. 1993. "Latin America's Fragile Democracies." In Larry Diamond and Marc P. Plattner, eds., *The Global Resurgence of Democracy.* Baltimore: Johns Hopkins University Press.

Halperín Donghi, Tulio. 1988. "Argentina: Liberalism in a Country Born Liberal." In Joseph L. Love and Nils Jacobsen, eds., *Guiding the Invisible Hand: Economic Liberalism and the State in Latin American History.* New York: Praeger.

Handleman, Howard. 1997. *Mexican Politics: The Dynamics of Change.* New York: St. Martin's Press.

Hansen, Roger D. 1980. *The Politics of Mexican Development.* Baltimore: Johns Hopkins University Press.

Harvey, Neil. 1998. *The Chiapas Rebellion: The Struggle for Land and Democracy.* Durham, N.C.: Duke University Press.

———. 1993. "The Limits of Concertación in Rural Mexico." In Neil Harvey, ed., *Mexico's Dilemmas of Transition.* London: Institute of Latin American Studies, University of London.

Hastings, Laura A. 1993. "Regulatory Revenge: The Politics of Free Market Financial Reforms in Chile." In Stephan Haggard, Chung H. Lee, and Sylvia Maxfield, eds., *The Politics of Finance in Developing Countries.* Ithaca: Cornell University Press.

Hausman, Ricardo. 1994. "Sustaining Reform: What Role for Social Policy." In Colin I. Bradford Jr., ed., *Redefining the State in Latin America.* Paris: Organization for Economic Cooperation and Development.

Hay, Colin. 1998. "The Tangled Webs We Weave: The Discourse, Strategy and Practice of Networking." In David Marsh, ed., *Comparing Policy Networks.* Buckingham: Open University Press.

Hellman, Judith Adler. 1994. *Mexican Lives.* New York: New Press.

Heredia, Blanca. 1996. "Contested State: The Politics of Trade Liberalization in Mexico." Ph.D. diss., Columbia University.

Hira, Anil. 1999. *Ideas and Economic Policy in Latin America: Regional, National and Organizational Case Studies.* Westport, Conn.: Praeger.

Hojman, David E. 1993. *Chile: The Political Economy of Development and Democracy in the 1990s.* London: Macmillan.

Hughes, Jane. 1991. "Actors in the Latin American Debt Crisis I: The Creditor Governments." In Scott B. MacDonald, Jane Hughes, and Uwe Bott, eds., *Latin American Debt in the 1990s: Lessons from the Past and Forecasts for the Future.* New York: Praeger.

Ikenberry, John G. 1990. "The International Spread of Privatization Policies: Inducements, Learning and 'Policy Bandwagoning.'" In Ezra N. Suleiman and John Waterbury, eds., *The Political Economy of Public Sector Reform.* Boulder, Colo.: Westview Press.

ILO (International Labour Office). Oficina Regional para América Latina. *Panorama laboral '99.* Anexo Estadistica. www.ilolim.org.pe/

IMF. *Article IV Consultations (Chile).* www.imf.org.

INDEC. www.indec.gov.ar

ISLA (Information Services on Latin America). Oakland, Calif. Various dates.

Izquierdo, Rafael. 1964. "Protectionism in Mexico." In Raymond Vernon, ed., *Public Policy and Private Enterprise in Mexico.* Cambridge, Mass.: Harvard University Press.

James, Daniel. 1988. *Resistance and Integration: Peronism and the Argentine Working Class, 1946–1976.* Cambridge, Eng.: Cambridge University Press.

James, Harold. 1996. *International Monetary Cooperation since Bretton Woods.* Washington, D.C.: International Monetary Fund and Oxford University Press.

La Jornada (Mexico City). Various dates.

Kafka, Alexandre. 1991. "Some IMF Problems after the Committee of Twenty." In Jacob A. Frenkel and Morris Goldstein, eds., *International Financial Policy: Essays in Honor of Jacques J. Polak.* Washington, D.C.: International Monetary Fund.

Kahler, Miles. 1992. "External Influence, Conditionality and the Politics of Adjustment." In Stephan Haggard and Robert R. Kaufman, eds., *The Politics of Economic Adjustment.* Princeton: Princeton University Press.

Kapur, Devesh, John P. Lewis, and Richard Webb. 1997. *The World Bank: Its First Half Century.* Vol. 1, *History.* Washington, D.C.: Brookings Institution Press.

Kaufman, Edy. 1988. *Crises in Allende's Chile.* New York: Praeger.

Kaufman, Robert. 1977. "Mexican and Latin American Authoritarianism." In José Luis Reyna and Robert J. Wienert, eds., *Authoritarianism in Mexico.* Philadelphia: Institute for the Study of Human Issues.

Kearney, Christine A. 1993. "The Creditor Clubs: Paris and London." In Thomas J. Biersteker, ed., *Dealing with Debt.* Boulder, Colo.: Westview Press.

Kelsey, Sarah, and Steve Levitsky. 1994. "Captivating Alliances: Unions, Labor Backed Parties and the Politics of Economic Liberalism in Argentina and Mexico." Paper presented at the XVIII International Congress of the Latin American Studies Association, Atlanta, March 10–12.

Kenworthy, Eldon. 1970. "The Formation of the Peronist Coalition." Ph.D. diss., Yale University.

Killick, Tony. 1995. *IMF Programmes in Developing Countries.* London: Routledge.

Kinney Giraldo, Jeanne. 1997. "Development and Democracy in Chile: Finance Minister Alejandro Foxley and the Concertación Project for the 90s." In Jorge I. Domínguez, ed., *Technopols: Freeing Markets and Politics in Latin America in the 1990s.* University Park: Pennsylvania State University Press.

Kleinberg, Remonda Bensabat. 1999. *Strategic Alliances and Other Deals: State Business Relations and Economic Reform in Mexico.* Durham, N.C.: Carolina Academic Press.

Kornhauser, William. 1959. *The Politics of Mass Society.* New York: Free Press.

La Botz, Dan. 1992. *Mask of Democracy: Labor Suppression in Mexico Today.* Boston: South End Press.

Lambert, Jacques. 1967. *Latin America: Social Structures and Political Institutions.* Berkeley: University of California Press.

Langston, Joy. 1997. "An Empirical View of the Political Groups in Mexico: The Camarillas." Centro de Investigación y Docenia Económica (CIDE), División Estudios Políticos, Documento de Trabajo, no. 15.

Larraín, Felipe. 1991. "Public Sector Behaviour in a Highly Indebted Country: The Contrasting Chilean Experience." In Felipe Larraín and Marcelo Selowsky, eds., *The Public Sector and the Latin American Crisis.* San Francisco: ICS Press.

Larrañaga J., Osvaldo, and Jorge Marshall R. 1990. "Ajuste macroeconómico y finanzas públicas, 1982–1988." Programa de post grado de economía. ILADES. Georgetown University, June 1–22.

Latin American Weekly Report. Various dates.

Lee, Boon-Chye. 1993. *The Economics of International Debt Renegotiation.* Boulder, Colo.: Westview Press.

Lehman, Howard P. 1993. *Indebted Development: Strategic Bargaining and Economic Adjustment in the Third World.* London: Macmillan.

Lewellen, Ted C. 1995. *Dependency and Development.* Westport, Conn.: Bergin and Garvey.

Lewis, Paul H. 1990. *The Crisis of Argentine Capitalism.* Chapel Hill: University of North Carolina Press.

Lichtensztejn, Samuel. 1983. "IMF Developing Countries: Conditionality and Strategy." In John Williamson, ed., *IMF Conditionality.* Washington, D.C.: Institute for International Economics.

Linz, Juan J., and Alfred Stepan. 1996. *Problems of Democratic Transition and Consolidation: Southern Europe, South America and Post Communist Europe.* Baltimore: Johns Hopkins University Press.

Loaeza, Soledad. 1994. "Political Liberalization and Uncertainty in Mexico." In Maria Lorena Cook, Kevin J. Middlebrook, and Juan Molinar Horcasitas, eds., *The Politics of Economic Restructuring, State-Society Relations and Regime Change in Mexico.* San Diego: Center for U.S.-Mexican Studies, University of California.

López Obrador, Andrés Manuel. 1999. *Fobaproa: Expediente abierto, reseña y archivo.* Mexico City: Editorial Grijalbo S.A.

Loveman, Brian. 1995. "The Transition to Civilian Government in Chile, 1990–1994." In Paul W. Drake and Iván Jaksić, eds., *The Struggle for Democracy in Chile.* Rev. ed. Lincoln: University of Nebraska Press.

———. 1988. *The Legacy of Hispanic Capitalism.* 2d ed. Oxford: Oxford University Press.

Lowenthal, Abraham F., and Jorge I. Domínguez. 1996. "Introduction: Constructing Democratic Governance." In Jorge I. Domínguez and Abraham F. Lowenthal, eds., *Constructing Democratic Governance: Latin America and the Caribbean in the 1990s, Themes and Issues.* Baltimore: Johns Hopkins University Press.

Loyola Díaz, Rafael. 1990. "La liquidación del feudo petrolero en la politica moderna, México 1988." *Mexican Studies/Estudios Mexicanos* 6 (Summer): 263–97.

Lüders, Rolf J. 1993. "El estado empresario en Chile." In Daniel L. Wisecarver, ed., *El modelo económico Chileno.* 2d ed. Santiago: Centro Internacional para el Desarrollo Económico.

Luke, Paul. 1991. "Actors in the Latin American Debt Crisis: The Commercial Banks." In Scott B. MacDonald, Jane Hughes, and Uwe Bott, eds., *Latin American Debt in the 1990s.* New York: Praeger.

Luna, Matilde. 1992. "Las associaciones empresariales Mexicanas y la apertura externa." Paper presented at the XVII International Congress of the Latin American Studies Association, Los Angeles, September 24–27.

Lustig, Nora. 1998. *Mexico: The Remaking of an Economy.* 2d ed. Washington, D.C.: Brookings Institution Press.

Maloney, William F. 1992. "Popular Capitalism in Chile." Paper presented at the XVII International Congress of the Latin American Studies Association, Los Angeles, September 24–27.

Mamalakis, Markos J. 1976. *The Growth and Structure of the Chilean Economy: From Independence to Allende.* New Haven: Yale University Press.

Manzetti, Luigi. 1993. *Institutions, Parties and Coalitions in Argentine Politics.* Pittsburgh: University of Pittsburgh Press.

———. 1991. *The International Monetary Fund and Economic Stabilization: The Argentine Case.* New York: Praeger.

Margheritis, Ana. 1999. *Ajuste y reforma en Argentina (1989–1995)*. Buenos Aires: Grupo Editor Latinoamericano S.R.L.

Marín, Gustavo, and Patricio Rozas. 1988. *Los grupos transnacionales y la crisis: El caso Chileno*. Buenos Aires: Editorial Nueva América.

Marsh, David, and R. A. W. Rhodes. 1992. "Policy Communities and Issue Networks, Beyond Typology." In David Marsh and R. A. W. Rhodes, eds., *Policy Networks in British Government*. Oxford: Clarendon Press.

Marshall S., Jorge, José Luis Mardones S., and Isabel Marshall L. 1983. "IMF Conditionality: The Experiences of Argentina, Brazil and Chile." In John Williamson, ed., *IMF Conditionality*. Washington, D.C.: Institute for International Economics.

Martínez, Gabriel, and Guillermo Fárber. 1994. *Desregulación económica (1989–1993)*. Mexico City: Fondo de Cultura Económica.

Maxfield, Sylvia. 1990. *Governing Capital: International Finance and Mexican Politics*. Ithaca: Cornell University Press.

Mayer-Serra, Carlos Elizondo. 1998. "Are Policy Makers Irrational? Currency Crisis in Mexico." Paper presented at the XXI Congress of the Latin American Studies Association, Chicago, September 24–26.

McGuire, James W. 1997. *Peronism without Peron: Unions, Parties, and Democracy in Argentina*. Stanford: Stanford University Press.

———. 1994. "Economic Reform and Political Shenanigans in Menem's Argentina." Paper presented at the XVIII Congress of the Latin American Studies Association, Atlanta, March 10–12.

———. 1992. "Union Political Tactics and Democratic Consolidation in Alfonsín's Argentina." *Latin American Research Review* 27:37–72.

McSherry, J. Patrice. 1997. *Incomplete Transition: Military Power and Democracy in Argentina*. New York: St. Martin's Press.

El Mercurio (Santiago). Various dates.

El Mercurio Internacional (Santiago). Various dates.

Mericle, Kenneth S. 1977. "Corporatist Control of the Working Class: Authoritarian Brazil since 1964." In James M. Malloy, ed., *Authoritarianism and Corporatism in Latin America*. Pittsburgh: University of Pittsburgh Press.

Mexico and NAFTA Report. Various dates.

Middlebrook, Kevin J. 1995. *The Paradox of Revolution: Labor, the State and Authoritarianism in Mexico*. Baltimore: Johns Hopkins University Press.

Migdal, Joel S. 1988. *Strong Societies and Weak States*. Princeton: Princeton University Press.

Ministerio de Economía. *Programa Economica Regional*. www.mecon.gov.ar

Ministerio de Economía y Obras Servicios Públicos. 1995. *Argentina en Crecimiento*. Buenos Aires: Ministerio de Economía y Obras Servicios Públicos.

Ministerio de Hacienda, Chile. 1995, August. *Estado de avance de las prioridades planteadas al país el 29 de 1994 por Ministro de Hacienda*.

———. 1995, October. *Exposición sobre el estado de la hacienda pública*.

Mizrahi, Yemile. 1992. "Rebels without a Cause? The Politics of Entrepreneurs in Chihuahua." Paper presented at the XVII Congress of the Latin American Studies Association, Los Angeles, September 24–27.

Molinar Horcasitas, Juan, and Jeffrey A. Weldon. 1994. "Electoral Determinants and Consequences of National Solidarity." In Wayne A. Cornelius, Ann L. Craig, and Jonathan Fox, eds., *Transforming State-Society Relations in Mexico*. San Diego: Center for U.S.-Mexican Studies, University of California.

Montecinos, Veronica. 1998. *Economists, Politics and the State: Chile, 1958–1994*. Amsterdam: CEDLA.

Mora y Araujo, Manuel. 1993. "Las demandas sociales y la legitimidad de la política de ajuste." In Felipe A. M. de la Balze, comp., *Reforma y convergencia: Ensayos sobre la transformación de la economía argentina.* Buenos Aires: Asociación de Bancos Argentinas.

Morales, Juan Antonio. 1996. "Economic Policy after the Transition to Democracy: A Synthesis." In Juan Antonio Morales and Gary McMahon, eds., *Economic Policy and the Transition to Democracy.* New York: St. Martin's Press.

Moreno, Francisco José. 1969. *Legitimacy and Stability in Latin America: A Study of Chilean Political Culture.* New York: New York University Press.

Mosley, Paul. 1987. *Conditionality as Bargaining Process: Structural Adjustment Lending, 1980–1986.* Essays in International Finance, No. 68. Princeton: Department of Economics, International Finance Section, Princeton University.

Mosley, Paul, Jane Harrigan, and John Toye. 1995. *Aid and Power: The World Bank and Policy-Based Lending.* 2d ed. London: Routledge.

Most, Benjamin. 1991. *Changing Authoritarian Rule and Public Policy, 1930–1970.* Boulder, Colo.: Lynne Rienner.

Muñoz, Oscar G., and Carmen Celedon. 1993. "Chile en transición: Estrategia económica y política." In Juan Antonio Morales and Gary McMahon, eds., *La política económica en la transición de la democracia.* Santiago: CIEPLAN.

Murillo, M. Victoria. 1997. "A Strained Alliance: Continuity and Change in Mexican Labor Politics." In Mónica Serrano, ed., *Mexico: Assessing Neoliberal Reforms.* London: Institute of Latin American Studies, University of London.

———. 1994. "Union Response to Economic Reform in Argentina." Paper presented at the XVIII Congress of the Latin American Studies Association, Atlanta, March 10–12.

Naim, Moisés. 1994. "Latin America: The Second Stage of Reform." *Journal of Democracy* 5 (October): 32–48.

Nelson, Joan M. 1992. "Good Governance, Democracy and Conditional Economic Aid." In Paul Mosley, ed., *Development Finance and Policy Reform: Essays in the Theory and Practice of Conditionality in Less Developed Countries.* New York: St. Martin's Press.

Newton, Ronald C. 1974. "Natural Corporatism and the Passing of Populism in Spanish America." In Fredrick B. Pike and Thomas Stritch, eds., *The New Corporatism.* Notre Dame: University of Notre Dame Press.

N'haux, Enrique. 1993. *Menem-Cavallo: El poder Mediterráneo.* Buenos Aires: Ediciones Corregidor.

O'Brien, Phil, and Jackie Roddick. 1983. *Chile: The Pinochet Decade, the Rise and Fall of the Chicago Boys.* London: Latin American Bureau.

O'Donnell, Guillermo. 1994a. "Delegative Democracy." *Journal of Democracy* 5:55–69.

———. 1994b. "Some Reflections on Redefining the Role of the State." In I. Bradford, ed., *Redefining the State in Latin America.* Paris: Organization for Economic Cooperation and Development.

———. 1977a. "Corporatism and the Question of the State." In James M. Malloy, ed., *Authoritarianism and Corporatism in Latin America.* Pittsburgh: University of Pittsburgh Press.

———. 1977b. "Estado y alianzas en la Argentina, 1956–1976." *Desarrollo Económico* 16 (January–March): 523–54.

———. 1973. *Modernization and Bureaucratic Authoritarianism: Studies in South American Politics.* Berkeley: Institute of International Studies, University of California.

O'Donnell, Guillermo, and Philippe C. Schmitter. 1986. *Transitions from Authoritarian Rule: Tentative Conclusions about Uncertain Democracies.* Baltimore: Johns Hopkins University Press.

OED (Operations Evaluation Department). 1996. *Argentina: Country Assistance Review.* Washington, D.C.: World Bank.

———. 1994. *OED Study of Bank/Mexico Relations, 1948–1992.* Washington, D.C.: World Bank.

————. 1990. *The World Bank, Program Performance Audit Report, Chile, First, Second and Third Structural Adjustment Loans.*

Oliveri, Ernest J. 1989. *Latin American Debt and the Politics of International Finance.* Westport, Conn.: Praeger.

Oppenheim, Lois Hecht. 1993. *Politics in Chile: Democracy, Authoritarianism and the Search for Development.* Boulder, Colo.: Westview Press.

Orlansky, Dora. 1994. "Crisis y transformación del estado en la Argentina (1960–1993)." *Ciclos* 4 (2d semester): 3–28.

Osorio, Victor, and Iván Cabezas. 1995. *Los hijos de Pinochet.* Santiago: Planeta.

Oxhorn, Philip, and Graciela Ducatenzeiler. 1999. "The Problematic Relationship between Economic and Political Liberalization: Some Theoretical Considerations." In Philip Oxhorn and Pamela Starr, eds., *Markets and Democracy in Latin America: Conflict or Convergence?* Boulder, Colo.: Lynne Rienner.

Pastor, Manuel, Jr., and Carol Wise. 1999. "The Politics of Second-Generation Reform." *Journal of Democracy* 10 (July): 3–48.

————. 1992. "Peruvian Economic Policy in the 1980s: From Orthodoxy to Heterodoxy and Back." *Latin American Research Review* 27:83–117.

Peralta Ramos, Monica. 1992a. *The Political Economy of Argentina: Power and Class since 1930.* Boulder, Colo.: Westview Press.

————. 1992b. "Economic Policy and Distributional Conflict among Business Groups in Argentina: From Alfonsín to Menem, 1983–1990." In Edward C. Epstein, ed., *The New Democracy: The Search for a Successful Formula.* Westport, Conn.: Praeger.

Peters, Guy. 1998. "Policy Networks: Myths, Metaphors and Reality." In David Marsh, ed., *Comparing Policy Networks.* Buckingham: Open University Press.

Petras, James, and Fernando Ignacio Leiva. 1994. *Democracy and Poverty in Chile.* Boulder, Colo.: Westview Press.

Petras, James, and Morris Morley. 1975. *The United States and Chile.* New York: Monthly Review Press.

Poder Ejecutivo Federal. 1999. *5 ° Informe de Gobierno.* Anexo. (September) (Mexico).

Polak, Jacques. 1997. "The World Bank and the IMF: A Changing Relationship." In Devesh Kapur, John P. Lewis, and Richard Webb, eds., *The World Bank: Its First Half Century,* vol. 2, *Perspectives.* Washington, D.C.: Brookings Institution Press.

Pollack, Marcelo. 1995. "The Right and the Transition to Democracy." In David E. Hojman, ed., *Neoliberalism with a Human Face? The Politics and Economics of the Chilean Model.* Liverpool, Eng.: Institute of Latin American Studies.

Porto, A. 1992. "Una revisión critica de las empresas públicas en la Argentina." In Pablo Gerchunoff, ed., *Las privatizaciones en la Argentina, Primera etapa.* Buenos Aires: Institute Torcuato Di Tella.

Powell, John Duncan. 1970. "Peasant Society and Clientelistic Politics." *American Political Science Review* 64 (June): 411–25.

Proceso. (Mexico City). Various dates.

Przeworski, Adam, Pranab Bardhan, Luiz Carlos Bresser Pereira, László Bruszt, Jang Jip Choi, Ellen Turkish Comisso, Zhiyuan Cui, Torcuato di Tella, Elemer Hankiss, Lena Kolarska-Bobińska, David Laitin, José María Maravall, Andranik Migranyan, Guillermo O'Donnell, Ergun Ozbudun, John E. Roemer, Philippe C. Schmitter, Barbara Stallings, Alfred Stepan, Francisco Weffort, and Jerzy J. Wiatr. 1995. *Sustainable Democracy.* Cambridge, Eng.: Cambridge University Press.

Purcell, John F. H., and Susan Kaufman Purcell. 1977. "Mexican Business and Public Policy." In James M. Malloy, ed., *Authoritarianism and Corporatism in Latin America.* Pittsburgh: University of Pittsburgh Press.

Purcell, Susan Kaufman. 1975. *The Mexican Profit Sharing Decision.* Berkeley: University of California Press.

Purcell, Susan Kaufman, and John F. H. Purcell. 1980. "State and Society in Mexico: Must a Stable Polity Be Institutionalized?" *World Politics* 32 (January): 194–227.

Puryear, Jeffrey M. 1994. *Thinking Politics: Intellectuals and Democracy in Chile.* Baltimore: Johns Hopkins University Press.

Qureschi, Moeen Ahmad. 1992. "Policy Based Lending by the World Bank." In Paul Mosley, ed., *Development Finance and Policy Reform: Essays in the Theory and Practice of Conditionality in Less Developed Countries.* New York: St. Martin's Press.

Raczynski, Dagmar. 1994. "Politicas sociales y programas de combate a la pobreza en Chile: Balance y desafíos." *Colección Estudios CIEPLAN* 30 (June): 9–73.

Ramamurti, Ravi. 1992. *Privatization and the Latin American Debt Problem.* New Brunswick, N.J.: Transaction.

Ramírez de la O., Rogelio. 1996. "The Mexican Peso Crisis and Recession of 1994–1995: Preventable Then, Avoidable in the Future?" In Riordan Roett, ed., *The Mexican Peso Crisis: International Perspectives.* Boulder, Colo.: Lynne Rienner.

Ramos, Joseph. 1986. *Neoconservative Economics in the Southern Cone of Latin America, 1973–1983.* Baltimore: Johns Hopkins University Press.

Remmer, Karen. 1996. "The Sustainability of Political Democracy: Lessons from South America." *Comparative Political Studies* 29 (December): 689–718.

———. 1995. "New Theoretical Perspectives on Democratization." *Comparative Politics* 28 (October): 103–22.

———. 1986. "The Politics of Economic Stabilization: IMF Standby Programs in Latin America, 1954–1984." *Comparative Politics* 19 (October): 777–800.

Reyes Esparza, Ramiro, Enrique Olivares, Emilio Leyva, and Hernández G. Leyva. 1978. *La Burguesía Mexicana.* Mexico City: Editorial Nuestra Tiempo.

Rhodes, R. A. W., and David Marsh. 1992. "Policy Networks in British Politics: A Critique of Existing Approaches." In David Marsh and R. A. W. Rhodes, eds., *Policy Networks in British Government.* Oxford: Clarendon Press.

Rodríguez, Allen M. 1991. "Actors in the Latin American Debt Crisis II: International Financial Institutions." In Scott B. MacDonald, Jane Hughes, and Uwe Bott, eds., *Latin American Debt in the 1990s: Lessons from the Past and Forecasts for the Future.* New York: Praeger.

Rondfeldt, Donald. 1989. "Prospects for Elite Cohesion." In Wayne Cornelius, Judith Gentleman, and Peter H. Smith, eds., *Mexico's Alternative Political Futures.* San Diego: Center for U.S.-Mexican Studies, University of California.

Roxborough, Ian, Philip O'Brien, and Jackie Roddick. 1977. *Chile: The State and Revolution.* London: Macmillan.

Rubio, Luis. 1998. "Coping with Political Change." In Susan Kaufman Purcell and Luis Rubio, eds., *Mexico under Zedillo.* Boulder, Colo.: Lynne Rienner.

Saba, Roberto Pablo, and Luigi Manzetti. 1997. "Privatization in Argentina: The Implications for Corruption." *Crime, Law and Social Change* 25:353–69.

Sachs, Jeffrey D. 1989. "Conditionality, Debt Relief and Developing Country Crisis." In Jeffrey D. Sachs, ed., *Developing Country Debt and Economic Performance*, vol. 1, *The International Financial System.* Chicago: University of Chicago Press.

Samstad, James G. 1998. "Mexican Labor after Fidel: Democratization and the Erosion of Corporatism during the Zedillo Administration." Paper presented at the XXI Congress of the Latin American Studies Association, Chicago, September 24–26.

Saragoza, Alex. 1988. *The Monterrey Elite and the Mexican State.* Austin: University of Texas Press.

Sarfatti, Magali. 1966. *Spanish Bureaucratic-Patrimonialism in America.* Berkeley: University of California Press.

Savas, E. S. 1987. *Privatization: The Key to Better Government.* Chatham, N.J.: Chatham House.

Schmitter, Philippe C. 1974. "Still the Century of Corporatism?" In Fredrick B. Pike and Thomas Stritch, eds., *The New Corporatism: Social-Political Structures in the Iberian World*. Notre Dame: University of Notre Dame Press.

Schvarzer, Jorge. 1995. "Grandes grupos-económicos en la Argentina: Formas de propiedad y lógicas de expansión." In Pablo Bustos, coord., *Más Allá de la estabilidad: Argentina en la época de la globalización y la regionalización*. Buenos Aires: Fundación Fredrich Ebert.

———. 1981. *Expansión económica del estado subsidiario, 1976–1981*. Buenos Aires: Centro de Investigaciones sociales sobre el Estado y la Administración (CISEA).

Seligson, Mitchell A. 1989. "Introduction: From Uncertainty to Uncertainty, the Institutionalization of Elections in Central America." In John A. Booth and Mitchell A. Seligson, eds., *Elections and Democracy in Central America*. Chapel Hill: University of North Carolina Press.

Serrano, Mónica. 1997. "Civil Violence in Chiapas: The Origins and Causes of the Revolt." In Mónica Serrano, ed., *Mexico: Assessing Neoliberal Reform*. London: Institute of Latin American Studies, University of London.

Shadlen, Kenneth C. 1999. "Continuity and Change: Democratization, Party Strategies and Economic Policy Making." *Government and Opposition* 34:397–419.

Siavelis, Peter M. 1997. "Executive-Legislative Relations in Post-Pinochet Chile: A Preliminary Assessment." In Scott Mainwaring and Matthew Soberg Shugart, eds., *Presidentialism and Democracy in Latin America*. Cambridge, Eng.: Cambridge University Press.

Sidicaro, Ricardo. 1995. "Poder político, liberalismo económico y sectores populares en la Argentina, 1989–1995." In Atilio Borón, Manuel Mora y Araujo, José Nun, Juan Carlos Portantiero, and Ricardo Sidicaro, *Peronismo y Menemismo avatores del populismo en la Argentina*. Buenos Aires: Ediciones El Cielo por Asalto.

Sigmund, P. E. 1977. *The Overthrow of Allende and the Politics of Chile, 1964–1976*. Pittsburgh: University of Pittsburgh Press.

Silva, Eduardo. 1996. *The State and Capital in Chile: Business Elites, Technocrats and Market Economics*. Boulder, Colo.: Westview Press.

———. 1995. "The Political Economy of Chile's Regime Transition: Radical to Pragmatic Neoliberal Policies." In Paul W. Drake and Iván Jaksić, eds., *The Struggle for Democracy in Chile*. Rev. ed. Lincoln: University of Nebraska Press.

Silva, Patricio. 1991. "Technocrats and Politics in Chile: From the Chicago Boys to the CIEPLAN Monks." *Journal of Latin American Studies* 23 (May): 385–410.

Smith, Martin J. 1993. *Pressure, Power and Policy: State Autonomy and Policy Networks in Britain and the United States*. Hemel Hempstead: Harvester Wheatsheaf.

Smith, William C. 1992. "Hyperinflation, Macroeconomic Instability and Neoliberal Restructuring in Democratic Argentina." In Edward C. Epstein, ed., *The New Argentine Democracy: The Search for a Successful Formula*. Westport, Conn.: Praeger.

———. 1989. *Authoritarianism and the Crisis of the Argentine Political Economy*. Stanford: Stanford University Press.

Smith, William C., and Roberto Patricio Korzeniewicz, eds. 1997. *Politics, Social Change and Economic Restructuring in Latin America*. Coral Gables: North-South Center Press at the University of Miami.

Stallings, Barbara. 1978. *Class Conflict and Economic Development in Chile, 1958–1973*. Stanford: Stanford University Press.

Starr, Pamela K. 1999a. "Capital Flows, Fixed Exchange Rates, and Political Survival." In Philip Oxhorn and Pamela K. Starr, eds., *Markets and Democracy in Latin America*. Boulder, Colo.: Lynne Rienner.

———. 1999b. "Monetary Mismanagement and Inadvertent Democratization in Technocratic Mexico." *Studies in Comparative International Development* 33 (Winter): 33–68.

Stern, Ernest. 1983. "World Bank Financing of Structural Adjustment." In John Williamson, ed., *IMF Conditionality*. Washington, D.C.: Institute for International Economics.

Stiles, Kendall W. 1991. *Negotiating Debt: The IMF Lending Process*. Boulder, Colo.: Westview Press.

Story, Dale. 1986a. *The Mexican Ruling Party: Stability and Authority*. New York: Praeger.

———. 1986b. *Industry, the State and Public Policy*. Austin: University of Texas Press.

Teichman, Judith. 1997a. "Mexico and Argentina: Economic Reform and Technocratic Decision Making." *Studies in Comparative International Development* 32 (Spring): 31–55.

———. 1997b. "Neoliberalism and the Transformation of Mexican Authoritarianism." *Mexican Studies/Estudios Mexicanos* 13 (Winter): 121–47.

———. 1995. *Privatization and Political Change in Mexico*. Pittsburgh: University of Pittsburgh Press.

———. 1988. *Policymaking in Mexico: From Boom to Crisis*. Boston: Allen and Unwin.

Tello, Carlos. 1979. *La política económica en México, 1970–1976*. Mexico City: Siglo XXI.

Thompson, Andrés A. 1994. "Think Tanks en la Argentina: Conocimiento, instituciones y políticas." Documento CEDES/102. Buenos Aires.

Torres, Juan Carlos. 1997. "The Politics of Transformation in Historical Perspective." In William C. Smith and Roberto Patricio Korzeniewicz, eds., *Politics, Social Change and Economic Restructuring in Latin America*. Coral Gables: North-South Center Press at the University of Miami.

Trejo, Guillermo, and Claudio Jones. 1998. "Political Dilemmas of Welfare Reform, Poverty and Inequality in Mexico." In Susan Kaufman Purcell and Luis Rubio, eds., *Mexico under Zedillo*. Boulder, Colo.: Lynne Rienner.

Tussie, Diana. 1988. "The Coordination of Latin American Debtors: Is There a Logic behind the Story?" In Stephany Griffith-Jones, ed., *Managing World Debt*. New York: St. Martin's Press.

Ugalde, Alberto J. 1984. *Las empresas públicas en la Argentina*. Buenos Aires: Ediciones El Cronista Comercial.

Urzúa, Carlos M. 1997. "Five Decades of Relations between the World Bank and Mexico." In Devesh Kapur, John P. Lewis, and Richard Webb, eds., *The World Bank: Its First Half Century*, vol. 2, *Perspectives*. Washington, D.C.: Brookings Institution Press.

Valdés, Juan Gabriel. 1995. *Pinochet's Economists: The Chicago School in Chile*. Cambridge, Eng.: Cambridge University Press.

Van de Walle, Nicolas. 1989. "Privatization in Developing Countries: A Review of the Issues." *World Development* 17 (May): 601–11.

Varas, Augusto. 1995. "The Crisis of Legitimacy of Military Rule in the 80s." In Paul W. Drake and Iván Jaksić, eds., *The Struggle for Democracy in Chile*. Rev. ed. Lincoln: University of Nebraska Press.

Velasco, Andrés. 1994. "The State and Economic Policy: Chile, 1952–1992." In Barry P. Bosworth, Rudiger Dornbusch, and Raúl Labán, eds., *The Chilean Economy: Policy Lessons and Challenges*. Washington, D.C.: Brookings Institution Press.

Véliz, Claudio. 1980. *The Centralist Tradition of Latin America*. Princeton: Princeton University Press.

Vellinga, Menno. 1998. "The Changing Role of the State in Latin America." In Menno Vellinga, ed., *The Changing Role of the State in Latin America*. Boulder, Colo.: Westview Press.

Vernon, Raymond. 1963. *The Dilemma of Mexico's Development*. Cambridge, Mass.: Harvard University Press.

Vilas, Carlos M. 1997. "Participation, Inequality and the Whereabouts of Democracy." In Douglas A. Chalmers, Carlos M. Vilas, Katherine Hite, Scott B. Martin, Kerianne Piester, and Monique Segarra, eds., *The New Politics of Inequality in Latin America*. Oxford: Oxford University Press.

Villareal, Juan M. 1987. "Changes in Argentine Society: The Heritage of the Dictatorship." In Monica Peralta Ramos and Carlos Waisman, eds., *From Military Rule to Liberal Democracy in Argentina*. Boulder, Colo.: Westview Press.

Villareal, René. 1986. "La empresa pública en el desarrollo de México: Mitos y realidades." *Empresa Pública* 1 (April): 27–51.

———. 1977. "The Policy of Import Substitution Industrialization, 1929–1975." In José Luis Reyna and Richard S. Weinert, eds., *Authoritarianism in Mexico*. Philadelphia: Institute for the Study of Human Issues.

Waisman, Carlos H. 1992. "Argentina, Revolution from Above: State Economic Transformation and Political Realignment." In Edward C. Epstein, ed., *The New Argentine Democracy*. Westport, Conn.: Praeger.

Waterbury, John. 1989. "The Management of Long-Haul Economic Reform." In Joan Nelson, ed., *Fragile Coalitions: The Politics of Economic Adjustment*. Washington, D.C.: Overseas Development Council.

Weyland, Kurt. 1997. "Growth and Equity in Chile's New Democracy." *Latin American Research Review* 32:37–57.

Wiarda, Howard J. 1998. "Historical Determinants of the Latin American State." In Menno Vellinga, ed., *The Changing Role of the State in Latin America*. Boulder, Colo.: Westview Press.

Wilkie, James W. 1967. *The Mexican Revolution: Federal Expenditures and Social Change since 1910*. Berkeley: University of California Press.

Wilks, Stephen, and Maurice Wright, eds. 1987. *Comparative Government-Industry Relations*. Oxford: Clarendon Press.

Williamson, John. 1994. "In Search of a Manual for Technopolis." In John Williamson, ed., *The Political Economy of Policy Reform*. Washington, D.C.: Institute for International Economics.

Williamson, John, and Stephan Haggard. 1994. "The Political Conditions for Economic Reform." In John Williamson, ed., *The Political Economy of Policy Reform*. Washington, D.C.: Institute for International Economics.

Winn, Peter. 2000. "Lagos Defeats the Right—By a Thread." *NACLA Report on the Americas* 33 (March–April): 6–10.

Witaker, Jorge, and Ismael Eslava. 1988. "Aspectos generales del régime legal aplicable a las entitdades parastatales." In Marcos Kaplan, Francisco Osornio, Beatriz Bernal, et al., *Regulación juridica del intervencionismo estatal en México*. Mexico City: Fondo de Cultura Económica.

World Bank. 1997. *World Development Report 1997*. Washington, D.C.: World Bank.

———. 1993. *Argentina: From Insolvency to Growth*. Washington, D.C.: World Bank.

———. 1991. *Poverty Alleviation in Mexico*. Washington, D.C.: World Bank.

Wynia, Gary. 1986. *Argentina: Illusions and Realities*. New York: Holmes and Meier.

Zeitlin, Maurice, and Richard Earl Ratcliff. 1988. *Landlords and Capitalists: The Dominant Class of Chile*. Princeton: Princeton University Press.